Bismi Llahi r-Rahmani r-Rahim
In the name of Allah the Most Compassionate, the Most Merciful.

"And convey unto them the story of Ibrahim."
- The Qur'an 26:69.

"Convey (my teachings) to the people, even if it be a single sentence, and tell others the stories of the Banu Isra'il (which have been taught to you) for it is not sinful to do so."
- Sahih Bukhari (4:56:667).

"We should be concerned with the things that make people connect to the heart of the Beloved, the Prophet Muhammad (sas), with love and praise, with respect and appreciation. This is what is important. **So relate the stories that perhaps they may reflect."** (7:176)
- Mawlana Shaykh Nazim al-Haqqani suhbah September 10, 2011.

Other Titles By This Author:

My Little Lore of Light
The Light of Muhammad
Links of Light: The Golden Chain
The Story of Moses
Who Are You? A Book of Very Serious Questions
The Animals of Paradise
The Animals of Paradise: Coloring Book
My Little Lore of Light: Coloring Book
Every Day A Thousand Times
As-Salamu 'Alaykum Ya Rasul Allah (sas)

Copyright © 2019 by Karima Sperling

All rights reserved. This book or any portion thereof may not be reproduced or used in any manner whatsoever without the express written permission of the publisher except for the use of brief quotations in a book review.

Printed in the United States of America ISBN 978-0-9913003-6-5

Little Bird Books littlebirdbooksink@gmail.com

Ibrahim Khalil Allah (as)

By Karima Sperling

Dedication

Our Lord! we have heard the call of the one calling to faith, "Believe in your Lord!" so we have believed. Our Lord! Therefore forgive us our sins and remit from us our evil deeds, and make us die in the company of the righteous. (3:193)

To Mawlana Shaykh Nazim Adil al-Haqqani and Hajja Amina Adil to whose call our hearts continue to respond.

Thanks

Thank you to Shaykh Mehmet Adil al-Haqqani for his wisdom, encouragement, and prayers.

Thank you to Hajja Rukiye Sultan always, for inspiration and for the many bits and pieces that have found their way into the book.

Thank you to Hajji Mehmet Nazim for answering so many questions and keeping things straight.

Thank you to Aminah Alptekin who, as always, listened to my endless worries and in the end miraculously turned a file into a book.

Thank you to my most patient advisors and supporters, Munir Sperling and Alia Nazeer.

Thank you to Sanaa Makhlouf, Mahmoud Shelton, Ranya Hassanin, Fatima Sperling. Thank you to Wafaa Sultan, Radhia Shukrullah, Akram Reda, Lamya Taher, and to Fatima Maringele and the water bearer.

Thank you to my loving family of book lovers – Haniya, Humayra, Layka, Ishaq, Jacob, Hamza, Ghalib, Khalil, Noura, Karima, Tarik, and Hala.

But most of all, thank You to the One who made them all.

Abbreviations

(sas) – *sall Allahu 'alayhi wa s-sallam*. The peace and blessings of Allah be upon him. Prayer said after the mention of the name of the Prophet Muhammad (sas).

(as) – *'alayhi s-salam*. On him be peace. Prayer said after the mention of the name of a prophet or archangel.

(ra) – *radhia Allahu 'an*. May Allah be pleased with him. Prayer said when the name of a male companion or family member of the Prophet Muhammad (sas) or other prophet is mentioned.

(rah) – *radhia Allahu 'anha*. May Allah be pleased with her. Prayer said for a woman from the family or companions of the Prophet Muhammad or of earlier prophets when her name is mentioned.

(q) – *qaddas Allahu sirrahu*. May Allah sanctify his secret. Prayer said when the name of a saint is mentioned.

Table of Contents

Introduction – The Father of Us All..1
1. When – The Heavenly Order...9
2. Where – The Earthly Setting..13
3. Who – The Tyrannical Pattern 19
4. It Always Begins with a Warning...23
5. The Return of the Light..27
6. Fathers and Forefathers..33
7. Ar-Rabb 37
8. The Cave of Fitra...41
9. Things That Set..47
10. Teasing the Gods 51
11. The First Lie – Too Sick to Sin...55
12. The Second Lie – A Bloodless Crime...61
13. Life and Death..65
14. Coolness and Peace... 67
15. The Companions of the Garden..75
16. From Whence You Don't Know..81
17. Becoming Khalil..85

18. Four Birds	91
19. Marriage	97
20. Salamun 'Alayk	101
21. The Language of Numbers	107
22. The Holy Land	113
23. The Third Lie – My Sister	119
24. Pharaoh's Gift	123
25. A Gift for Lut (as)	127
26. A Leader of Men	131
27. Welcome Guests	137
28. Sarah's (rah) Gift	141
29. The Good News	149
30. The Bad News	155
31. Allah's Wrath	159
32. God Forbid	165
33. Planting the Seed	167
34. The Hijra of Hajar (rah)	173
35. The Well That Suffices	177

36. The Sacrifice of Isma'il (as)..185
37. Ibrahim (as) Had Two Sons..191
38. The Sacrifice of Ishaq (as)... 199
39. What Difference Would It Make?..207
40. A Clear Test... 215
41. The Great Sheep..221
42. The *Qibla* of Ibrahim (as)... 229
43. Ibrahim's (as) Call...239
44. The Book of Ibrahim (as)... 247
45. Isma'il (as): The Rest of the Story..251
46. Ishaq (as): The Rest of the Story..259
47. Two Rivers.. 265
48. Three Images of Ibrahim (as)... 273
49. The Unwelcome Guest..281
Conclusion – Our God Is One..287
Glossary..294
Bibliography..301
Picture Credits..306

Our father Ibrahim (as) holding his children: Jews, Christians, and Muslims. 12th century French, Bible de Souvigny.

INTRODUCTION
The Father of Us All

"O Allah grace Muhammad and the family of Muhammad as You graced Ibrahim and the people of Ibrahim, truly only You are worthy to be praised and glorified.

O Allah bless Muhammad and the family of Muhammad as You blessed Ibrahim and the people of Ibrahim. In all the worlds only You are worthy to be praised and glorified."

When the Prophet Muhammad (sas) was asked in what way those who love him should petition Allah to bless him, he replied with the above words (Muslim and Bukhari). He asked to be mentioned together with Ibrahim (as), the Friend of the Merciful, the Father of the faithful. And so every day, a minimum of five times, Muslims around the world repeat this request asking Allah to bless both Sayyiduna Muhammad (*sall Allahu 'alayhi wa s-sallam*) and Sayyiduna Ibrahim (*'alayhi s-salam*) and those who follow them; to bless the one like the other.

This prayer is called the *Salatu l-Ibrahimiyya* and is also used as a *dhikr*, litany, outside of the prayer. It is repeated thousands of times on the breath of Muslims around the world in order to please Allah and to bring benefit for themselves. It is said to heal, to protect, to enlighten, to save. It can be recited at any time, anywhere and in any state. Saying it purifies, erases sins, is a charity, increases love, paves the way to Paradise. Reciting it attracts the attention of the Prophet (sas) himself and brings his prayers for us in response. It is the remembrance most recommended by the Prophet (sas) himself and by the shaykhs for attaining higher stations and ultimate salvation.

Muslims may wonder why it is that Muhammad the Beloved of Allah (sas) asked to be remembered in the same breath as Ibrahim the Friend of Allah (as). There is a strong connection between the two prophets, both familial and spiritual. Sayyiduna Muhammad (sas) said that every prophet has an ally among the past prophets and his ally is his forefather Ibrahim (as). After rebuilding the House of God, the Ka'ba, Ibrahim (as) prayed, **Our Lord! And raise up in their midst a messenger from among them who shall recite unto them Your revelations, and shall instruct them in the Scripture and in wisdom and shall purify them. Surely, You only You are the Mighty, Wise** (2:129). Muslims believe that Ibrahim (as) was aware of the presence of the Prophet Muhammad (sas) among his descendants and that he prayed specifically for his coming as the last prophet, to seal and complete the religion. The Prophet (sas) himself said that he is the prayer of his father Ibrahim (as) (Hadith Ibn Hisham).

The Prophet (sas), from the moment of his birth until the Last Day, continues to ask Allah's blessing and mercy for those who follow him, his *Ummah*. He was particularly touched and thankful, therefore, for the concern shown by his father Ibrahim (as) who, out of all the prophets, prayed for the *Ummah* of Muhammad (sas) both after his first Hajj and again when they met on the Night Journey in the seventh heaven. So when Ibrahim (as) asked Allah to **grant me a mention of honor among the later generations** (26:84), Allah made sure that his prayer was answered.

Daily remembrance of Ibrahim (as) is not reserved just for the Muslims, however. Observant Jews around the world

The perhaps unintended resemblance between the Muslim and his forefather Ibrahim (as).

also mention the name of Ibrahim (as) in prayer three times a day. In the essential portion of their three daily ritual prayers that were established by the Rabbis after the Babylonian exile, they begin by praising God with the words: "Praised are You Lord, Shield of Abraham - *Magen Abraham*" (Genesis 15:1). In actuality Sayyiduna Ibrahim (as) has become their shield. It is on account of their filial connection to his goodness and his faithfulness and his love that they hope they will be forgiven the consequences of their ordinary human failings. It is said that the mid-day prayer is in the manner of Ishaq (as) whose attribute is awe and the night prayer is in the manner of Ya'qub (as) whose attribute is said to be mercy. The morning prayer, however, is said to be in the way of Ibrahim (as) and its attribute, like his, is love.

Ibrahim (as) is also mentioned daily in the Catholic ritual, the Liturgy of Hours, which is the framework of daily prayer in the Church. He is remembered and referred to as 'our father in faith'. He is one of only a few Old Testament prophets who are part of the Christian ritual and, of these, his name is mentioned the most often. The Christians continue to trace their spiritual descent from him. Jesus (as) was, of course, a direct blood descendant of Sayyiduna Ibrahim (as) through the house of David (as). However, most Christians are not his blood descendants. They, instead, draw their spiritual descent from the words of Paul: "If you belong to Christ, then you are Abraham's seed and heirs according to the promise" (Galatians 3:29). They picture Paradise being in proximity to Ibrahim (as) where they will be received as small children, "carried by the angels into the bosom of Abraham" (Luke 16:22). It is into the loving arms of Ibrahim (as) that all souls are drawn. On the Night Journey the Prophet Muhammad (sas) saw Ibrahim (as) in the seventh Heaven surrounded by the souls of children.

So we must ask, who was Ibrahim (as) that four thousand years after his passing the people of the three major religions, who seem to be able to agree on very little else, continue to praise him, pray for him, obey him, follow him, remember him, and compete to be considered among his legitimate descendants? And what did his faith look like that it is established as a model for all people of faith in all times, everywhere?

First of all, simply, he is our father and his love is important. However we reckon our descent, whether spiritual or physical, we all find solace and support in being among his children. Like a perfect father he is loving and supportive at all times, under all circumstances. He would never leave any of us behind.

And yet, paradoxically, he is the one who is remembered for being willing to kill his own son if that was the order of his Lord. Much of his life can be defined by fatherhood. First he was tested by the idolatry of his own father, then he was tested by not being a father. Finally, he was tested by being too loving a father. Even his name means father (*Ab*). The Jews call him *Abraham Abinu* (Ibrahim our father). He was the actual ancestor of all their prophets and of the Jewish nation, the Banu Isra'il. The Christians say that by virtue of being a grandfather of Jesus (as), "He is the father of us all" (Romans 4:16) and trace their spiritual descent from him. He is also an ancestor of the Prophet Muhammad (sas) through his son Isma'il (as) and Allah says in The Qur'an **the faith of your father Ibrahim is yours**. (22:78).

All three religions revere Ibrahim (as) as one of the greatest of Allah's servants. They also all characterize him as the Friend of God, a man of such strength of faith, and such exalted capacity that even the Almighty took him as His friend. He has the station, unique to him and to the Prophet Muhammad (sas) of being **Khalil Allah** (Qur'an 4:125), the Friend of God (Isaiah 41:8) (James 2:23) (Chronicles 20:7). He is the father of us all and our model for what is required in order to establish an intimate relationship with God.

The stories of the prophets that are introduced in The Qur'an and elaborated in the Hadith and Tafsir are not bedtime stories and they are certainly not just for children. They could be characterized as part of the instruction manual with which our most generous Lord has sent us into the world. They can serve as guides for us to discover on our own the answers to the big questions in life - who we are and why we were created, where we came from and where we are going. They should be given to children to be processed slowly over a lifetime. It is important in this day of so many pointless stories, movies, and books, to recognize those stories that actually carry meaning and lead to correct understandings. They are not to be passed over lightly.

In Islam before beginning any task or action we must consider carefully and express clearly our intention (*niyyat*). Intention is everything.

We are rewarded for our intention and we are answered according to our intention so we must try to be clear before acting, what exactly we intend. If the outcome turns out to be contrary to our sincere intention, then Allah has promised to reward the intention regardless.

The first intention of this book is to present an interesting and compelling retelling of the familiar story of Ibrahim (as) to a Muslim audience. It doesn't matter how often it is told, each telling is unique to the teller and unique to the hearer as well. It reveals a little more every time it is encountered and casts its light on the issues of the moment. The Prophet Muhammad (as) had a special connection and similarity to Sayyiduna Ibrahim (as) and so the events of his historical life are used to flesh out some of Ibrahim's (as) less detailed history. Hopefully it increases understanding and love for both of them.

The second intention of this book only developed while it was already in progress. It is to provide non-Muslims a way to travel inside Islam instead of being on the outside looking in. Abraham (as) has recently been the subject of some popular books written for the purpose of bringing understanding and peace to a world split with misunderstanding, fear, and violence. However, it is rare to find much depth or positive information about the Islamic view of things. We all want peace but we also want respect and understanding.

This book, however, is not meant to be ecumenical in that the intention is not to please everyone. The intention is to express, as openly and honestly as possible, one side of a many sided issue but to do it with respect and love.

Islam does not claim to be a new religion. It is simply a fresh restatement of the message with which all the prophets have been sent. But just because it is the newcomer in the group and its revelation came last does not mean that it borrowed or copied from those that came before. It would be ridiculous to say that a younger brother looks similar to his older siblings because he stole from them or copied them. In fact, the older traditions were just as likely to have borrowed and learned from the newer one. The Torah remained without vowels, for instance, until its scholars recognized the efficacy of the voweling system developed by the Muslims to ensure the accurate preservation of The Qur'an. Maimonides (a prominent Jewish scholar of the 12th century) was heavily influenced by the Muslim community in which he prospered even to the extent that some of the books with which he is credited were actually translations of earlier Muslim texts. Saint Francis is known to have had beneficial contact with Muslims and with Sufi ideas and practices. Among people of religious sincerity there has always been interested communication and shared learning.

Islam does, however, claim to be the most recent and most intact of the divine revelations and the one that was sent specifically for this time. The Qur'an is the latest message from our Lord and the most historically well preserved. There has been no politically motivated tampering, no losing and restoring, no choosing and discarding, nothing anonymous or amended. It still is as it was delivered from God – whole and intact. This is not saying that it is easy to understand. It is a revealed book and to some degree it needs to be revealed anew to everyone who opens it. But if we give it a chance, surely Allah will open it for us as we need it.

Unlike Judaism, Christianity, Buddhism or Hinduism, Islam is not named after either a nation or a prophet. Muslims are niether the Banu Isma'il nor have they ever consented to be called Muhammadans. Islam means submission and it means peace. The only way for mankind to have a true relationship with God is to be at peace with His Authority, not to fight or object or even wish other than He wishes. This is the way of all the prophets, all the saints, all the men of God everywhere since the creation of Adam (as) and it is illustrated particularly clearly in the story of Ibrahim (as).

God willing, this book conveys an invitation from our father Ibrahim (as), the best of hosts, the one who loves us, to sit down together in his company, to experience his hospitality in a slightly new way, and to let him share with us his story.

Map of the area in which this story takes place.

Adam's (as) Peak in Sri Lanka where Muslims believe the prophet Adam (as) first landed on earth. He stood on one foot for 300 years seeking forgiveness until his huge footprint became imbedded in the rock.

CHAPTER ONE
When: The Heavenly Order

As with most stories our story begins at the beginning, or if not at the very beginning, then at least at one of the beginnings. Allah Almighty was as He is and always will be, without beginning or ending, without mate or partner, without equal or similar – One. It is said that He wanted to be known so He created the creation to know Him, to reflect Him back to Himself.

First He created the Throne of His dominion, then the Pen to design the creation, then the Tablet on which to inscribe it, then Mind with which to witness it. Then He pulled light from the darkness and from this light He created the light of Muhammad (sas). From that light He created the lights of all the other prophets and, from them, the lights of everyone else. Then Allah created the Heavens and their inhabitants. Then He made the Earths and drew the dry land out of the sea and populated it with plants and animals. For all of this Allah simply said to it "Be" and it became, in six very long days.

In the last hour of the sixth day Allah began to create something different. He made a clay out of the dust of the Earth and the waters of

Paradise. He molded it with His own hands into a perfect shape. Then He blew into it some of His own breath. The form became soft and warm. Breathing on its own, it awoke with a sneeze. Allah placed the light of Muhammad (sas) on its forehead and gave it Mind and self, which is ego. This was Adam (as) the first human and the first prophet. From him Allah made his wife, Hawwa (rah), and they were happy together in Paradise. Allah gave them only a single commandment. They must not eat from one of the trees in an orchard of uncountable trees. Their enemy, shaytan, made them afraid. In their fear they forgot this one command and so began to think for themselves. No longer able to stay in Paradise, they fell into the world Allah had made for them. Now they needed to learn how to use their minds to remember and find their way back.

Adam (as) landed in Serendip (Sri Lanka) on the top of Mount Nudh. Standing on one foot for three hundred years, he wept for forgiveness. His tears filled the valleys with water and his foot left an imprint in the rock for all to see. Hawwa (rah) landed in Jeddah (which means grandmother) in Arabia. Guided by Allah, Adam (as) finally went off in search of his wife. He found her in Mecca. He stood on the hill of As-Safa and she on Al-Marwa and they looked at each other but were forbidden to come closer. Allah ordered His angels to bring the Heavenly House (*al-Baytu l-Ma'mur*) to Earth to serve as a reminder of their heavenly home. Jibra'il (as) descended to teach them the rites of pilgrimage. They circled the heavenly House seven times, as the planets circle around the sun. Then they went out to the plain of 'Arafah (meaning to know). They stood all day on the Mount of Mercy under the blazing sun praying for Allah to forgive them for what they knew they had done. Leaving quickly before the light was gone they spent the night on the Mash'ar (which means to understand). At Muzdalifa (which means to draw close) in the darkness they came together. As the sun rose they moved to Mina (a wish granted) and knew they were forgiven. In a new state of awareness, they rejected the devil who had misled them and they sacrificed (*qurban* - drew close) to the One who had guided them. They returned to Mecca to start their earthly life together as husband and wife.

Allah created Adam (as) as His first prophet and He honored him (17:70). He placed the Light of Muhammad (sas) on his forehead to illuminate his way like the full moon and He ordered all of the creation to honor him as well (2:34). Then Allah taught him the names of everything.

Some say this means that Adam (as) was given the alphabet and taught to write. Allah drew out and arrayed before Adam (as) all of his children to be and He took a promise from them that they would remember and worship only Him. Then He ordered Adam (as) to write on a scroll of leather the names, or some say draw the pictures, of each of the 124,000 prophets and He instructed Adam (as) to keep it safe in a chest (*Tabut* or Ark) made from wood.

Adam (as) and Hawwa (rah) began to have many children, who also had many children but only some of them remembered their promise to their Creator. Gradually the number of those who remembered became less and less. The word for mankind in Arabic, *insan*, comes from the root meaning to forget. Surely man is forgetful and needs frequent reminding (20:115). When Adam (as) died he left the Light of Muhammad (sas) and the Ark to his son Seth (as). From him it passed to Idris (as) and from righteous son to righteous son for ten generations until it came to the prophet Nuh (as).

Nuh (as) and his parents alone of all his nation remembered Allah. For 950 years he patiently called his people to truth but only eighty of them listened. He gave up and asked that the earth be cleaned of all the unbelieving people. Allah answered His prophet by sending water raining down from the sky and surging up from the ground, until the earth was inundated. Nuh (as) built a boat of 124,000 planks of wood. On each board was written the name of one of the prophets. It was a huge floating Ark. Three of his sons, their wives and the eighty believers boarded the ship along with two of every animal and they were carried safely through the storm of Allah's anger. Sayyiduna Nuh's (as) wife (66:10) and fourth son (11:42) perished in the flood. The Holy House was rescued from the waters and taken back into Heaven. After sailing seven circles around the spot where it had been, the Ark was brought to land far from Mecca on a mountain called Judi, the generous. Here they descended from the Ark and began a new life. At the foot of Mount Judi, in the town of Cizre, sits the tomb of Nuh (as) from which Al-Mas'oudi in the ninth century CE wrote that the Ark was still visible.

Nuh (as) is the second father of mankind since all the other children of Adam (as) were washed away. His three sons, Sam, Ham, and Japheth (ahs) came down from the mountain and began to build homes and have children. The other believers were too old to have children. The *Tabut* and the light were passed to Sam (as) and then from father to son for another ten generations until most of the people had again forgotten their Lord. They set up stones and began to worship them. Some say they made gods of the angels who came to them as messengers or of their ancestors whom they idolized. However it happened, they were once more in desperate need of a heavenly reminder. The light of Muhammad (sas) and the *Tabut* of Adam (as) were waiting to be carried by another of Allah's chosen messengers and the Heavenly House needed to be rebuilt on Earth.

The footprint of Adam (as) is now covered and only open for viewing once a year.

CHAPTER TWO

Where: The Earthly Setting

The area where the Ark landed is now a part of Turkey and is the uppermost limit of what is called Mesopotamia, the land between the rivers. The Tigris and the Euphrates originate in the mountains of which Judi is a part and gather water as they flow all the way south to the Persian Gulf. At the southern tip, where the rivers met the Gulf at that time, was the capital city of a great kingdom, called Ur. At the northern tip was a border city of some size called Urfa. One of these cities was to be the birthplace of the next of Allah's great reminders, the prophet Ibrahim (as).

In the Torah it says that Ibrahim (as) was born in Ur of the Chaldees but there were no Chaldeans at the time of Ibrahim (as). It is much more likely that the place of his birth was Urfa in southern Turkey. Even the Torah agrees that he later moved with his family to live in Harran, a town just a little south of Urfa. Urfa is one of the oldest continuously inhabited sites in the world, believed to have been a place of human settlement since at least 7,000 BCE and human habitation many thousands of years before that. Six miles distant from Urfa at Gobekli Tepe, circles of large delicately carved stones have been unearthed: layers and layers of vertical

Mount Judi in Turkey, where The Qur'an states the Ark of Nuh (as) landed. In the foreground is said to be the outline of the fossilized Ark itself.

stones, similar to the more famous Stonehenge in Britain but built 6,000 years earlier dating back to at least 10,000 BCE. Since it lies a little to the west of Mount Judi some have suggested that this ancient temple site was founded by the sons of Nuh (as) after they descended from the Ark but it could date even earlier to the time of the first sons of Adam (as). And there is no evidence that it was used for the worship of Allah.

Its discovery has, however, changed the theory of the development of civilization. It used to be thought that it was only the advent of agriculture that enabled people to congregate in towns freeing some of them from having to produce their own food and affording them the spare time to develop art and religion. It was assumed that man's first concern was to establish a secure source of food and only then did he consider his spiritual and creative needs. However, since Gobekli was built many hundreds of years before the advent of agriculture in the region, the new theory is that the need to gather for religious purposes instead encouraged the development of agriculture and all the other varied aspects of what we call civilization. It was later in this region that wheat was first cultivated and that goats, sheep, and cows were first domesticated. It was the desire to worship their Creator that drew human beings together and it was the act of servanthood that was in fact the initial impulse for all other human endeavors.

This region, where it is believed that the world was first re-peopled after the destruction of the flood, is also the area where it is said that the world will finally come to an end. On the plain of Amuq to the southwest of Urfa, it is foretold that the Mahdi (as) will lead the forces of good against the forces of evil in the last battle, known as Armageddon. It is in this historically significant area that the prophet Ibrahim (as) was most probably born. In fact, those who take the Bible literally think that Sam (as) the son of Nuh (as) lived 600 years and may well have still been living in the area at the time our story begins around 2,000 BCE. The Qur'an clearly states that **of his** [Nuh's] **followers was Ibrahim.** (37:83).

The Assyrian, Sumerian and Akkadian empires alternatively ruled the area at that time. They were agricultural civilizations with extraordinary art, and advanced writing systems. They governed extensive trading networks with large commercial centers, roads, cities, and organized law. These people were neither backward nor primitive.

Today we take for granted many of the things they were the first to discover and develop: wheeled vehicles, the plow, cuneiform writing, the sail boat, irrigation, measurement of time, astronomy, mathematics, and much more. And yet, however advanced and creative they were, they had managed to forget about their own Creator.

The Akkadians, who were probably the ones in power at the time of our story, were a Semitic people (descendants of the prophet Nuh's (as) son Sam (as)) originally pastoral nomads who assimilated to Sumerian civilization and became urbanized. Their form of government was theocracy. This should have meant that the state was governed by God but meant in fact that the gods were governed by the state. Religion belonged to the government and so belief was a matter of loyalty to the state and disbelief was traitorous.

They remembered that there was one supreme God, whom they called El, the name by which He is known in the Hebrew scriptures. Although El was the Creator, they believed He had become remote and beyond reach. Instead they worshiped gods whom they called the children of El. Their deciphered religious texts describe a creation story similar to that told in the Torah and The Qur'an. They also relate the story of the great flood that washed away most of life on earth. This could be the preserved traces of the religion of Adam (as) and of Nuh (as).

The gods they actively worshiped were Sin - god of the moon and wisdom; his son Shamash - god of the sun and justice; and his daughter Inanna - goddess of Venus and fertility. These they represented by statues in human form and ascribed to them human needs and emotions. The people of Sumer built large multi-level stone temple complexes in their honor which dominated the urban landscape. In Ur one of the wonders of the ancient world was a ziggurat, a tall truncated pyramid-like structure with steps up the outside. At the very top was a temple with a large statue of the god Sin and at the bottom were kitchens to cook his daily meals. Inside the mosaic halls there were larger-than-life statues of their imagined deities. There were priest attendants whose only job was to clothe, bathe, and cook special meals to feed the statues. It is said that at night they lay the gods down in special beds for them to sleep comfortably like huge dolls. And they didn't question of what benefit it was to have a god who sleeps.

Two of the towering Stonehenge type stones unearthed at Gobekli Tepe outside of Urfa Turkey.

A 3m high carving found in the hills of northern Iraq, thought to be Naram-Sin.

CHAPTER THREE

Who: The Tyrannical Pattern

It is said by the Muslim historians that only four men have ruled all of the area of Mesopotamia. Two of them were faithful: the prophet Sulayman ibn Dawud (as) and Dhu l-Qarnain (as) (who may or may not have been Alexander the Great and may or may not have been a prophet). And two of them were faithless: Namrud and Nebuchadnezzar (who ruled Babylonia around 1500 years after Namrud). Some commentators tell us that some four thousand years ago there were kings of Sumer, Akkad, and Babylon, who represented themselves as lions and were all called Namrud.

The historian Muhammad al-Kisai (8th century) says that the Namrud of our story was so dark, disagreeable, and unpleasant even as a baby that his parents could not wait to get rid of him. As an infant they had him thrown into a fast flowing river. Instead of being drowned he was washed ashore and adopted by a ferocious mother tiger who suckled him along with her cubs. Tiger in Arabic is *nimr*. When he was grown and had rejoined human company, he continued to exhibit the savage characteristics of his tiger upbringing. Most of the kings of this time period are known from the written records to have been ruthless and heartless.

Some had all of their own sons killed for fear of losing power to them. While they were busy trying to be lions, many of them in fact became beasts. And the gods who supported and inspired them were created in their image, stony and vain, hardly heavenly.

This tyrannical pattern is repeated for a number of the great prophets of God. As Namrud was the tyrant of Sayyiduna Ibrahim (as), so Pharaoh was the tyrant of Sayyiduna Musa (as), and King Herod of Sayyiduna 'Isa (as). They were all temporal rulers whom Allah had established in the land and whom He tested with wealth and power. They are examples of the real dangers of being tested with too much worldly good fortune. **Your wealth and your children are but a trial and a temptation, whereas with Allah there is a tremendous reward.** (64:15-16). And they stand in direct contrast to the prophets they opposed who willingly gave up everything of this world in order to attain to the tremendous reward.

Each tyrant was warned; they each had a dream or were informed by the wise that there was a true king coming who would establish God's kingdom on the earth. If they heard, they did not listen. If they listened, they did not accept. Allah's kingdom is not a matter of palaces and parades. Each one of them thought they could impose their will over that of Allah by killing the messenger who was sent to them while he was still a baby. In so doing, they were directly responsible for the killing of hundreds, if not thousands, of innocents.

The parents of all three of these prophets had to flee or abandon their homes or, in the case of Musa (as), their child. The mother of 'Isa (as) fled to Egypt. The mother of Ibrahim (as) fled to the cave, and the enslaved mother of Musa (as), unable to flee, cast her son onto the waters of the Nile. Each of these tyrants was really fighting against God, and each of them, in the end, lost. The patterns they exhibit are unfortunately not just symbolic or mythic but totally real and still going on in the world around us. Consider the modern tyrants and the atrocities they commit in order to mold their world into whatever form they think it should be, eliminating those elements they find threatening or polluting or offensive in some way; men who have appropriated for themselves the authority and judgment that is God's. They scheme their schemes, **but Allah brought their scheming to naught – for Allah is the best of schemers.** (8:30).

Naram-Sin was the name of one of the Akkadian kings who ruled around 2,000 BCE. It is believed he was the first ever to call himself a god. Among the many titles by which he honored himself were, God of Akkad, Ruler of the Four Directions, and Ruler of the Universe. The crown with which he crowned himself had two horns like the crescent moon and he considered himself the earthly incarnation of Sin the moon god. A narrative poem written a hundred years after his death, called The Curse of Akkad, has been unearthed and deciphered. It relates that Naram-Sin angered the gods and in consequence they destroyed him and leveled his beautiful capital city of Akkad. They laid a curse on the city so that it could never be inhabited again. To this day no one has found a trace of Akkad and where it lies nobody knows.

It could be that Naram-Sin was Namrud. The story, as it is related in the Holy Books, gives us only a few clues as to the actual historical setting because the intention is less to inform about the outward events than it is to inform about the inner significance. As the historical record, created by kings and tyrants, makes no mention of the men of God, so God's Book, finding nothing good to say, barely makes mention of Namrud and the other tyrants. Our story could very well take place in almost any land, at any time, ancient or modern, without affecting either its significance or its truth.

A mosque built over another spot thought to be the birthplace of Ibrahim (as) with what remains of a ziggurat in the distance, Borsippa, Iraq.

CHAPTER FOUR

It Always Begins with a Warning

There was a man in ancient times in the land between the rivers, Mesopotamia, who was called Namrud. He was showered with favors by Allah. He was rugged, strong, and tall. He seemed to tower over most of the men around him. He was athletic, agile and fast, a hunter who always hit his mark. He had never lost in battle and had never considered showing mercy to an opponent. He was adequately clever and not unobservant and, although he lacked true wisdom, there were many people who sought his counsel and many who accepted his judgment. He plowed his way through life finding that wherever he went the doors swung open in front of him. Success courted him. He did not seem capable of failure. Higher and higher he rose among his people, until, following an inspiration, he had the goldsmiths make him a jeweled crown that he proceeded to set ceremoniously upon his own head, the first to have ever done such a thing.

After this he ruled his people with an iron fist. Whether they lived or died was in his hand and he didn't for a moment doubt his ability to choose. Nor did he question his good luck or feel he owed thanks to anyone for the favors he enjoyed. He didn't know his Creator. He thought that everything was his by right. He had never been sick or needy, alone or helpless. He thought these things were for other people and had no relevance to him. He could never fail and so would possibly never die. He thought he was truly godly, and even perhaps that he was a god. The only gods he knew were carved statues that could neither move nor talk, made by the hands of men. He knew that he was certainly better than they and if they represented some higher powers he was confident that he spoke and acted on their behalf. He had no fear of any living thing and because of this, all living things had reason to be in fear of him.

Unlike the tyrannical Pharaoh of Musa (as), who is mentioned numerous times in The Qur'an, Namrud is mentioned only once and he is simply called the *kaffir*, the one who persists in denying truth (2:258). He is neither referred to by name nor by title. It is explained that, until Pharaoh's rejection of Musa (as), he was a just and beneficent ruler. For this reason, Allah gives him the indirect honor of mentioning him in The Qur'an by his kingly title. There is, however, apparently no good that can be said of Namrud. Muslims only received knowledge of his name from Hebrew sources.

One night Namrud had a dream in which a light appeared suddenly in the night sky. It began as a speck and, as he watched with his sleeping eyes, it grew rapidly brighter until it was the brightest thing in the whole sky. He continued to watch, unable to turn his horrified eyes away. The intensity of the light increased, pulsing against the darkness that encircled it. First the pinpoint sparkle of the guiding stars slipped beneath the tide of light. Then the soft glow of the sacred moon was swallowed whole. As the blessed sun rose, it too was quickly submerged in the sea of radiant light until nothing else existed in all his dream universe but the waves of light that appeared to be coming straight for him. He shot awake, his heart pounding. He felt fear for the first time in his life and he didn't like it. A strange thought entered his mind that maybe he would one day actually be gone and that everything he had built and amassed and arranged would be erased without trace. Maybe there was something bigger than him.

He called the wisest men in his kingdom to his side and asked them to interpret his dream, to interpret it in a way that would restore his confidence and his sense of power. They told him that a boy was to be born who would, if allowed to live, replace him and efface him. They had a plan. They must extinguish this bringer of light while he was still a baby, before he could defend himself or fulfill his destiny. Because the king didn't believe there was any power above his own or any creative will beyond his own, the destiny of all things must consequently lie firmly in his hands. Therefore, he could take action and feel like himself again.

So he sent messengers running down every alley and lane in the kingdom announcing his mighty decree. Husbands and wives must keep away from each other for the whole of the coming year. If they failed to do this and a boy child was born, he would be killed without recourse whoever he was. Women already pregnant would be imprisoned until they delivered and then sent home clutching to their breasts only the baby girls. Like an old lion raging against the inevitable, he lashed out to kill any of the cubs who might be a threat to him.

The king kept his male courtiers on duty in his many palaces attending to his many needs. He sent his soldiers to faraway lands on contrived campaigns to pillage and lay waste. His governors he kept busy with trials and petitions, exacting taxes and changing policy. The women were bound to their homes to tend to their domestic affairs alone. The poor farmers and their wives, who worked the land together, were ordered to double their production so that they labored in the fields from dawn to dusk. By the time they sank onto their sleeping mats they were too exhausted to care who lay beside them. And when a mistake happened, which it naturally did, the outcome was death.

The father of Ibrahim (ra) worked for Namrud but he did not worship him or mistake him for a god. He was a descendant of the children of Nuh (as) and he had not forgotten his Lord. One day Namrud sent him on an important mission that happened to take him in the vicinity of his own home. He asked for, and was given, permission to visit his wife and family as long as he kept strictly to the recent command of his king to avoid intimate relations. He had no doubt that he would have the strength to keep his promise and stay at a distance. His wife, Usha (rah), was also dutiful and she kept herself carefully concealed under voluminous skirts and heavy shawls. But as Allah willed, a garment shifted and a veil fell, and Abu Ibrahim (ra) lay with his beloved just one time.

An overview of the remains of houses one of which is said to be the house of Ibrahim's (as) family. In the background is the great ziggurat of Ur. Iraq.

CHAPTER FIVE
The Return of the Light

A few months later Usha (rah) discovered she had conceived a child. She did not know what to do. Since it was a clear sign that she and her husband had broken the law, Abu Ibrahim (ra) might lose his job or even his life. If they found out, the priests would keep a watchful eye on her to see what sort of child she might deliver. If it was a boy he would certainly be killed. Some say that she kept the news a secret from everyone. Some say that she found a way to send word to her husband. His immediate reaction was joy until he realized the consequences. He advised his wife to keep her secret from everyone else, even the members of her household and family. She confided in none of them and no one guessed that she was pregnant. The commentators say that perhaps she was still very young herself and had yet to mature, so her household noticed no changes. Others say that she was already old and her people considered her past the possibility of bearing children and so they thought nothing of her growing girth. Whether old or young it is not so unusual to be able to conceal a pregnancy for many months. Some say this was the first child for Usha (rah) but most say they had two boys already half grown, named Harran and Nahor.

When her time came due and she felt her labor beginning, Usha (rah) retreated to a cave that her husband had prepared for her. Others say, however, that she wandered into the wilderness in desperation, not knowing where to go. A being of light appeared before her and guided her to a cave hidden deep in the mountainside. There she was delivered of a son. Some have said he was born on the tenth of Muharram, the day on which many of Allah's signs have been revealed and the trials of the prophets have been relieved. Adam (as) was forgiven, the Ark of Nuh (as) found dry land, the sea split open for Musa (as), and Yunus (as) emerged from the fish, all on that auspicious day.

He was a beautiful boy. It was as if a light shone from his forehead illuminating the cave and he smiled sweetly at his mother. Usha (rah) drifted in and out, not sure if she was dreaming or awake. The cave seemed at times like a royal palace. There were soft pillows and rugs to cushion the cold floor. There were hangings of brocade and silk to cover the rough rock walls. Figures of light moved gently around her bringing refreshing drinks and whatever she needed. She rested peacefully with the small infant nestled close to her.

The father of Ibrahim (ra) came to see the baby soon after he was born. As he held this precious child close in the thick shadow of the cave, he was awed by the Light of Muhammad (sas) shining from the little face resting on his arm. According to the Torah he was inspired to name him Abram. In Hebrew '*ab*' means father and '*ram*' means high. Since Allah in Hebrew is also referred to as '*Ab*' the name can be translated as either Exalted Father or child of the Most High.

When he was almost a hundred years old, the Torah says that Allah changed his name from Abram to Abraham (as). The Torah explains this new name as meaning "the father of multitudes", the father of many tribes of believers, but there is no Hebrew word that still exists to support this meaning. The Old Testament scholars look to the closely related Semitic language of Arabic. There they find *raham*, which means soft continuing showers, the kind of rain that soaks everything gently and thoroughly. It is a rain that nourishes and encourages growth. There is a derivative word *ruhaam* that can mean abundance probably because the drops of this kind of rain are small and abundant but also because the result of such a rain is to gently generate abundance. Ibrahim (as) was to be the origin of showers of regenerating blessings for all the world. His spiritual children would grow and spread and hold fast to the worship of God. The Torah says he would be a blessing for all people.

In The Qur'an he has only one name, Ibrahim (as). However, in one traditional style of recitation (the *qira'a* of Ibn 'Amir) it is written and pronounced Ibraham (as). And in another traditional scriptural variation, it is pronounced Ibrahim but spelled differently for the fifteen times it appears in the first long chapter, *Suratu l-Baqara*. This is said to be a subtle indication of the name change that is mentioned more explicitly in the Torah.

The thirteenth century classical commentator, al-Qurtubi said that Ibrahim stands for *ab rahim*, meaning merciful father. In both Arabic and Hebrew, although the h of Ibrahim and the h of *rahim* are not the same, the meaning is most appropriate. This tiny baby who would first be tested by being nobody's father and then be tested by his fatherly love and end up being considered the father of over half of the world, was appropriately named for what he would become – the father of the faithful.

When Usha (rah) was strong enough, after her forty days had passed, she returned to her house. They knew that if the officials found out they would kill the baby so she swaddled him tightly and left him in the protection of Allah in the cave. She blocked the entrance with a stone to prevent wild animals and other intruders from entering. The cave was actually quite far from her house but she was carried smoothly and swiftly over the long path in such a way that she did not feel or realize the length of the journey. Every morning and every night, when she could, she visited the cave to nurse her child. She always found him sucking on the fingers of his right hand. She noticed that he was growing plump and strong more quickly than other babies. One day she gently pulled his fingers from his mouth and found that the first one dripped butter, the second honey, from the third ran pure water, and from the forth he sucked milk. It was as if all the sacred rivers of Paradise were flowing through his little body. Others say instead that he nursed from the tip of the wing of the Archangel Jibra'il (as). Either way he was raised on heavenly provision.

Ibrahim (as) grew quickly. Each day was like a week, each week like a month, perhaps each month like a year. He had never seen any human being other than his mother and father and he had never been outside the cave, but he was not stunted or forgotten. His Lord protected him, raised him, nurtured him. **And, indeed, long ago We bestowed right judgment on Ibrahim and We knew him well.** (21:51).

The reconstructed great ziggurat of Ur on which sat a temple to the gods.

The blessed tree in Jordan under which the Prophet Muhammad (sas) sat as a young man and where he met the monk Bahira. The last living sahaba.

CHAPTER SIX
Fathers and Forefathers

At some point during this time Abu Ibrahim (ra) must have died. Perhaps he only saw his infant son once. Usha (rah), as was the custom, was offered marriage by one of his older kinsmen, maybe even his older brother. She chose to accept this offer because it would mean she and her children would be taken care of by family rather than by a stranger who might resent having to raise another's child. Probably this is the man who is called Azar in The Qur'an. He was a very successful craftsman, and he took on the responsibility of raising and fathering Abu Ibrahim's (ra) sons. He was not a bad man but he was not on the straight path which is why *azar* means crooked. Azar, though descended from the family of prophets, had abandoned worship of the one God. He served Namrud and he served Namrud's gods with pride and devotion. He worked as a carver of idols. He actually made with his own hands the gods his people adored and he must have believed that he had a special inspired ability to translate their divinity into stone or wood. He was perhaps the best carver in the kingdom and Namrud brought him close and trusted him and made him carver to the king. He was supposed to in turn memorialize Namrud as he wanted to be remembered and to set his legacy in stone to endure for all time, or so they thought.

The parents of prophets are clean and god-fearing, without exception. The Prophet Muhammad (sas) said about his own lineage that, going back to Adam (as), his ancestors were pious believers, the best of their generation in virtue and morality. He said that all prophets have the same pure descent. "Allah continued moving me [Muhammad (sas)] from the pure backs of fathers to the pure wombs of mothers. Never would a family line branch out into two except that I was in the best of the two." (Hadith Bukhari). Since Ibrahim (as) and his parents are in the lineage of the Prophet (sas) this must describe them also.

Abraham in Hebrew.

In the Torah, the father of Ibrahim (as) is called Terah or Tarakh. In the Talmud he is sometimes called Zahar. In a work by the third century Christian historian Eusebius he is called Athar. In The Qur'an Allah calls the father of Ibrahim (as) Azar (6:74). The 'th' easily turns into 'z'. According to The Qur'an Azar made his living by carving idols with his own hands. If we are to believe the hadith quoted above, Azar could not have fathered a prophet. The early historians explain this by saying that Azar was only the stepfather of Ibrahim (as) although The Qur'an explicitly calls Azar his father. Often in Arabic, as in English, 'father' can denote an ancestor or other male relative. Allah speaking to the Prophet Muhammad (sas) in The Qur'an tells him to follow the religion of **your father (*abikum*) Ibrahim** (22:78) although here the meaning is forefather not actual father. In addition, when the prophet Ya'qub (as) is dying he asks his sons who they will worship when he is gone and they reply: **We shall worship your God and the God of your fathers (*aba'ika*) Ibrahim, Isma'il, and Ishaq, one God.** (2:133). Ya'qub's (as) grandfather, uncle, and actual father are collectively called his fathers. Sayyida Maryam (rah) is called the daughter of Imran (66:12) although he was an ancestor not her actual father. In addition, there is a Hadith of the Prophet (sas) in which he relates the meeting between Ibrahim (as) and Azar in the hereafter. In this Hadith the Prophet (sas) refers to Azar as the farthest father, *abi l-ab'adi*, of

Ibrahim (as). (Bukhari). When Abu Talib (ra) took the Prophet Muhammad (sas) to Syria as a boy, they met a monk on the way who asked about the boy and his father. Abu Talib (ra) replied that he was the boy's father. But Bahira (ra) the monk knew that the father of that very special boy could not be living. Only then did Abu Talib (ra) say that he was actually the uncle of Sayyiduna Muhammad (sas) and his guardian.

Ibrahim in Arabic.

Another way some of the early Muslim historians explain this is to say that Terah, whose name is found only in the Torah, was the actual biological father of the prophet Ibrahim (as) and Azar, whose name is found in The Qur'an, was his stepfather. But in the Torah (Joshua 24:2) Terah is identified as an idol worshiper. Trading one name for the other doesn't seem to make much of an improvement. It could be that Terah and Azar are different names for the same man. Azar was his first name, a description of his character, derived from the Sumerian meaning crooked. Terah was his last name, his family or clan name derived from the Hebrew, meaning wild goat or wanderer. In the genealogies found in the Torah, Terah was the son of Serug, who was the son of Nahor who was descended from Arpachshad the son of Sam (as) the son of Nuh the prophet (as). Terah was the name of a clan of Semitic speaking pastoral nomads. Whether they were one man or two men, neither was the biological father of a prophet.

Azar is the name of a male relative of Ibrahim (as), his *ab*. We have to conclude that perhaps we do not know the name of the biological father, *walid*, of Ibrahim (as). For the purposes of this story we will simply call him Abu Ibrahim (ra), father of Ibrahim, and guess that he died soon after the birth of his third son. Terah or Azar are the interchangeable names of either the relative or step-father of Sayyiduna Ibrahim (as), the one who raised him. None of the other five major prophets were raised by their birth fathers either. Adam (as) of course had no birth father or mother and was not raised by anyone since he was created full grown. Musa (as) was raised by Pharaoh as an adopted father or master. 'Isa (as) also had no biological father and was raised by his stepfather Saint Joseph (ra). The father of the Prophet Muhammad (sas), 'Abdullah (ra), died a few months before his only son was born and Muhammad (sas) was raised by his grandfather Abdu l-Muttalib (ra) and then by his uncle Abu Talib (ra). Perhaps it can be said that these remarkable men were removed from their parents to be raised instead under the eye of Allah, as it is said about Musa (as): **And [thus early] I spread My own love over you – in order that you might be formed under My eye.** (20:39)

Abu Ibrahim (ra) was a direct descendant of the Prophet Nuh (as) through his son Sam (as), ten generations of grandfathers and grandmothers who were pure and righteous, all of them believers in the One God, the God of Nuh (as) and of Adam (as). His wife, the mother of Ibrahim (as), is not named in the Torah but she is called Amtilai or Amathlai (rah) in the Talmud and Ednah in the Book of Jubilees. The Muslim biographers call her Usha (rah). She was also a believer and most probably a girl from the same family. May Allah bless them both.

CHAPTER SEVEN
Ar-Rabb

Ibrahim (as) spent many years alone in the cave, mostly in the company of angels. He must have delighted in the lights that sparkled and danced on the dark walls as they bent to bow and prostrate in prayer and he was lulled to sleep by the beautiful praises they sang of their Lord. He played happily in their gentle company. They were the best of caretakers. And all the while he kept growing quickly.

As his mind developed there were certain truths that he took for granted. He knew he was not alone. He knew there was someone outside of himself who cared for him, who watched over him, who was deserving of his thanks and his service and he wanted to confirm it with the people closest to him. Once when his mother came to visit he asked her, "Who is my master?" Of course she answered, as all mothers hope, "I am your master." "Then who is your master?" Ibrahim (as) continued. And she answered as all husbands hope, "Your father is my master". "Then who is my father's master?" "The king Namrud" Usha (rah) replied. "Then who is the king's master?" asked the innocent boy. "Be quiet" said his mother.

This word 'master' is the translation of the Arabic *rabb*. However,

Arabic Calligraphy – Ya Rabb – O Lord, Master, and Cherisher.

there is not a single English word that covers the full scope of this word. *Rabb* in Arabic has three levels of meaning. The first level means lord and master, owner; the one with authority over you as a master has authority over a slave. The second level means the one who nourishes and cherishes, the one who takes care of and sustains. A *rabb* is the one who provides for and watches over what belongs to him. The third level means to raise or to grow, as a parent raises his child, as a farmer cares for his crops. It implies helping something to reach its full potential, to mature and bloom. But whereas the parent and the farmer, however kindly and unselfish, have some degree of self interest in the result of their efforts, Allah has none. Allah, as *Ar-Rabb* of His creation, is only concerned for the sake of the creation. He neither benefits nor profits from the outcome. So His role of caretaker is unique. All the *du'a* mentioned in The Qur'an begin with addressing Allah as *Ar-Rabb*, Master, Owner, and Cherisher. Allah is not only a Master to be obeyed but also a Caretaker whose only goal is to help his servant fulfill his personal destiny. He is the one whose displeasure we should fear and whose pleasure is our only hope.

The child Ibrahim (as) did not wonder who is his master – who has authority over him. If it were so then the answer to his first question would properly be his father. Instead his first *rabb* was his mother, who gave birth to him and nourished him and gently raised him. He was asking who is the one taking care of him, who is the one he knows, who loves him, the one to whom his heart responds?

Usha (rah) went home and told Azar. The next time he went to the cave Ibrahim (as) asked him the same series of questions. "Who is my *rabb*?" he asked. "Your mother" replied Azar. And who is the *rabb* of my mother?" "I am" replied his father. "So who then is your *rabb*?" asked the curious boy. "Namrud, the king" said Azar in a sharp but proud way, hoping to put an end to the questioning. But Ibrahim (as) continued in his childish voice, "Then who is the *rabb* of Namrud?" "Be quiet" shouted Azar and in his fear he slapped the child.

Did Namrud have a master? Namrud like Pharaoh said, **I am your lord most high** (79:24). Was there anyone above him in power or authority? If there were, His name could not be spoken or His existence whispered. That night Usha (rah) and Azar gave each other distressed looks. Each knew what the other was thinking. This boy, Ibrahim (as), was the very boy about whom the soothsayers had warned. He was the bright star, the radiant light that would overwhelm Namrud and the darkness that surrounded him. Azar worried about his job and his position. Usha (rah) worried about her son. Namrud himself, however, seemed to have all but forgotten about the dream. After many years nothing had come of the prophecy. The kingdom was still intact. Namrud still ruled unchallenged. He assumed that the threat had been taken care of, that the dangerous baby had been dealt with. No mention had been made in many years of the boy babies, a hundred thousand of them according to some narrators, who had lost their lives for nothing.

Azar was not interested in changing destiny or affecting the big picture. He was probably a kindly but misguided man who wanted to protect his family and his social status. He hoped he was wrong and that his brother's indiscretion would go unnoticed, and be without consequence. He hoped that somehow he could integrate this son into the community without making even the smallest wave. But just as Pharaoh had known in his heart that the baby Musa (as) he was adopting was the prophet he feared, so Azar knew. But Allah's plan was not only to make the efforts of all tyrants in vain, but also to bring the very thing they feared right up to the threshold of their house.

CHAPTER EIGHT

The Cave of Fitra

Allah made man with His own hands and breathed into him from His spirit. Mankind was made in His likeness and enlivened with His holy breath. We know Allah as we know ourselves. We have love for Him imbedded in our every cell. We belong to Him and our purpose is to serve Him. This is how we were made. It is our *fitra,* our natural state. **And so, set thy face steadfastly towards the [one ever-true] faith (*dini hanifa*), turning away from all that is false, in accordance with the natural disposition (*fitra*) which Allah has instilled into man: [for,] not to allow any change to corrupt what Allah has thus created this is the [purpose of the one] ever-true faith; but most people know it not** (30:30).

Allah Almighty questioned the souls of all people while they were still inside their father Adam (as), on the day called the Day of Promises. **'Am I not your Lord?'** He asked. **To which they answered, 'Yes, indeed, of that we bear witness'.** (7:172). The Prophet (sas) said that all children are born in this state of *fitra*. This is their natural state in which they still remember their Lord and their promise to Him. *Fitra* is our original state and that state is submission to Allah. The Arabic word for this state of

The entrance to the Halilu r-Rahman Mosque in Urfa Turkey, that leads to the cave in which Ibrahim (as) was born and runs along side the Paradise pool.

acceptance or submission, is - Islam. So the hadith states that all children are born Muslim. Their parents make them Jewish, Christian or other. To this could be added - or 'Muslim' - because someone's group affiliation or what they write on government forms is not what is meant. The meaning of Muslim in this context is the uncorrupted state of Islam, at peace with and in full acceptance of, the ultimate Truth, the way in which Allah made us all.

Ibrahim (as) was born in this state, as are all children, but unlike most children he continued to live in this state until he was well past infancy. In the cave, away from the pressures and influences of society and family, he grew as a tree grows freely in an open field, bathed in the divine light and nourished on heavenly mercy. He was not bent or bound by trying to please others or trying to fit in. This allowed his heart to guide him on its natural path. **Like a good tree, its root firm and its branches in the sky, yielding its fruit at all times by permission of its Lord.** (14:24) Some of the great saints were also like this; the veil of forgetfulness that falls over the hearts of most of the children of Adam (as) never descended to blind their hearts. They lived as if confined within the stone walls of a cave, pure and protected. Ibrahim (as) is said to have remained in the solitary sanctuary of the cave of *fitra* until he was at least ten, until he had almost reached the age of responsibility.

And someone like this, whose heart has not been veiled but who retains his state of *fitra*, is called *hanif*. So Ibrahim (as) is called Ibrahim the Hanif repeatedly by Allah in The Qur'an. Sometimes this word is translated into English as, 'by nature upright' (Pickthall); sometimes as 'one who rejects falsehood' (Muhammad Asad), 'true in faith' (Yusuf Ali and Abdel Halim), "a man of pure faith" (Ali Unal), "ever inclined to Him" (Sher Ali), "a monotheist" (Khalifa). In all cases, however, it is a rare and remarkable person who is *hanif*. Despite his environment and his upbringing, despite all the pressures on him to conform to whatever is the current ideology, he remains true to the certainty of his heart, true to the form in which he was made by his Creator. He simply knows what is right and what is wrong as clearly as he knows night from day. And, perhaps without even knowing why, he makes his life decisions based on this fundamental certainty. **Ibrahim was indeed a model, devoutly obedient to Allah, true in faith (*hanif*), and he joined no gods with God.** (16:120).

This was not a new concept introduced by The Qur'an. It is an age-old concept of which Sayyiduna Ibrahim (as) is the prime and most perfect example. It can also be found mentioned in the pre-Islamic poetry of the Arabs. At the time of the birth of the Prophet Muhammad (sas) there were at least two men who were known as *hanif* in Mecca. One was the uncle of Sayyida Khadija (rah), the Prophet's (sas) wife, whose name was Waraqa ibn Nawfal (ra). He was able to read the scriptures of the Jews and Christians. After the Prophet's first encounter with Jibra'il (as), Sayyida Khadija (rah) took him to talk to Waraqa (ra). Waraqa (ra) recognized and confirmed immediately the prophethood of Muhammad (sas) and lamented the fact that he was old and would probably not live to support the Prophet (sas) in his mission. It was Qutayla (rah), the sister of Waraqa (ra), who had seen Abdullah ibn Abdu l-Muttalib passing by on his wedding night and had recognized the Light of Muhammad (sas) shining from his father's forehead and desired its blessing for herself.

The second *hanif* was Zayd ibn 'Amr ibn Nufayl (ra) who left Arabia in search of the true religion. He discovered from both Christianity and Judaism that there was something called the religion of Ibrahim the Hanif (as) and he dedicated himself to find and follow that. Asma bint Abi Bakr (ra) said that as a young girl she had seen him standing with his back against the Ka'ba declaring strongly his belief in the one God to the idol worshipping Quraysh. He would refuse to eat the meat sacrificed in the name of idols saying, "Allah created the sheep, grew the grass to feed it, sent the rain to water it, how then can you sacrifice it in the name of other than Allah?" At that time the Arabs had a reprehensible practice of killing their girl babies thinking it a waste of resources to raise girls. Zayd (ra) would take these babies and raise them in his own household. When they were grown he would offer them back to their fathers if they chose. He was banished from Mecca by his uncle al-Khattab, the father of Sayyiduna 'Umar (ra). Sadly, he died returning to Mecca to meet Muhammad (sas). With his last breath he prayed that his son Sa'id (ra) would follow the Prophet (as). Sa'id ibn Zayd (ra) was one of the first Muslims and one of the ten guaranteed Paradise. He was married to the sister of Sayyiduna 'Umar (ra) and it was in their house that Sayyiduna 'Umar (ra) first read The Qur'an and where Islam entered his heart.

The Prophet Muhammad (as) was kept pure from having anything to do with the idols his people worshiped and from the indecencies they practiced. He said that at one time he was thinking to go to a wedding party but, on the way from the pasture where he was taking care of the sheep, Allah caused him to fall asleep. In this way he was protected from committing even this one possible indiscretion. Without following any master or any scripture, he used to climb the mountains above Mecca to fast and pray for many years before The Qur'an was revealed to him. He knew with certainty that there was a right way to live and to believe. He was determined to cling to that way. It was as if he had a sixth sense that enabled him to always choose the straight way. When his mission was delivered, Allah ordered him to follow the way of the Prophet Ibrahim (as). **And lastly, We have inspired thee, [O Muhammad, with this message:] Follow the creed of Ibrahim, who turned away from all that is false (*hanif*), and was not of those who ascribe divinity to aught beside Allah (*mushrik*).** (16:123)

Inside the cave in which Ibrahim (as) was born, Urfa.

A clay impression made from a cylindrical seal dated to 2,000 BCE, showing the Akkadian gods. Inanna (Venus) is on the left. Shamash (the sun) is cutting his way through the mountains in order to rise for the day. The conical hats with horns indicate they are gods.

CHAPTER NINE

Things That Set

When Ibrahim was around ten years old, Azar decided to take him out of hiding. The cave was actually quite far from where they lived. When she had been going to nurse Ibrahim (as) Usha (rah) hadn't noticed but she had been carried swiftly on invisible wings. But now that they were bringing Ibrahim (as) out into the world they had to travel in the regular fashion and they found the journey much longer than they had anticipated. They took him out of the cave in the late afternoon hoping to reach the outskirts of the city as it grew dark so that their arrival would go unnoticed. Ibn Abbas (ra) says that as they walked, Ibrahim (as) looked with wonder and curiosity at all the things and animals they passed. He asked his father about each of them: "What is that father? What is that?" And Azar patiently answered him: "That is a cow my son. That is a sheep, a dog, a horse." All the things of the wide world were new to Ibrahim (as).

The journey was long. It was the middle of the month and as it got dark the first bright light to show on the horizon was Venus. And perhaps Ibrahim (as) asked about it or perhaps Azar volunteered the information that this was his god Inanna rising in the night sky. **When the night grew** dark over him he [Ibrahim] saw a star and said, 'This is my Lord,' but when it set, he said,' I do not like things that set.' (6:76)**

As it got darker suddenly Ibrahim (as) saw an even brighter light appear on the opposite side of the sky. **And when he saw the moon rising he said, 'This is my Lord,'** (6:77). They continued to walk slowly by the light of the full moon, taking turns supporting the child. The way seemed much longer than they remembered and many times they thought they had lost the path. They found a soft spot and rested there. The three of them lay and looked at the vast sky, appreciating the sight in a new way through the wondering eyes of their child. Azar informed his son that this was the great god Sin whose temple dominated their city and whose many forms and faces Azar himself had carved into countless blocks of wood. And perhaps he told him stories of the exploits of Sin and of his wives and children.

They started walking again, picking their way among the bushes and stones partially lit by the glow of the moon. Slowly the lovely moon also made its way across the sky and disappeared just as Venus had done earlier. **When it too set, he said, 'If my Lord does not guide me, I shall be one of those who go astray'** (6:77). And Ibrahim (as) categorically rejected the idea that the moon was God. More significantly he realized immediately that his limited ability was not enough to answer a question that was clearly beyond the scope of his five senses. He needed help. He turned instinctively to the only One who could really help, the only One who actually knew the answer, the One he had come to trust. And since he turned in the right direction he received clarity and certainty.

A new brightness spread across the sky. Little Ibrahim (as) watched in wonder as the huge orb of the sun rose above the distant horizon in a pool of color. "What is this father?" he must have asked in astonishment. "This is Shamash, god of the sun, son of the moon, sister of Venus, the one who watches over us in the day" said Azar with misplaced piety. And Ibrahim (as) for the first time thought that his father might be right. **Then he [Ibrahim] saw the sun rising and cried, "This is my Lord! This is greater"** (6:78).

His mother and father sighed with relief. His father was relieved because he thought he had communicated his religious beliefs to his child. His mother was relieved because she did not want her son to be the one

Namrud was hunting. They approached their house from the garden side and slid noiselessly through the back door before any neighbors saw them. They ate a little and slept. That evening from a crack in the closed door Ibrahim (as) watched as the darkening sky again broke into streaks of color and Shamash followed his father and sister below the horizon and out of the world. **But when the sun set, he said, "My people, I disown all that you worship beside Allah. I have turned my face as a true believer towards Him who created the heavens and the earth. I am not one of the polytheists"** (6:78-9).

Whether in one night or over a period of years, in a relatively short space of time and while very young, Ibrahim (as) considered, and then thoroughly rejected the world view of all of those around him. He had been shown something quite different. The God he knew intimately in the quiet of his heart was not one of the ones they worshiped. Allah says that He **showed Ibrahim the kingdom of the heavens and the earth that he might be of those possessing certainty** (6:75). Some believe that this means that Allah took Ibrahim (as) on a journey similar to the Night Journey (*mi'raj*) of the Prophet (sas). Allah showed him the dominion (*malakut*), the angelic realms and the reality behind physical appearances, the Cause behind all causes. When he later tells his father, **knowledge has come to me that has not come to you, so follow me.** (19:43), it is a simple statement of fact without pride or exaggeration.

The difference between the Creator and the created is neither subtle nor esoteric. It is clear and obvious. By looking at the creation perhaps a sense of who created it can be divined, as scholars analyze a text in order to psychoanalyze the author. But a creation on the scale of the universe posits a Creator of unimaginable power and knowledge. Looking within our own selves, creatures of great psychological and physical complexity, how much greater and how much more complex must our Creator be? Ibrahim (as) could not help but wonder how it was possible for the act to be mistaken for the Actor, the expression to be mistaken for the Speaker, the creation mistaken for the Creator. Clearly the two are just not the same category of thing. And he saw no sense in relying on something that is here today and gone tomorrow. He said with great wisdom and yet with the simplicity of a child: **I do not like things that set, that pass away** (6:76). He would only worship the One who is eternal and unchanging.

An Assyrian king's head on the body of a divine bull.

CHAPTER TEN

Teasing the Gods

They faced no problems it seems introducing Ibrahim (as) into society. We don't know what reason they gave for his late appearance. Perhaps they said that they had left him with some relatives. He had been too young to travel and only now had his relatives found a way to send him. He seemed so much older than he actually was that no one thought he was from the generation of sacrificed children and no one really wanted to remember Namrud's dream and the terrible nightmare it had engendered.

Azar labored hard at his carving. He had a workshop with many men working under him turning out statues big and small, friezes, cylindrical seals and historical steles. He employed his older sons to hawk the smaller statues in the marketplaces. They would carry sacks of them on their backs, maybe just the ones made of wood, and try to interest people in buying their own personal idol to set up on altars in their houses. Azar expected Ibrahim (as) to help. But Ibrahim (as) was not interested in getting people to spend their hard-earned money on useless things and for certain he thought the statues were useless. Instead he would take the idols down to the river where he would swim and play with them, teasing them like naughty dolls. He would offer them food and then shout at them for not eating. He would hit them and ask them to fight back. Sometimes it is said, he tied strings around their necks and dragged them through the dusty streets like children's pull toys. Who then would buy a dirty, chipped statue? And when the other boys returned with all their wares sold and money in their pockets, Ibrahim (as) would return as he had left. Or worse, he would return with nothing, neither statues nor money. From Azar's point of view, he was really quite rebellious, a shame for the community and a trial for the family.

As he grew older Ibrahim (as) didn't just play with the idols or refuse to sell them. He became more bold and would hang around the marketplaces talking to whoever would listen. He would tell them about the majesty of Allah to whom they owed everything. He would try to explain what was flawed in their understanding. He pointed out the uselessness of talking to, or expecting help from lifeless things. He used to say, "Why do you worship what causes you no harm and brings you no good?" But of course the idols did cause harm because they diverted worship from its true object, just as a man with a curable disease is harmed by taking a placebo. And they bring no good because they are man-made things with no life of their own, no power and no sense. But talking to the men in the town was like talking to the statues themselves. **Deaf are they, and dumb, and blind: for they do not use their reason** (2:171).

The thing was that Ibrahim (as) was not a crazy person. He was not wild or rude. He was not ranting or raving. He was an intelligent young man, serious, gentle, and kind. The Prophet Muhammad (sas) saw him while on his Night Journey in the seventh heaven and described him as being most like himself. Allah describes him as *awahun halim* – **compassionate and mild mannered** (9:114). He, like the Prophet Muhammad (sas), was admirable in every way, reasonable and personable, honest and trustworthy, clean and noble. In Islamic spiritual literature Ibrahim (as) is the prime example of a *fata* (21:60)– a spiritual knight, a noble youth, exhibiting all the fine qualities of a true hero. He was sure of his path, sure of his guidance, and sure of his Guide. The absolutely only thing about him that was not acceptable to the people around him and that caused problems, was his belief in Allah, the one God and Creator.

The Qur'an cites several of the conversations he had with his people as examples of the thousands that must have actually taken place. There was no stopping him. There was no pleading with him to keep his ideas to himself. There was no argument that even remotely swayed him or gave him pause. He knew what Allah had given him to know. He knew it with a certainty that could not be shaken. Ibrahim (as) asked his father and his people: **'What do you worship?'** (26:70) **They said, 'We worship idols, and are constantly in attendance on them'** (26:71). **He asked, 'Do they hear you when you call? Do they help or harm you?'** (26:72-3). **They replied, 'No but this is what we saw our fathers doing'** (26:74). **Ibrahim said, 'Those idols that you have worshipped, you and your forefathers, are my enemies; not so for the Lord of the Worlds who created me. It is He who guides me; He who gives me food and drink; He who cures me when I am ill; He who will make me die and then gives me life again; and He who will, I hope, forgive my faults on the Day of Judgment.'** (26:75-82).

The people admonished him and tried to argue with him. They said he should be afraid to talk in this fashion. He should fear what the gods would do to him for they were angry, jealous, haughty little gods who took retribution for any small slight – just like their representative Namrud. Ibrahim (as) replied to them: **'How can you argue with me about Allah when He has guided me? I do not fear anything you associate with Him: unless my Lord wills [nothing can happen]. My Lord encompasses everything in His knowledge. How can you not take heed?'** (6:80). **'Why should I fear what you associate with Him? Why do you not fear to associate with Him things for which He has sent you no authority?'** (6:81). **Such was the argument We gave to Ibrahim against his people – We raise in rank whom We will – your Lord is all wise, all knowing** (6:83).

The people knew about El, the god of the sky and they knew He was the Creator but they did not believe that He cared about them or that He responded to their prayers any more. He had retreated far into the heavens, they said, chased away by younger, stronger gods; deposed and discarded by His own children in the manner in which they were accustomed to see their leaders behave. In other words, they accepted that He was *Ar-Rabb* the Creator but rejected Him as *Ar-Rabb* the One who cherishes and nourishes. For those qualities they looked to many smaller gods and goddesses, to help them, to heal them, and to soothe their hearts.

Al-hamdu liLlahi Rabbi l-'alamin – Praise be to Allah, Cherisher of the worlds.

And they did not hear or appreciate or thank the one God who continued to provide for them and call to them and hope that they would finally turn to Him. And they did not realize that standing before them, in the form of an ordinary young man, was in fact an extraordinary kindness - a Messenger sent specifically for them from Allah, the Cherisher of the Worlds (*Rabbu l-'Alamin*).

CHAPTER ELEVEN
The First Lie – Too Sick to Sin

People began to talk about Azar's strange son. Some thought there was wisdom in what he said and they listened, but most dismissed him as a child and paid no attention. When word reached his father of the unusual behavior of Ibrahim (as), at first Azar beat him thinking that fear would help change him. But nothing changed the faith and conviction of Ibrahim (as). Usha (rah) cried and reproached Azar for his harshness. It was, after all, their own fault for leaving Ibrahim (as) so long by himself in the cave, she said. How could they expect him to be as other children? How could they expect him to adjust perfectly to being in society? So Azar became softer and took the blame on himself and apologized to the people for the disturbing words of his son. He decided to send Ibrahim (as) to the temple to serve the priests. He hoped he would learn first hand about the religion and slowly be convinced. This turned out in some ways to be a perfect environment for the young man. It was quiet and clean. No one bothered him or disturbed his thoughts. He could contemplate and worship Allah in peace. No one questioned to whom his prayers were directed. No one guessed to whom his heart was turned. But he had to watch first-hand and up-close the pathos and absurdity of people asking for help from stones

Akkadian figurines of worshippers from Eshnunna dating to 2,000 BCE.

and clay. And he had to witness the cruelty and immorality committed in the name of worship. He did not last long in that position.

This went on for a while until one day it was time for the great festival when all the people leave the city to cavort and get drunk for the sake of their gods. Inanna, the goddess of fertility and the goddess of war, was also the patron of both beer and prostitution. Perhaps the people had the decency to leave their young ones at home while only the adults attended these orgies. But this year Azar felt it was time for his son to join them at the festival and he insisted Ibrahim (as) attend with them. Ibrahim (as) tried to be respectful and obedient although he found it sickeningly distasteful. He set out with his father and townspeople but after walking a little way he had to talk to them about what they were doing. **He said to his father and his people, 'What are these images to which you are so devoted?"** (21:52) **They replied, 'We found our fathers worshipping them'** (21:53) **He said, 'You and your fathers have clearly gone astray.'** (21:54) **They asked, 'Have you brought us the truth or are you just playing around?'** (21:55) **He said, 'Listen! Your true Lord is the Lord of the heavens and the earth, He who created them, and I am a witness to this.'** (21:56).

He was a witness. He had been taken on a journey to the seven heavens and the seven earths. He had seen with his own eyes some of the mysteries of creation and the indescribable greatness of its Maker. He was trying with all his heart to communicate and share what he knew to be true but there was no one who would take him seriously. At this point something changed. He realized that words were getting him nowhere. He could not do as his father wanted. He could not pretend to be what he was not. He must find some other way to awaken his people. They had not gone very far when he dropped to the ground in pain. It was all he could think of. His family gathered around him. Ibrahim (as) told them that he could not go any farther because he felt sick. This was not a complete lie for he did indeed feel sick at heart. He told his family to go on without him, he would make his way home when he felt better. So, anxious to be on their way, they left him in the middle of the road and continued on. (37:89). And as they left he said quietly to himself: **'And by Allah, I will surely plot against your idols after you have turned and gone away!'** (21:57).

Ibrahim (as) sat by the side of the road watching the crowds of townspeople passing, laughing excitedly, and behaving badly. He thought about where they were going and what they were doing. How far they were from the cleanliness and uprightness that Allah wanted for them. How far they were from any truth whatsoever. He waited until most of the crowds had passed and then rose unsteadily to his feet and made his way slowly back to the the great temple. He felt tired and full of disgust. There must be something he could do that would make his people open their eyes and see their lies and deceit and ugliness for what they were.

Back in the temple, Ibrahim (as) looked around him. In the large main room there were figures of every size and description, half naked men and fully naked women, half animal half human, of wood and stone, gilded with gold and silver, jeweled crowns on their empty heads, good food going to waste at their flat unmoving feet. There was one very large statue of Sin on the high place and then medium and small ones gathered around it on all sides and in every corner. Each one was adorned with costly things it could not use, bestowed with gifts it could not appreciate by some poor man or woman in desperate need. In the half light of the setting sun and the smoldering oil lamps, their faces leered at him with wordless mouths and huge sightless eyes. Empty emptiness wherever he looked.

There was an axe that was used for chopping firewood to keep the temple warm in winter. He went and got it. *"Bismillah"*, he said, "In the Name of Allah", and he began swinging the axe. **He struck them with his right arm.** (37:93) Wooden heads went rolling. Stone bodies crashed to the ground in pieces, their backs broken. Arms and hands shattered and splintered. Ibrahim (as) went on swinging the axe, destroying falsehood with every swing until all the stony crowd lay in pieces at the feet of the big statue of Sin. Sin, his arms folded against his chest, clutching the symbols of his imaginary rule in his huge hands, towered above his ruined realm. A small self pleased smile was fixed on his impassive face. From those proud and useless hands Ibrahim (as) hung the axe. And then he turned his back on them all and went home. **He broke them all into pieces, but left the biggest one for them to return to** (21:58). As he turned he said: **'I am clear of that which you worship apart from Him who created me, and He will surely guide me'** (43:26-27). **'My people, I disown all that you worship beside Allah. I have turned my face as a true believer towards Him who** created the heavens and the earth. I am not one of the polytheists (idol worshippers)' (6:78-9).

Central Asian miniature of a young Ibrahim (as) smashing the idols. Al-Biruni 10th century.

Nemrut's Mountain outside of Urfa Turkey. Built in the first century BCE by King Antiochus of Commagene, it illustrates the end result of false pride.

CHAPTER TWELVE
The Second Lie - A Bloodless Crime

In a few days the people returned from their festival outside the city somewhat tired and hungover. The priests and notables went first to the temple to visit the gods before they returned to their homes. They went in order to take the offerings of food and valuable items that had been laid at the feet of the idols days before. Even they knew that the statues had no possible use for these valuable things. They complemented themselves on their own generosity in giving the items and then took them back saying that the gods had blessed them and returned them as gifts. It was probably only the priests and their families who made away with the offerings. It was their share of the bounty.

When the heavy temple doors were unlocked and pulled open the priests and nobles found spread before them a frightful sight. The protectors of their families, the guardians of their city, the defenders of their nation, lay in chips and splinters, strewn about the marble floor, hacked to pieces in a bloodless crime. Some of the men were too stunned to utter a word. They sucked at the air in horror and could not find the breath to breathe out. They sank to the floor on their knees in soundless shock. Others immediately found voice for their anguish. They shrieked and wailed as if their whole family had been cut down in front of their eyes. They ran about frantically checking to make sure all the valuable items were accounted for. It must have been a dramatic spectacle.

When they had collected themselves a bit they began to investigate the destruction around them. They saw the axe hanging from the hands of the large statue of Sin and realized that this act had to have been perpetrated by someone. Who? **"Who has done this to our gods?"** (21:59). This was the question on all their lips as soon as they had recovered some sense. Some of them had heard Ibrahim (as) threaten the gods when they had left him sick on the road and all of them had heard the things he had been saying in the marketplaces for years. They said: **"We heard a youth mention them who is called Ibrahim"** (21:60). So then go bring him to us they said: **"Then bring him in front of the eyes of the people that they may testify"** (21:61). They set off for the house of Azar. They knocked on the door and asked Azar to bring out his son so they could talk to him. They were upset but they had not decided that Ibrahim (as) was the culprit, they just wanted to question him and see what he had to say. Azar accompanied him, not sure what was happening or why, trying to understand what had caused all these people, his friends and associates, to gather excitedly at his house. Ibrahim (as) knew the reason, however, and he did not cower or hide. They returned to the temple and faced the priests who him asked: **"Have you done this to our gods, O Ibrahim?"** (21:62). Confronted by the angry crowd Ibrahim (as) stood his ground. He was not surprised and he was not without an answer and a plan. He said: **"Rather, that one, the biggest of them did it. So ask them if they are able to speak!"** (21:63). Ibrahim (as) accused the big statue of Sin of having chopped up its rivals. Didn't they see the axe still in its hand? Didn't they see it was the only one left standing? Why didn't they ask it first if they thought it is a living god that can hear and respond to them? And so by divine inspiration Ibrahim (as) had caught them in the web of their own deceit.

Now they were confused for they knew that these statues could neither speak nor wield an axe. Caught off guard, at first it seemed that what Ibrahim (as) was telling them was reasonable and **They turned back to themselves and said, "Indeed you are the ones who are misguided"** (21:64). Either they began to question the basis of their beliefs or they were ashamed not to have turned to the gods first before looking for answers from a human being. But then The Qur'an says they quickly reversed themselves again. Perhaps some reasonable people were ready to accept that the gods they worshiped in fact had not even the power to protect themselves let alone others. They might have been open to listening to some other explanation of the world and of truth. But something happened. Those who had an invested interest in keeping things as they were, those with political power which they said they inherited from these gods, threatened or convinced the people and soon **They reversed themselves** [literally they were turned on their heads] **and said, "You know very well that these cannot speak"** (21:65). This is a perfect image. These people, like the wooden statues they worshipped, were metaphorically turned upside down. They reversed their intellectual position. Heads in the dirt, feet waving helplessly in the air, they were totally confused. They accused Ibrahim (as) of not fearing to destroy the idols because he also knew that the statues could not testify against him. Whether they could speak or not was no longer the issue. He had assaulted objects, these poor helpless idols, that they and their fathers before them cherished. Ibrahim (as) said: **"Then do you worship, instead of Allah, something that cannot benefit you, in any way, nor harm you?"** (21:66). **"Shame on you and what you worship other than Allah! Will you not then use your mind?"** (21:67). Their final answer was simply: **"Burn him and avenge your gods, if you are going to do the right thing"** (21:68).

The people had judged him. They no longer were going to tolerate his dissension. He was a neighbor, the son of a respected member of the community, but they were afraid to let him continue freely. He had power and had almost convinced some of the people of the truth of his position. They could no longer laugh or look the other way. Ibrahim (as) had become seditious. His religious views threatened civic order and the authority of the state. They would press charges with the powers that be. They would now turn him over to the royal court to try him and judge him and enact the appropriate punishment. He was taken to the court of Namrud, the tyrant king, the one who walked the earth as if he owned it, the one who presented himself to the people as their master and their god, the one who felt accountable to no one.

The victory stele of Naram-Sin, shows the king, wearing the horned hat of a god, in triumph over his enemies.

CHAPTER THIRTEEN
Life and Death

It is recounted that the entrance to Namrud's throne room was built low to the ground, forcing those entering to duck their heads and bend double. This ensured that everyone entered the presence of the king bowing almost to the ground whether they wanted to or not. Ibrahim (as) watched as the guards prostrated and entered. Quickly he thought of a way to avoid bowing to the tyrant. When his turn to enter came, he spun around and entered the low doorway backwards so that he bowed in the opposite direction to the king and presented himself bottom first in what must have been a very disrespectful, if not outright rude, attitude.

Namrud was surprised but was secure enough to laugh it off. He was used to having crazy people brought up before him. "Why do you not bow to me in the proper fashion?" was his first question for Ibrahim (as). The prophet answered that he bowed before no one but his Lord and Creator, Allah. Namrud had never heard of this before and so he asked "Who is this Allah, who is your Lord instead of me?" Ibrahim answered: **"My Lord is the one who grants life and deals death"** (2:258). Namrud replied: **"I grant life and deal death"** (2:258). Then he called for two prisoners who had just been tried before the royal court. One had been judged innocent but had not yet been released and the other had been found guilty and had yet to be sentenced. Namrud took his spear and summarily took the life of the innocent man and then he ordered the guilty one to be set free. He had reversed the judgment of the court by his whim and dealt death where there should have been life and granted life where there should have been death. Then he looked at the horror stricken Ibrahim (as) with satisfaction and triumph.

Poor Ibrahim (as) who had to witness such atrocity. Strengthened by his Lord, he replied with another challenge: **"Verily, my Lord causes the sun to rise from the East, cause it then to rise in the West"** (2:258). This was a direct challenge to Namrud's divine authority for he claimed to be the earthly representative of Shamash the god of the sun and Sin the god of the moon. He called himself Lord of the East and the West, shouldn't he be able to choose the place of his rising and his setting? If he couldn't even do that, then what power did he actually have? He could only accept things as the Creator had made them and continued to make them, just like everybody else. **The disbeliever** [Namrud] **was dumbfounded. Allah does not guide those who do evil** (2:258).

Judgment was swift. This young man Ibrahim (as) was a dangerous rabble rouser. He had potential for disrupting the political establishment. The power of the government rested on the backs of the lifeless idols that Ibrahim (as) had so brazenly smashed. If people doubted their power, they would doubt the power of the king as well. Although Ibrahim (as) had no interest in taking over the government, his beliefs presented a powerful threat to the legitimacy of the state and could not be tolerated. Ibrahim (as) was sentenced to death.

CHAPTER FOURTEEN
Coolness and Peace

It is said that the first punishment that Namrud tried was to chain Ibrahim (as) on a mountaintop where he was exposed to the scorching sun during the day and the freezing wind in the night. Every day they brought him only a little bit of barley bread and salt but they never brought him water. Whenever he asked for water they would offer to bring it only if he would renounce his belief in his Lord and agree to follow their religion. The very thought of doing this caused Ibrahim (as) to shudder and feel so ill that he lost all interest in either food or water. For one whole year he was kept on the mountain and never did he for a moment consider renouncing or pretending to renounce his faith. They say that the angels brought him sustenance from heaven. After a year Namrud gave up on this plan. Or it could be that it was the way they devised to hold Ibrahim (as) until they could gather enough firewood to make the furnace in which to burn him.

According to the close companion of the Prophet Muhammad (sas) Salman al-Farsi (ra), Namrud had in his possession two untamed lions. He kept them in cages to frighten the poor ones who came to him hoping for charity or justice. Sometimes he even let the lions eat one or

Ottoman miniature of Ibrahim (as) at peace in the fire.

two. He ordered the keepers of the lions to stop feeding them. For two weeks they kept the lions hungry. Roaring and growling the beautiful beasts grew hungrier and angrier. When they brought Ibrahim (as) down from the mountain, they locked him in the cage with the lions. But wild animals know their Lord often better than people do and they are faithful to their promise never to harm someone beloved by Allah. There are many accounts of wild animals behaving like domestic cats in the presence of prophets or saints. Daniel (as), Yusuf (as), and the Prophet Muhammad (sas) are some examples. Although they were starving, the lions lay beside Ibrahim (as) peacefully. Soothed by his holy presence, they no longer even felt the pangs of hunger. In any case after a year on nothing but a slice a bread Sayyiduna Ibrahim (as) could not have looked too tasty.

Now Namrud was determined to do away with this threat, to do away with the truth at all costs. He declared that Ibrahim (as) was to be publicly burned to death. But this was not going to be an ordinary fire. He had tried twice to finish Ibrahim (as) in the usual ways and twice he had failed. He was not going to lose face by failing a third time. He ordered all the people of his kingdom to donate wood. It was like a tax on the people that they had no choice but to pay. And he declared that the gods would find favor with whoever brought wood. So it is said that when someone wanted to please the gods or ask a favor from them, he vowed to collect more wood for the fire. The people chopped their beautiful forests into piles of firewood but the horses and even the stubborn little donkeys refused to carry it for they knew instinctively that it was an action hated by their Creator. So people had to carry it on their own backs. Those who could not gather or carry wood, spun wool or did small jobs to earn money to pay others to gather wood for them. Everyone contributed something.

When Namrud had amassed literally a mountain of dry firewood, he felt he was ready to try for the third time. They threw bitumen and sulphur onto the pile to get it going. The dry wood flared up. The blaze was so hot that people from miles away held their hands in that direction to warm them. And the people who lived closer had their bread baked before it was risen. And the people who lived even closer had to move. Birds could not fly over it. Big trees wilted like delicate sprouts. Even the sun hid its face behind clouds. However fierce, the flames of ignorance and arrogance cannot consume the truth.

Namrud now faced a challenge. How was he to get Ibrahim (as) into the middle of this inferno? As they were debating what to do, shaytan entered among them, as he often did for he was at home in their company. He suggested that they build a catapult and fling Ibrahim (as) into the raging inferno in that way. The people liked this novel idea so that is what they decided to do. Others say, however, that Namrud had not been so shortsighted and had built a small enclosure in the center in which he imprisoned Ibrahim (as) first and then they piled the firewood over him.

As Ibrahim (as) was being loaded onto the catapult all the creatures of the world cried out to their Lord to save His beloved prophet. Each animal, from the tiniest crawling thing to the largest beast, every blade of grass and every leaf on every tree pleaded in its own way for the life of Ibrahim (as). **For, before Allah prostrates itself all that is in the heavens and all that is on earth – every beast that moves, and the angels: [even] these do not bear themselves with false pride** (16:49). Every living thing on the face of the earth cried out to save the life of Ibrahim (as) – except the men and the jinn. These pride themselves on being independent of God and of being His rival in the creation of all things, even of their own destinies.

The angels on high heard the cries of the natural world and they in turn asked their Lord if they might go and be of service for they were afraid that if Ibrahim (as) died there would be no man left on earth to worship the Creator. Allah answered them that they had permission to do only what Ibrahim (as) asked of them. If he asked them for help, they could help him but if he asked only from his Lord then they must leave him for his Lord.

The angel of the wind spun down in a surge of air and whispered in his ear that if Ibrahim (as) asked, with one fan of his mighty wings he would extinguish the fire and scatter its coals and ashes over the entire surface of the earth. Ibrahim (as) declined the offer for he said that he was content with whatever Allah willed. Then the angel of the water eddied down to try his luck. His eyes moist with tears he pleaded with Ibrahim (as) to let him put out the fire. At his command all the waters of the world, from below and from above, would swell and pour and drown the fire. He would wash the world clean of any trace of it. Ibrahim (as) also declined his offer, refusing to accept help from any but Allah. Then lastly the angel of the earth roused himself and pleaded with Ibrahim (as) in his rocky voice to let him shake out his crusty wings until the fire and those who rejoiced in it were smothered and buried in dust. Ibrahim (as) thanked him but continued to insist that only the Maker of the wind and the water and the earth had any power to save him. No doubt Ibrahim (as) realized that the angels were offering help on their own accord. They had permission but they were not being sent by Allah Almighty to deliver His help and so Ibrahim (as), as Allah knew he would, waited for what his Lord would send.

Ibrahim (as) was catapulted into the air, and went spinning in the direction of the center of the blaze. The mighty Archangel Jibra'il (as), who was described by the Prophet Muhammad (sas) as reaching from horizon to horizon, descended to catch him in mid-flight. He asked for permission to deliver Ibrahim (as) from the terrible torture that awaited him. But even then Ibrahim (as) would not agree to accept his help. Jibra'il (as) sternly advised him that his situation was, in fact, dire. His soul was safe but if he hoped for his body to survive he should pray to his Lord without delay. To this timely advice Ibrahim (as) listened and he turned to his Lord and said, **On Allah I rely and He is the best of caretakers - *hasbun Allah wa ni'ma l-wakil*** (3:173).

Ibrahim (as) was a prophet whose reliance on and love of his Lord was firm and unchanging. He would ask help from no one but Allah, for he knew without doubt that no one else has any power and because Allah's pleasure was his only desire. But still the Archangel Jibra'il (as), the chief prophet of the angelic world, had to grab him in midair and remind him that he has a duty too. His duty and the duty of all of us, is to do our part. As the famous hadith says: "If you take one step towards Allah, He takes ten towards you. If you turn to Him walking, He comes to you running." First we must step, or walk, or run. We must do what we can with the resources that Allah has so generously afforded us. Sometimes that is simply to admit we are weak and in need. Then we must turn to our Creator and ask for help. We cannot just sit back and say that Allah knows everything and He can do as He wants. That goes without saying, of course He will do as He wants. But it is our part to ask of Him what we want and to trust that He is our *Rabb* and whatever He sends is exactly what we need.

In what is called the year of sadness, when his beloved wife Khadija (rah) and his uncle and protector Abu Talib (ra) both died, the Prophet (sas) found himself without visible support in this world. He sent emissaries to other lands looking for a safe haven in which to worship Allah. He traveled alone to visit relatives in the city of Ta'if to see if Allah would open a door there. When that door was slammed in his face, he literally had nowhere to turn. He was alone in the desert between two cities which both rejected him and rejected his message with active hatred. He was essentially in the catapult with nothing before him but fire. At that point he turned to his Lord and made this moving prayer which is essentially an expansion and explanation of the prayer of Ibrahim (as). He said: "O Allah to You alone do I cry of my weakness and helplessness and lowliness before men. O Most Merciful of the merciful, You are the Lord of the weak and You are my Lord ... I don't mind anything as long as You are not angry with me ... I take refuge in the light of Your countenance by which all darkness is dispelled and by which all things of this world and the next are put right ... There is no power or might except in You."

Shortly thereafter Allah brought coolness and peace to the heart of the Prophet (sas) by inviting him on a journey to the seven heavens and beyond. After that experience the world itself did not perceptibly change. The people of Mecca still wanted to kill him. They amassed three armies and countless smaller forces to try to physically stop him. They continued to oppose him with their hands and their hatred. And yet he never experienced it in quite the same way because Allah had answered his prayer first by changing him, not by changing the world.

When the way seems closed we have to continue to look for an opening. And all the while we must turn to Allah and ask and ask and ask some more. Never stop asking because Allah has said that He loves to fulfill the prayers of His servants and never gets annoyed by their pleas. So Ibrahim (as) asked and His Lord immediately, replied: **O Fire, be coolness and peace for Ibrahim** (21:69). It is a fact that if there is a situation in life that is causing pain, if the feeling of the pain can be altered, the situation can be tolerated. Allah did not change the fact of the fire. He changed only the affect it had on Ibrahim (as).

Others say that if Allah had not said 'peace' as well as 'coolness', the fire would have become so cold that Ibrahim (as), instead of being burned, would have been frozen to death. Upon hearing the command of Allah Almighty, all the fires around the entire world, all the ovens, all the candles, even the volcanos, burned without heat. Each flame feared that Allah's mighty word was addressed specifically to it. In consequence, therefore, for that day no person on earth had a hot meal.

Two Corinthian pillars from a Roman 3rd century fort built on the ruins of the temple of Sin in Urfa. These pillars appear in the previous miniature as the catapult that hurled Ibrahim (as) into the fire.

Persian miniature of the nightingale on the rose.

CHAPTER FIFTEEN

The Companions of the Garden

Jibra'il (as), still holding Ibrahim (as) in his mighty arms, brought him down gently into the middle of the forest of flames. When they dropped under the blanket of smoke they found in the center, like the quiet eye of the hurricane, a peaceful garden. Israfil (as) had brought, by his Lord's command, a piece of the Paradise garden and set it in the midst of the flames. There a spring, born from the rivers of Paradise, gathered in a rippling pool. Some say that as Ibrahim (as) and the angel passed over the fire, the dry logs and branches swelled again with sap. They sprouted leaves and roots until they became a shady forest. Jibra'il (as) set Ibrahim (as) down on the mossy bank where the heavenly water swirled at his feet. He lay on thick piled carpets, his head rested on silk embroidered cushions and the angel of shade sat beside him to keep him company. All the comforts that await the soul of the worthy servant were provided for Ibrahim (as) in the midst of the blazing inferno. Others say simply that when the Lord Almighty commanded the fire to be coolness and peace, all the heat fled from the flames and only the radiant light remained. In that light the prophet of God rested.

When life gets difficult just remember the prophet Ibrahim (as) sitting peacefully in the center of the raging fire. Abdul Qadir al-Jilani (q) says that hardship can be either a punishment or a test from Allah. The way to tell the difference is that when it is a punishment the heart continues to burn but when it is a test, however painful, the heart remains at peace. If the heart is at peace, then the aggressions of the world cannot disturb. We can walk through the turmoil of life quietly. Not distracted by concern for our own safety, we can take care of others and become a source of peace and goodness to all.

Angels brought Ibrahim (as) three cups of water from each of the streams of Paradise because he had not had water in many months. He drank the first and one drop fell from his lips. From that drop the cypress tree grew with its beautiful teardrop shape. He drank the second cup and another drop fell. This drop grew into the little wild white rose or some say the narcissus. He drank the third cup and when a drop of water fell to the ground it grew into the most fragrant red rose.

All the animals in the area, not knowing the secret of the garden, rushed in where they thought the angels had failed. Each one in his own way followed his heart in an effort to save Ibrahim (as). The ant scurried, her thread-like legs carrying her lightly over the ash, with a small drop of water in her mouth to spit at the blaze. The deer, the wild donkey and horse, did whatever they could to stomp out the flames with their hard little hooves. The lion and wolf, the rabbit and mouse, rolled with their thick furry coats to try to smother the flames. The small birds tried to drown it with water which they carried in their beaks or in nutshells held tightly in their talons. The large birds tried to blow the fire out with the beating of their wings. But the heat was much too intense and they were not able to reach the heart of the fire before they feared their feathers would burst into flame. Even the little honey bee released her precious nectar, drop by drop, in a futile attempt to quench the fire. Only the transparent gecko blew air at the blaze from his small, sharp mouth with the intention of fanning the flames. The Prophet Muhammad (sas) called him the little evil one.

The nightingale, in the intensity of her love for Allah's prophet, propelled herself fearlessly into the flames. If Ibrahim (as) were to burn she would only be content to burn with him. She alone made it to the center of the inferno. There she saw the cool garden with Ibrahim (as) sitting peacefully inside. She fluttered down to him, singed but unhurt, and he set her on a twig of the red rose that had sprung from the drop of Paradise water. And there she sang of her love for Allah. Since then the nightingale has loved the rose because it was on the rose that she first set eyes on the beautiful face of Allah's prophet. And in her song she repeats the ninety-nine names of Allah because that is what he taught her while they sat together in the garden of fire.

They say the fire burned for forty days and then cooled for another forty before people could see through the smoke and flickering flame. What they saw astounded them. Ibrahim (as) was sitting with another man who looked exactly like him, both of them alive and well. It is said that Namrud climbed a nearby mountain in order to be able to see down into the center of the enormous fire. It is also said that he had a lofty tower built just so he could peer down while the flames were still burning. Some say that his daughter one morning looked out of her window high in the tower and spied Ibrahim (as) where a clearing in the smoke had been made by a stray wind. Overwhelmed by the obvious miracle she ran to her father and pleaded with him to accept the religion of Ibrahim (as).

We know that the daughter of the Akkadian ruler Naram-Sin was the high priestess of the temple of Sin and so in charge of the idols that Ibrahim (as) was accused of destroying. Her name was Enmenanna and she was a very powerful woman. Her defection from the religion of the state would have been taken very seriously. The stories state that Namrud had her killed for apostasy. However, it happened, eventually Namrud had to face the fact that all his effort and expense had been without success. Unless Allah Almighty willed, all his efforts were in vain.

Sayyiduna Ibrahim (as) walked out of the fire as he had gone in. Not one thread of his garments had been scorched, not one hair on his body had been singed. The only thing on him that had burned were the ropes that had bound him. However you understand the fire, trial, test, Ibrahim (as) had survived it and risen above it. He had kept his eyes fixed on his Lord and accepted without a struggle what He gave him. And so it had not been a struggle but instead a garden. And the bonds that held him to the darkness of this material life were released and he was set free.

The narrators go on to relate that Namrud asked Ibrahim (as) about his companion in the fire. When he looked he had seen two identical figures, two Ibrahims. Ibrahim (as) told him that this was an angel that Allah had sent to shade him. He was his shadow, identical in appearance, his double. The Qur'an talks about a *qarin*, an inseparable companion who accompanies all the children of Adam (as) for all of their lives. In most cases it is understood as a personal devil or jinn who encourages the doing of things that are wrong. The Prophet (sas) said that all men are accompanied by their shaytan. When asked if he also had one, he replied that he did but Allah had made his shaytan Muslim, meaning that he had control over it and it no longer even tried to tempt him. Some of the hadith say that each person has both a personal shaytan and a personal angel. Some identify them with the recording angels who sit, one on the left shoulder and one on the right, recording all a person's good and bad deeds. Perhaps this is what Namrud saw. Only the prophets have this shaytan in their service, to keep them company in the fire and shade them from the heat of the world. As Allah says in His Qur'an: **Verily, you [shaytan] will have no power over My servants** (15:42).

When Namrud saw Ibrahim (as) still alive and well, he called to him above the crackling and hissing of the dying fire: "If you can come to me, then come." Ibrahim (as) picked his way across the wasteland of charred wood and burning embers until he reached the king. And Namrud and all the people who had been dancing and rejoicing around the fire were shocked and speechless. For a brief moment they were impressed enough to consider believing in the God of Ibrahim (as) who could enact such a clear miracle, just as Pharaoh had considered such a thing when he feared Musa's (as) staff that turned into a dragon. But fear is momentary and when it passes so does the desire and need for accepting change. If there is only one God, it cannot be either Namrud or Pharaoh. They are reduced to the status of a servant like all other men and that is ultimately not acceptable. Once they have raised themselves so high they are unlikely ever to be willing to step down.

And so Namrud, unable to do away with Ibrahim (as) or to change him or to believe in him, sent him away. He had tried to kill him but his God had saved him and Namrud had understood from this that Ibrahim (as) was just a servant of a much more powerful God. It is not proper for kings to fight with servants, he thought. If he would fight with anyone it should be with the Lord of Ibrahim (as). So he ordered his men to build for him a tower and his intention was to climb it high into the sky and challenge Allah Himself. So Namrud lost interest in Sayyiduna Ibrahim (as) and set his sights on higher things.

The Halilu r-Rahman mosque, Urfa Turkey, showing the paradise pool that was left when the fire burned away and the logs turned into fish.

Stone relief of an Assyrian king shooting with bow and arrow, Nineveh Iraq.

CHAPTER SIXTEEN

From Whence You Don't Know

It is said that Namrud climbed the tower that he had built and, bow and arrow in hand, he challenged the Lord of Ibrahim (as). Allah says in The Qur'an: **But Allah came at their structure from the foundations, so the roof fell upon them from above, and the punishment came upon them from whence they did not perceive** (16:26).

After the punishment of Ibrahim (as) the kingdom of Namrud suffered from disasters and fell to its enemies. There are more than one story relating the terrible end of the tyrant Namrud. In the poem called the "Curse of Akkad" the historical Naram-Sin angered the gods who then put a curse on him. His kingdom was torn apart by invaders, and he was captured. His grand capital city, Akkad, was leveled so that no one could ever live there again. In another account he climbed the tower that he had built, a tower like no other that had ever been built or conceived in that area before, just as the historical Naram-Sin was the first to build the ziggurat step mounds. When it was finished he climbed to the top and shot an arrow into the sky. Alternative narratives say that the tower was not tall enough so his engineers devised a sort of plane – a box whose corners were attached to four great eagles that carried him so high into the sky that he could no longer see anything either below him or above him. Then he deemed himself high enough to take aim at the God of Ibrahim (as). In either case it is said that Jibra'il (as) grabbed the arrow and used it to pierce a fish that he had taken from the ocean for this purpose. The arrow was thrown back to earth covered in blood and so Namrud assumed his assault had been successful. He strutted around in triumph. The great hunter had hunted the gods in the sky.

Ibrahim (as) of course was disgusted with this exhibition of arrogance and immediately denounced the victory as a farce. So Namrud challenged Ibrahim (as) again, this time to a battle. Namrud gathered his army and made them ready. Sayyiduna Ibrahim (as) went to pray with his few faithful followers. The next day Namrud advanced to the battlefield and laughed at the sorry sight of the handful of believers who stood staunchly facing him. But Allah is the best of planners. From out of the sky came an army of mosquitoes or gnats, tiny flying soldiers bent on obeying their Lord. They got inside the armor of Namrud's army and they stung and they itched, they annoyed and they bit. Many of the soldiers killed themselves or each other flailing about trying to get rid of the pests. Many died throwing themselves into rivers to end the itching. Others simply ran as far away as they could. But the mosquitoes followed them and made their way through the cracks in their armor and bit and sucked their blood until nothing remained.

Namrud had set himself a throne on a hill overlooking the battlefield so he could savor the victory he was sure was about to take place and he could revel in the final horrible massacre of his enemy. Spread out before him he saw the tidy ranks of his massive army suddenly dissolve into chaos but he wasn't able to see why. The insects were too small to detect from a distance. Afraid for his life, he ran from the enemy he couldn't see sent by the God he couldn't see. He threw himself into the private windowless apartments in the heart of his palace that he had prepared for the time when all those who hated him might rise up against him. He locked the door with a special twisted lock and left the key inside so he was sure that not even a tiny opening to the outside remained.

There was a very small mosquito with only one good wing. He couldn't fly fast and he couldn't fly straight. He came limping and dodging through the air long after his companions had launched their attack. He cried weakly to his Lord because he wished also to be of service in defending Allah's prophet. Allah heard his prayer and chose him for a special task. With determination and divine guidance this poor creature wobbled through the air until it reached the palace. It squeezed itself into the keyhole, past the key, and through the twisted space for which its small broken body turned out to be the most perfect fit. Inside the king's bedroom, it buzzed its labored way. Namrud in terror swatted at it but it evaded his hand. For several hours they played this game until Namrud was exhausted and beyond caring. As he lay on the bed, he looked up and saw the little insect poised to dive.

It landed on the great curly beard of the proud hunter and before Namrud could swat it away, it propelled itself into the tyrant's nostril. Then, tiny bite by tiny bite, the insect made its way into Namrud's brain. There it feasted and buzzed. The pain was extreme and the noise was unbearable. Namrud found a stick and proceeded to hit himself on the head with it. Each time he hit, the insect would pause in his merry munching. So Namrud gave the stick to his nobles and commanded that they take turns to continuously hit him on the head as this was the only relief available to him.

For many months this agony continued until it was the turn of the strongest nobleman in Namrud's court. He hit the tyrant with such a blow that his skull finally split in two. Out of his head, like a chick from an egg, flew the inspired bug. And that was how the biggest, proudest tyrant was defeated by the weakest and most insignificant of Allah's creatures **and the punishment came upon them from whence they did not perceive** (16:26).

La ilaha ila Allah Ibrahim Khalil Allah. There is no god but God and Ibrahim is the friend of God. Ottoman calligraphy carved in stone above the Jaffa gate, Jerusalem.
Courtesy Akram Reda.

CHAPTER SEVENTEEN
Becoming Khalil

Ibrahim (as) was born in *fitra*, the natural state of submission to Allah in which all children are born. He had maintained that state into adulthood becoming *hanif*, someone who turns away from anything that is not purely for Allah. He was chosen for the honor and responsibility of being a prophet (*nabi*). In addition, he was given the even more exalted task of being a messenger (*rasul*), the carrier of Allah's Word. Allah now drew him even closer in His love to a place of extreme intimacy.

It is said that in the very beginning of the world, on the sixth day of creation, Allah Almighty ordered his Archangel Jibra'il (as) to descend to Earth and bring back a handful of soil in order to form the very last of His creatures, man. Immediately the foremost angel flew down in obedience. But shaytan had already informed Earth of what an aggressive master this last creature would be, tearing her apart to extract her treasures, and drenching her pure soil in blood. Earth was so afraid and upset that when Jibra'il (as) asked politely for a handful of her skin (adam means skin), she shrieked and cried so pitifully that out of compassion he would not touch her. He returned to his Lord ashamed and empty handed. So Allah asked the other Archangels to perform the task but they fared no better. One by one each Archangel returned to his Lord downcast and empty handed. Then Allah ordered the last of His Archangels, 'Azra'il (as), to try his hand at fulfilling the divine command. When Earth began her piteous wailing, 'Azra'il (as) thundered back at her for daring to object to her Creator's request. Despite her lamentations, 'Azra'il (as) was unmoved. He took handfuls of earth from every place, of every sort and color, and brought them all to his Lord. Because of his strength of heart and unflinching obedience, Allah appointed him to be the one to take the souls of men when their time on earth is done. So 'Azra'il (as) became the Angel of Death and from that day on he has never been seen to smile.

'Azra'il (as), although busy with his heavy responsibilities, came to hear of Ibrahim's (as) new closeness because all the heavens were abuzz with the news - as the Prophet (sas) said that the prayer of angels sounds to us like the humming of bees. 'Azra'il (as) had been keeping a close watch on Ibrahim (as) for a long time. First as a baby when his parents had left him alone in the cave. Then as a young man, a warrior on the path of Allah who never sidestepped an opportunity to confront falsehood. Then through the various tortures of the tyrant: starvation, exposure, lions, and finally fire. Ibrahim (as) had been walking a line delicately close to death for many years. 'Azra'il (as) had remained on the alert, grim and determined to obey his Lord no matter whose soul required taking. His sympathies were of course with Allah's prophet. He loves the ones his Lord loves and takes their souls gently with extreme deference and delicacy. Now, to his surprise, 'Azra'il (as) found himself feeling something he had not experienced in a very long time – perhaps it was joy. He had a great desire to, just this once, be the herald of good news. He felt compelled to ask his Lord for this favor and it was granted. 'Azra'il (as), the Angel of Death, was given permission to be the one to announce to Sayyiduna Ibrahim (as) the great news of Allah's gift of friendship.

Ibrahim (as) also was no stranger to this mighty angel. He had been aware of his presence many times already in his young life. As 'Azra'il (as) approached, Ibrahim (as) greeted him with familiarity and prepared to return his soul to its Maker. But 'Azra'il (as) convinced him, if not with a smile then at least with a lightness of spirit, that he had not come for this purpose. The Sufi's say "die before you die" meaning leave ego and love of this world behind and be filled with your Lord. So it was not inappropriate for 'Azra'il (as) to be the bearer of this news. It indicated certainly a kind of death, death of the selfish ego. But whereas physical death puts an end to the possibility of striving and attaining, death of the ego brings spiritual rebirth and renewed power to pursue the path.

The Lord and Creator of the Worlds, the Unseeable, Unknowable, the One beyond the scope of human understanding, beyond time and space, beyond names and images, who always was and always will be, without beginning or end, Allah Almighty chose Ibrahim (as) to be His intimate friend. **Allah took Ibrahim as khalil** (4:125). This title, the Friend of God, also appears in both the Torah/Old Testament, (Chronicles II 20:7 and Isaiah 41:8) and in the New Testament (James 2:23). It is the description by which all the Peoples of the Book know Ibrahim (as). He is referred to more specifically as *Khalilu r-Rahman*, the friend of that aspect of the Lord that is called the All Merciful.

One of the primary meanings of the Arabic root kh-l-l, from which the word *khalil* is derived, is to penetrate, to transfix, to permeate. So one derivation from this root means to pickle or marinate. Ibn 'Arabi (q) uses this meaning when speaking about the particular prophetic quality of Ibrahim (as). He is soaked, drenched, permeated with His Lord. One of the reasons it is said that Allah created the world in the first place was to reflect His self to Himself. When He gazed in the mirror of His servant Ibrahim (as) He saw Himself reflected perfectly in His attribute of the Merciful. And this is, after all then the fulfillment of the purpose of creation.

In Arabic saints are called *awliya Allah* which is also translated as Allah's friends. But the root, w-l-y, means to protect, to support. Allah is their patron and they are His servants. They are protected under His 'domes' and they act as protectors for the rest of us. The relationship is close and dear, but not equal. *Khalil* however denotes an intimate friend, someone with whom love is shared on a more equal basis. The only other human we know who was blessed and dressed with this honor was the Prophet Muhammad (sas). Although he is more commonly known by the title *Habib Allah*, the Beloved of Allah, there is a Hadith in which he said: "If I were to take a *khalil* among my companions I would have taken Abu Bakr (ra) because no one has benefited us more in every way. However, your companion [the Prophet (sas)] is the *khalil* of Allah." (Bukhari).

This Hadith suggests that in the relationship between Abu Bakr (ra) and the Prophet Muhammad (sas) we will see an example of what *khalil* looks like, at least between human beings.

A *khalil* always brings benefit. The Prophet (sas) said that when most people accepted Islam there was a little bit of hesitation or doubt except in the case of Abu Bakr (ra). He surrendered to Allah and to His Messenger (sas) fully and completely with his sword and his word. Sayyiduna 'Umar (ra) said that he could never compete with the dedication and generosity of Abu Bakr (ra). On the occasion of his having given in charity half of his entire weath, he found that Abu Bakr (ra) had already given all of his. When the Prophet (sas) announced that Allah had taken him to visit Jerusalem (*Isra*) and the seven Heavens (*Mi'raj*) in the space of a few hours, all the people, even the Muslims, had trouble accepting and believing. But Abu Bakr (ra) did not for one second entertain any doubt. He confirmed without hesitation that if that is what the Prophet (sas) said, then that is what had happened. He knew with certainty that the Prophet (sas) spoke only truth. Although the Prophet (sas) could not give Abu Bakr (ra) the title of *khalil*, because this was reserved only for his relationship with his Lord, he honored him with the title of *as-saddiq* which means the one who testifies to truth and is also another word for true friend.

To put it clearly, a *khalil* is someone whose love you can depend on. He will remain certain of your goodness under all circumstances. He will not betray you by ascribing to you intentions which are either base or selfish. For God this means that Ibrahim (as) would never doubt His Goodness, His Fairness, His Mercy. When asked to do something that from all angles was logically wrong and morally sinful, as later he was asked to kill his own son, Ibrahim (as) never doubted for a second that Allah had any intention other than goodness. The outcome of following God's command can only be goodness even if Ibrahim (as) could not imagine how that would come to be. The fact is, he did not even try to imagine it at all. He just did it. He did not even stop to question because of his certainty in his Friend's absolute Goodness. Some way, somehow, Allah would turn sacrifice into reward, fire into coolness, death into life, mud into gold. And that is why all the People of the Book also call Ibrahim (as) the Father of Faith.

But it was not just Ibrahim (as) who was a *khalil* towards God. After all Allah is the one God, He is ultimately Reliable, absolutely Trustworthy,

Wise and All-Seeing. One can imagine perhaps, the possibility of being totally reliant on Him. But Allah also had the same certainty about Ibrahim (as). Allah was also confidant that when He spoke to His servant Ibrahim (as) He would be understood. Allah could count on Ibrahim (as) under all circumstances to be merciful and loving – to his Creator and to His creation. He had been tested heavily and he had not failed. In response to difficulty he returned love. In response to rejection he returned love. In response to deprivation he returned love. There was no circumstance which could shake his unfailing love for his Lord and what other attribute could better reflect the Most Merciful of the merciful - *Arhamu r-rahimin* (12:64)?

The Prophet (sas) and Abu Bakr (ra) in the cave of Thawr. 16th century Ottoman miniature.

Ottoman miniature of the prophet Ibrahim (as), the four birds, and the corpse of the donkey, to demonstrate how Allah brings life to the dead.

CHAPTER EIGHTEEN
Four Birds

After 'Azra'il (as) had delivered the news, Ibrahim (as) in awe and humility, asked what this honor might mean. It is said that 'Azra'il (as) answered him that he could now ask for whatever he wanted and his Friend would gladly give it him. He could say to a thing "Be" and by Allah's will, it would become.

So Ibrahim (as) asked something from his Friend. He said: **'Show me how You restore life to the dead'** (2:260). Allah replied to him: **'Do you not believe?'** (2:260). Did he not already believe in Allah's words? Did he need to see with his eyes? **'I do'** believe answered Ibrahim (as) **'but just so that my heart might be at ease'** (2:60).

If he had no doubt, then why would seeing put his heart at ease? This is a prophet speaking to his Lord. He knows he cannot hide something from his Lord. He knows that the deepest secret of his heart is a clear book for his Lord. He must be completely sincere. There is a difference between believing and seeing, between seeing with the heart and seeing with the eyes and Allah promises us that after we die we will see in this way: **In the end you will see most surely with the eye of certainty** (102:7). Ibrahim (as) believed but he wanted to see in this way while he was alive. He was asking for the station of certainty: **And worship your Lord until He grants you certainty** (15:99). And this is what was granted to him. **We showed Ibrahim the kingdom of the heavens and the earth that he might be of those possessing certainty** (6:75).

There is some disagreement about when Ibrahim (as) was told that Allah Almighty had chosen him for an intimate friend. Most of the Christians and Jews say that this honor was revealed to him later when the angelic guests descended to announce the imminent birth of Ishaq (as). The change of his name from Abram to Abraham was the sign of it. Some of the Muslim commentators say, however, that it happened much earlier. In The Qur'an this request for witnessing resurrection follows almost immediately after the account of the meeting with Namrud. Perhaps Sayyiduna Ibrahim (as) needed to ease his heart after seeing the innocent man put to death before his eyes. Perhaps he needed to fully see and understand in order to face his own immanent execution. He needed to know in a deeper way the reality of his own words: **'My Lord is the one who grants life and deals death'** (2:258).

But others say that the request was made independent of these events and that Ibrahim (as), having received the stupendous news that Allah Almighty was returning his love with His friendship, felt compelled to reach out to Him. He wanted to feel his Lord's closeness with all of his senses. He wanted his eyes and his ears to be full of his Lord in just the way that his heart already was. In other words, he wanted to be completely permeated with his Lord, *khalala*. He wanted to taste the sweetness of the communion with his Beloved that had just been offered him and so he reached out to make contact by asking a favor and savoring the response.

Allah instructed him: **Take four birds and make them obey you, then place them separately on every hill, then summon them** (2:260). Ibn Kathir (14th century *Tafsir*) says that Allah is telling Ibrahim (as) to take four birds and train them to come to him. Then he should cut off their heads, chop up the bodies, and mix the meat all together. He should put a portion of this grisly mix on the top of each of four or seven mountains then return to his place with the heads and call the birds to come. **They will come flying to you in haste** (2:260). Then he would witness how the dead are revived as the bits reassembled themselves in midair; every bone, feather and piece of flesh uniting to form the original four birds. They would fly without their heads to the spot where he stood and take from his hand the head that belonged to them and in this way he would be an eyewitness to the creation of life from death.

Certainly this would be a most convincing demonstration if perhaps unnecessarily graphic. So there is an additional story which explains the context. When walking by the sea, Sayyiduna Ibrahim (as) saw the carcass of a donkey lying half in the water and half out. The predators of the sea were eating it on one side and the predators of the land on the other. Then he asked his Lord how a body like this, its meat eaten by different animals, its bones washed away or left to dry and turn to dust, how it could possibly assemble itself once again as a whole living body? And his Creator showed him how simple an act it was for Him Almighty and then He said: **And know that Allah is Almighty, Wise** (2:260).

Allah showed the same lesson many centuries later to the prophet 'Uzayr (as) who had expressed doubt that Allah would be able to rebuild the Temple in Jerusalem as it was before its destruction by the Babylonians in 589 BCE or restore the Torah that had been burned and forgotten during the fifty years of exile. Allah put 'Uzayr (as) to sleep for a hundred years. When he woke he watched in wonder as the bones of his little donkey reassembled themselves and grew meat, skin and hair and came to life before his eyes. And he looked farther and saw the Temple being rebuilt as it had been and his heart was inspired with the whole text of the Torah. In fact, to the Jews 'Uzayr (as) is like a second Musa (as) in that the Torah we have today is the result of it's second revelation through him.

Abu Muslim, (10th century *Tafsir*) says, however, that it would be enough of a lesson for Ibrahim (as) to see the four birds winging their way from all directions with the single purpose of answering his call. The chopping up is not mentioned directly in The Qur'an and is not necessary to its understanding. Just as four homing pigeons will take the fastest, most direct route home from wherever they have been released, so the soul and substance of man will fly to their Lord from wherever they have been buried, thrown, washed, or strewn. Simply, they are His; they belong to Him. Nor is it necessary for every element of a body to be present in order for Allah to recreate the whole of it for Judgment Day. Some say one bone is enough and Allah will grow the rest fresh around it as He did in its first creation and as He did with the donkey of 'Uzayr (as). Others say that even if it was completely destroyed without a trace, if it is Allah's intention, it will be restored. **When He wills a thing, He but says to it 'Be' - and it is** (2:117).

The desire of flying home to the one we love is so strong in us that, like the steadfast homing pigeon, we will ignore the call of the world and fly to our Creator if He just breathes our name. There is no doubt that the body will do the same. In fact, it is said that it will be in just this way, on the Resurrection Day, that our *Rabb* will call us home. And the sight of the birds' determined flight gave certainty to the heart of Ibrahim (as).

Because this is such a powerful image it has inspired many different interpretations. The Sufis say that each of the birds represents a different veil that must be torn or discarded before the servant can see with certainty. As-Suyuti (15th century) says he took a rooster, a peacock, an eagle and a raven. Al-Kashani (14th century) says the four birds were a peacock representing wonder, the rooster representing passion, the dove representing love of the world, the duck of covetousness, or the raven of ravenousness. Al-Qashani (13th century) says the four birds were a peacock representing the allure of the world, a crow representing greed, a rooster representing pride, and a duck representing the desire to hoard provision for the future. Once Ibrahim (as) had killed these passions within himself he would experience certainty and his own rebirth. But then why would he call them to return to him after he had finally gotten rid of them? Because they are aspects of the ego, the *nafs*, and when they have been tamed they no longer call to forgetfulness and sin. Once they have died and been resurrected they are heavenly and serve the righteous servant on the path to God. Physical passion becomes spiritual devotion, *himmat*. Pride lets go of vanity and becomes righteousness. Greed becomes generosity, and love of the world becomes caring and compassion for Allah's creation.

Like the lovesick suitor who has just received a positive response from his beloved, he will run to be with her. And perhaps, in his incredulous joy he will test to see if she could truly, honestly love him. So As-Suyuti says that Ibrahim (as) was testing by making this request and Al-Qashani says that he just wanted to be immersed in the new closeness. Either way it is also said that from this request arose an unspoken understanding that when the time came, Ibrahim (as) would have to grant his Lord a similar proof. As Allah showed him with certainty that He revives the dead, Ibrahim (as) could not refuse to give the life of the one dearest to him in certain trust in the resurrection.

Another miniature with four different birds and the prophet Ibrahim (as).

Byzantine icon of Ibrahim (as) and Sarah (rah).

CHAPTER NINETEEN
Marriage

Around this time Ibrahim (as) married Sarah (rah). We don't know much about her before her marriage other than that she was a believer in Allah and His prophet (as), she was related to Ibrahim (as) in some way, and that she was a remarkably beautiful and noble woman. It is said that her beauty was second only to that of Hawwa (rah) the wife of Adam (as) who was the most beautiful woman ever created.

The name Sarah itself means a high born woman and is often translated as princess. Some even say she was the daughter of the king of Harran. But the Torah says she was the half sister of Ibrahim (as), the daughter of his father Terah by a different mother. The Jewish scholars have claimed that this marriage was not forbidden before the Torah of Musa (as) was revealed, as the sons of Adam (as) had also married their sisters. But the children of Adam (as) had no other choice than to marry a sister. Until the single birth of Seth (as), Hawwa (rah) only gave birth to twins, a boy and a girl. They were careful, however, never to marry their own twin. This was part of the reason Cain (Qabil) killed Abel (Habil) (as) – he was jealous and wanted to marry his own twin although it was forbidden. So even at the very beginning, some sort of incest prohibition was recognized and observed. The fact that Sarah (rah) is said to be the daughter of Terah should serve as conclusive proof that Terah was not the birth father of Ibrahim (as). Rather he was a male relative and guardian who might have married his own daughter to his stepson.

It is basically inconceivable that a Prophet of God would commit incest even if it was before the law had been written down. First cousin marriage is preferred in the Muslim world and is almost as close a relationship as brother and sister and sometimes even referred to as such. Therefore, some say that Terah had a brother named Haran who had two daughters, Sarah (rah) and Milcah. Ibrahim (as) married Sarah (rah) and his brother Nahor married Milcah. Allah knows best. Bible scholars point out that in the Song of Solomon the phrases "my sister, my bride" and "my sister, my spouse" are used to indicate social status rather than relationship. The use of the word sister denotes a woman of equal status. In much the same way the Pharaohs of Ancient Egypt called their wives their sisters in order to raise their status so that the children would be of pure divine lineage.

After being tried and punished by Namrud it is unlikely that anyone other than a family member would consent to give him their daughter as a wife. It is surprising that even an uncle consented. But perhaps it was the right of first cousins to marry like it is today in the Muslim world. And the parents hoped that despite their differences the family would stay together. Maybe they hoped that marriage and children would change Ibrahim (as) and make him more interested in conforming to the society around him.

The Torah says that Sarah (rah) was ten years younger than Ibrahim (as) in which case, if she was a stepsister, she would have been born to Azar and a second wife just around the time that Ibrahim (as) was brought home from the cave. As either a cousin or a stepsister, she would have grown up essentially in the same household and have been familiar with the character and the beliefs of Ibrahim (as). She would have heard him speak persuasively and eloquently about his Lord to her parents. She would have witnessed every day the honorable way he behaved, treating everyone with kindness, gentleness and patience. Because her heart was true, she would have responded in sympathy with his way. Most likely she had grown up always loving him.

Soon after their marriage, the family or clan of Terah decided to leave Urfa or Ur and emigrate to the city of Harran. "Terah took Abram his son, and Lot the son of Haran, his son's son, and Sarai his daughter-in-law, his son Abram's wife; and they went forth with them from Ur of the Chaldees to go to the land of Canaan; and they came to Harran and dwelled there." (Genesis 11:31). This verse from the Bible has been the source of much commentary and supposition by the Jews and Christians. Some say that Ibrahim's (as) brother Haran died in a temple fire in Ur, perhaps even a fire set by Ibrahim (as) himself. He left behind him his young son Lut (as) orphaned. In order to forget the sorrow of their loss, Terah moved the family to a town far to the North of Ur that was called Harran. Some read into this verse that God chose Terah first to be the one to emigrate to Canaan but that he got stuck in Harran, lost his faith and returned to making idols. So the command was passed on to his son Ibrahim (as) whose determination was strong enough to complete God's order. But we know from The Qur'an that this did not happen, that Azar/Terah did not change and never followed the way of Ibrahim (as). He persisted in worshipping idols until he died as an unbeliever.

In addition, if Terah was heading to Canaan by way of Harran it was certainly an unnecessarily long and indirect route. They traveled 1,000 km north along the eastern edge of the Fertile Crescent to reach Harran in order to turn around and travel the same distance south along the Mediterranean coast to Canaan. If their intention was to go to Canaan, then it seems much more likely that they were living in Urfa and traveled only 50km south to Harran which was directly on the way to Canaan. Ur of the Chaldees, *Ur Kasdim* as it is called in the Torah, did not even exist as such at the time of Ibrahim (as). Therefore, many scholars believe that the word Chaldees is an anachronism that was added later and that the real Ur where Ibrahim (as) was born is the city that is now called Urfa.

The Turkish city of Urfa has several places still deemed holy for their association with the Prophet Ibrahim (as). One is a cave in which the prophet was supposedly born. A mosque has been built near it and a place for prayer walled off inside. There is a 13th century mosque built next to a large rectangular pool. This pool is reported to be what remains of the spring fed from the rivers of Paradise that Israfil (as) brought to comfort

Ibrahim (as) in the fire. It remained as a sign for mankind after the fire of Namrud had long burned itself out and vanished. In the pool are large carp believed to be the fish of Paradise. There is a local tradition that says that the flames turned to water and the logs turned to carp. There is also a soup kitchen in the mosque which feeds hungry pilgrims in the tradition of the first most generous host, Sayyiduna Ibrahim (as).

The old town of Harran Turkey with its characteristic beehive shaped houses, where both the Bible and The Qur'an say Ibrahim (as) lived for many years. In the background is the minaret of the 8th century Islamic University of Harran built over the remains of the temple of the moon god Sin.

CHAPTER TWENTY
Salamun 'Alayk

Harran was a large town not far from Urfa and is still inhabited today. At that time, it was a border city which like both Ur and Urfa was devoted to the cult of Sin the moon god. Ibrahim (as) had spent a long time in Urfa trying to revive in his people the monotheism of their ancestors. At this he was mostly unsuccessful even though they had just witnessed a clear miracle. But Ibrahim (as) continued to obey his Lord and call the people to the truth. He hoped their hearts would open and they would come to their senses. He continued to talk to whoever would listen but his message became more of a warning than an enticement. He said: **'you have chosen idols instead of Allah. The love between you is only in the life of the world. Then on the Day of Resurrection you will deny each other and curse each other, and your abode will be the Fire, and you will have no helpers'** (29:25).

They had chosen to worship idols rather than Allah just to please each other and to fit in, even though they could see it made no sense. It was what their fathers had done so it was easier to follow along than to change. Changing meant rejecting and disrespecting those they claimed

Above is a Kufic calligraphy, *As-salamu 'alaykum*. Below is an aerial photograph of the foundations of the temple of the moon god Sin on the ziggurat of Sagmatar 30 miles from Harran, Turkey.

to love. Nobody said it was easy, but when the truth becomes clear, hiding from it is not an option. There is a choice to be made and the wrong one will lead to nothing either cool or peaceful. And their ancestors would actually take more benefit if their children became believers.

Ibrahim (as), full of love and concern tried one last time to talk sense into Azar. Their conversation is recorded in The Qur'an. Ibrahim (as) pleaded: **"O my father, why do you worship that which neither hears nor sees, nor can bring you any benefit? O my father, knowledge has come to me that has not come to you, so follow me. I will guide you to the right way. O my father, do not worship shaytan. Shaytan has rebelled against the Lord of Mercy. O my father, I fear that a punishment of the Lord of Mercy may touch you and that you may become a companion of shaytan"** (19:42-45). Each phrase begins with the heartbreaking endearment in Arabic, *ya abati*, O my father, please listen to me.

Azar tried to find a reply to this boy whom he had raised since he was an infant, whom he had protected and tried to make his own; this young man who had brought the anger of the king down on the whole family, who had disgraced his parents, who never listened to what his elders said. Azar, unmoved and unloving, pushed to his limit, thundered: **"Ibrahim, do you reject my gods? I will stone you if you don't stop. Leave me for a long while"** (19:46). Azar threatened Ibrahim (as) with physical harm and scholars say that by 'a long while' he meant forever. Sayyiduna Ibrahim (as) answered with great dignity and sadness: **"Salamun 'alayk, peace be with you. I will ask my Lord to forgive you, He has always been gracious to me. I will leave you and what you pray to other than Allah and I will call upon my Lord. I hope that my prayer will not be unsuccessful"** (19:47-48).

His father may have disowned him and sent him away in anger but Ibrahim (as) did not give up on his father nor answer him back in anger. He left him with a promise to continue to pray for forgiveness for him. And he did continue to pray for him as it is mentioned five times in The Qur'an. It is said that even after Azar died without having changed his faith, Ibrahim continued to pray for him until he was commanded to stop. Allah has said that there is no way an idolater can gain entry to Paradise, even with the prayers of a prophet. **The Prophet and the believers should not ask forgiveness for the polytheists – even if they are related to them**

– after having been shown that they are the inhabitants of the blazing Fire. Ibrahim asked forgiveness for his father because he had made a promise to him, but once he realized that his father was an enemy of Allah, he disavowed him [although] **Ibrahim was tender-hearted and forbearing** (9:113-114).

The Muslims were not forbidden to pray for their fathers while they lived and there was still a chance they could have a change of heart and accept Islam. But when they died actively opposing Allah's Prophet (sas), the believers were instructed to no longer plead with Allah to forgive them. The verse above clearly connects the plight of Ibrahim (as) with that of the early Muslims who were forced to leave their prospects, their homes, their loved ones in Mecca and emigrate to Medina with nothing but what they could carry. They had to put aside the natural love of a child for his family and take only God's servants as their brothers. At this time Ibrahim (as), as the Prophet Muhammad (sas) and his companions would do so much later, turned his back with sorrow on his family, his people, and his country. He turned his face inwardly towards Allah and said: **"I shall go to my Lord, He will guide me"** (37:99).

Ibrahim (as) had certainly done his best. Even though his people had for the most part rejected him and his message, he had not failed. It is only by Allah's will that someone becomes Muslim or not. It was only the prophet's duty to speak the truth, to warn and to testify. He had fulfilled his mission. He had succeeded. His people were the ones who had lost. **And whereas they sought to do evil to him, We caused them to suffer the greatest loss** (21:70). As evidence of the stubbornness of the people of Harran, they persisted in their worship of Sin the moon god despite the later wide acceptance of Christianity in the area. Well into the Islamic period, they falsely identified themselves as Sabians in order to be accepted by the state as People of the Book (2:62) and be permitted to continue their pagan traditions.

There were some who believed in Allah and His prophet Ibrahim (as). Among them were his mother Usha (rah) but as far as we know she did not leave with him. Some, however, stood beside him and turned their backs on their idolatrous kinsmen and what they idolized. Lut (as) the son of Ibrahim's (as) brother who had died earlier, stood beside his uncle and prepared to leave with him. There were also other people whose names we do not know because The Qur'an tells us: **Ibrahim and those with him said to their people: "We are done with you and all that you worship besides Allah. We deny the truth of what you believe. And between us and you has risen enmity and hatred until you come to believe in the One God." The only exception was Ibrahim saying to his father: "I shall pray for your forgiveness although it is not in my power to do anything for you against Allah"** (60:4). It is recorded in the History of At-Tabari that one of those who left with Ibrahim (as) might have been the father of the man who is known in all traditions as the Green Man, Al-Khidr (as).

And We rescued him and Lut [and brought them] **to the land which We have blessed for all peoples** (21:71). And Ibrahim (as) and his followers left the land in which they had been raised and all that was familiar and set out for the unknown, committing themselves to serve God and to go where He would guide them. Their prayer was: **"O our Rabb, in You we have placed our trust, and to You we turn, and to You is the journey"** (60:4).

So Ibrahim (as) became the leader of a small band of believers who set out with him in the direction Allah would guide them. It could be that Azar continued to live another 60 years after Ibrahim (as) left and that he died in Harran at 209 having never seen his son again. There is a shrine built for Terah/Azar in Harran that is still visited by pilgrims today praying for the forgiveness of the father of Ibrahim (as). In a Hadith narrated by Ibn Abbas (ra) it is recorded that Ibrahim (as) will see his father Azar on the Day of Judgment and he will say to him, "Didn't I tell you not to disobey me?" And his father will reply sadly, "Today I will not disobey you." Ibrahim (as) will say, "O Lord, You promised not to disgrace me on the day when all people are resurrected, so what disgrace is greater than that of my furthest father?" Allah will answer saying, "I have made Paradise forbidden for the unbelievers." (Bukhari) And Allah knows best if Azar will then have another chance at forgiveness. Ibrahim (as) was later to pray: **'O my Lord, these [idols] have led many of mankind astray. But whoever follows me, he is truly of me. He who disobeys me – for truly You are forgiving, merciful'** (14:36). So Ibrahim (as) also had hope that in the end Allah would forgive the misguided.

It is said that Ibrahim (as) was 75 years old when he left Harran and Sarah (rah), his wife, was 65. They had spent at least 20 years married and so far had not had any children. Sarah (rah) was the best of wives. In all her life she never disobeyed her husband. She was content with what he gave her and she supported him in every way. She always had food waiting for him and had gotten used to the fact that he never came home without a guest or two. The only thing that marred their married life was that they had been unable to have a child. And now Sarah (rah) was getting older and the chances of conceiving were even less likely. They contented themselves in giving their attention and affection to the children and adults who had put their lives in their hands and chosen to emigrate with them but they had not given up hope for children of their own. Leaving Harran, Ibrahim (as) prayed to Allah to grant them a child. He was now disconnected in a world in which relations and kinship were everything. Only family provided protection, support, and the promise of a continuing posterity. Raising his hands to his generous Lord, he prayed: **'Grant me a son from among the righteous'** (37:100).

CHAPTER TWENTY-ONE

The Language of Numbers

Something needs to be said at this point perhaps about the ages of the people in this story. Certainly they bear no resemblance to the ages of people today. Sarah (rah) married at 39 and was still hoping for children at 65. Ibrahim (as) embarked on a new life at 75. Azar lived to be 209. Ibrahim (as) himself lived to 175 and Sarah (rah) to 127. Some people say that all the early prophets lived very long lives. Adam (as) is said to have lived 960 years, Nuh (as) 950. Life spans got shorter after the flood but they were still much longer than we know of today. The prophet Sulayman (as) lived 150 years, the prophet Musa (as) 120. They were also, it is said, taller than people are today and they stayed youthful their entire lives.

As their years progressed they got neither frail nor aged. It is said that Ibrahim (as) grew the first white hairs known to man when he was over one hundred as a gift from his Lord. The Prophet Muhammad (sas) was only 63 when he left this world but he appeared like a man of 30. The prophets continued to live rugged, active lives up until the end and many of them were not ready to die even then because they felt they still had so much energy left for serving God. Certainly we know that it is possible

ARABIC

Letter	ا	ب	ج	د	ه	و	ز	ح	ط	ي	ك	ل	م	ن
Name	Alif	Ba	Jim	Dal	Ha	Waw	Za	Ḥa	Ṭa	Ya	Kaf	Lam	Mim	Nu
Value	1	2	3	4	5	6	7	8	9	10	20	30	40	50

Letter	س	ع	ف	ص	ق	ر	ش	ت	ث	خ	ذ	ض	ظ	غ
Name	Sin	ʿAyn	Fa	Ṣad	Qaf	Ra	Shin	Ta	Tha	Kha	Dha	Ḍad	Ẓa	Gha
Value	60	70	80	90	100	200	300	400	500	600	700	800	900	1000

HEBREW

Letter	א	ב	ג	ד	ה	ו	ז	ח	ט	י	כ
Name	Aleph	Beth	Gimel	Dalet	Heh	Vav	Zain	Chet	Tet	Yod	Kaf
Value	1	2	3	4	5	6	7	8	9	10	20

Letter	ל	מ	נ	ס	ע	פ	צ	ק	ר	ש	ת
Name	Lamed	Mem	Nun	Samekh	Ayin	Peh	Tzaddi	Quf	Resh	Shin	Tau
Value	30	40	50	60	70	80	90	100	200	300	400

Arabic and Hebrew numerological charts.

to live longer than a hundred years because even in our day a very few people do so. However, one hundred and twenty seems to be the limit and in all cases these people both look and act old. Was it possible that the early prophets had a different genetic makeup or that proper diet and lifestyle could have prolonged their youth? This is possible, because Allah can do anything but they would have had to have had a very different biology than modern man because our cells will not reproduce often enough to keep us alive that long and certainly not youthful and strong - definitely not for the 950 years that the prophet Nuh (as) is recorded as having lived. One fact supporting this possibility is that the Prophet Muhammad (sas) traveled in his body through time and space on the Night Journey ('*Isra* and *Mi'raj*). An ordinary body could not have performed such an extraordinary journey.

There is a custom in some parts of the world to exaggerate a person's age in order to reflect their wisdom and their worth. So it is said that a saint lived to three hundred years while a common man who died of old age may have been spiritually only three. In a Hadith transmitted by Abu Hurayra (ra) he explained that the size of the Prophet Adam (as) of forty meters was his original size in Paradise. Once he landed on Earth he had shrunk to a normal human size. So there is a measure of size and time that relates to heavenly conditions not to earthly ones. The prophets accomplished so much in their lives that it is as if they lived many lifetimes and their importance and influence extends until today. It can be said that due to their continuing affect on the world, they are still alive. In Indonesia even today they increase someone's age out of respect for them. This is the opposite of Western etiquette in which a person is always told they seem younger than they actually are. But this would not, however, explain why the life of Azar/Terah is so much longer than that of the prophet Ibrahim (as).

Or it could be simply that there was another method of counting time. The Sumerian counting system at the time of Ibrahim (as) was based on 60 instead of 10. We derive 60 seconds in a minute and 60 minutes in an hour from this ancient system, as well as 360 days in a lunar year and degrees in a circle. The Egyptian system of that time period, however, was based on 10 like our own. The special number of the highest god El was 60, which would correspond to our 100. The moon god Sin was 40 even though one would think that the moon god would be 30 for the average of days in the lunar month.

The Jews also counted the sacred year by jubilees. A Jubilee is the year that comes after a period of 49 years, seven sets of seven years. It is the fiftieth year and a year of rest for man and land, accompanied by celebration. And they have two new years six months apart. So it might have been that things were counted by sets of seven moon cycles making the counting almost double what it would be if counting by twelve months. But of course there were no Jews at the time of Ibrahim (as), there were only the followers of Nuh (as) and of Adam (as). The Jews are the descendants of Ibrahim's (as) grandson Ya'qub (as).

Some commentators, Jewish and Christian, have posited that the numbers themselves have a hidden meaning and were chosen as a kind of secret spiritual code. They have found patterns in the ages of the prophets mentioned in the Torah that they say statistically could not be random. The Hebrew numerical system is based on an alphabet of twenty-two letters. Each letter represents a sound and also a number. The first ten letters are the numbers 1-10 and after that each letter stands for a multiple of 10 – 20, 30, 40 until 100 and then continues to increase by hundreds until it reaches 400. This is called *Gematria*. Arabic has a similar system called *Abjad*. But since Arabic has twenty-eight letters it can assign numerical values all the way up to 1,000. Originally Arabic, like Hebrew, used its letters as numbers. In the ninth century the Muslims adopted Indian (what we usually call Arabic) numerals, unique symbols to represent numbers exclusively. *Gematria* allows each of the numbers mentioned in the Torah to also spell a word. But usually it is practiced the other way around. They derive a number from a word and then find amazing patterns of these numbers throughout the sacred text. *Abjad* has been traditionally used to try to figure out the meaning of the mysterious individual letters that begin some of the chapters in The Qur'an (*al-Muqatta'at*).

Because at the time of Ibrahim (as) letters and numbers were represented by the same symbols, they carried shared meanings that were understood easily by the people of the past. People were not confronted by so many large numbers as we are today, lists of prices for everything from ice to islands, census data, star counts, inventories, billionaires and budgets. The exact number of things was important in trade but was less important in daily life. Rather numbers could serve as adjectives to describe the nature of the thing being discussed, its quality as well as its quantity. In much the same way that matter can be reduced to its atomic structure, it is thought that the reality of all things can be described numerically.

In both Arabic and Hebrew systems, 1 and its multiples - 10, 100 - stand for unity and for Divinity.

2 is duality - Adam (as) and Hawwa (rah), the forces of good and evil, night and day, the nature of the world.

3 is the resolution of the duality by including the upper point, the heavenly reality. Each side of the triangle holds the secret of the others, the pyramid, the spiritual way. Its multiples give us 33 and 99, the Names of Allah. They also say that there are 201 names of the Prophet Muhammad (sas) which, when added together, make 3.

4 is double 2, indicating a worldly completion or balance.

5 is for the nature of humanity, 5 prayers, 5 pillars, 5 senses, 5 points of the human star – head, two arms and two legs.

6 is double 3.

7 are the levels or layers of existence, the veils, the divisions. Allah created the world in 7 days and from that we derive the 7-day week. There are 7 earths and 7 heavens. 70, 700 seem to mean simply a long and perfect period of time, or a great amount without being specific as to the actual number.

8 is stability and peace, there are 8 Paradises, and it is the sign for infinity.

9 is the closest to 10, to God. 99 names of Allah are revealed to mankind. The hundredth name is a secret.

The number 40 is a special number indicating some sort of completion or perfection, 4 being balance and 10 being divinity, it is the symbol of completion for the inner reality. Musa (as) spent 40 days on Mount Sinai, the Bani Israil spent 40 years in the wilderness, Isa (as) spent 40 days in the desert, many of the Prophets were 40 when they received their missions, including the Prophet Muhammad (sas). There is a Hadith related by Abu Ayyub al-Ansari (ra) that the Prophet (sas) said: "When a person devotes himself purely, or sincerely, to Allah for 40 days, wisdom will pour from his heart and appear on his tongue." Numerology is a science in itself that is said to have been perfected by Sayyiduna Ali ibn

Abi Talib (ra) but it is not open to everyone.

It is interesting, and there is sufficient evidence to be confident in assuming, that these very large and often very specific numbers, such as 127 or 960, indicate something other than actual lifespan. The divine Author of these sacred books was more than an accountant or scribe. But what His purpose is, other than to amaze and impress mathematicians, we cannot say. So we leave it to Allah as something tantalizing that we don't understand and as something that when it becomes useful knowledge for us, will undoubtedly be unveiled.

CHAPTER TWENTY-TWO

The Holy Land

Slowly the group made their way south, herding their animals as they went from pasture to pasture, from watering place to watering place along the land we call Bilad as-Sham, an area defined as six days by camel in every direction from Damascus. It is the land that stretches along the Mediterranean coast from Urfa in Turkey south all the way to Egypt. And it is considered to be what Allah was referring to when He said: **the land which We have blessed for all people.** (21:71) It is the land that was called Canaan, what we now call Palestine. It is where the prophets of the Bani Israil lived and died and where Isa (as) will return at the end of time and the Mahdi (as) will fight the last battle between good and evil.

There is a tradition that on their way, this small band of believers crossed the Euphrates at what is now the Turkish-Syrian border and proceeded to Aleppo, one of the oldest inhabited cities. In Arabic the name for Aleppo is Halab as-Shahba. *Halab* comes from the root meaning 'to milk'. The explanation is that Ibrahim (as) camped there for a while and every morning he would milk his grey cow whose name was *ash-Shahba*, the Grey. Ibrahim (as) offered this milk as *sadaqa*, charity to the poor. The

The well at Beer Sheba that was dug by Ibrahim (as) and near which he lived.

inhabitants of the city would call out to each other, "He is milking *as-Shahba*" so that the needy would know to come with their bowls to collect their portion of milk. It is thought that the place of his encampment was near or within the ancient citadel walls that comprised, until recent events, the oldest standing castle in the world. There is also a mosque built over the rock where it is said that Ibrahim (as) stayed on his way out of the city, called *Maqam Ibrahim*.

Then he continued his southward journey, moving slowly with pack and herd animals. He would stop for pasture and for watering. The country there was different. The languages of the area were still Semitic but from the southerly branches and he may have had some difficulty understanding. The religion was different also but not in kind, only in the details. They were still polytheists but with a slightly different pantheon of gods and goddesses. The people were mostly nomadic pastoralists rather than farmers so their places of worship were natural outdoor sites. There were altars set up near sacred trees. Stones set up, as the biblical phrase goes, as places of libation or sacrifice. People passing by poured some milk or fat over the stones in the name of one god or another. The father of all their Gods was still known as El, the earliest form of Allah but, like the Akkadians, the people of Canaan had mostly forgotten His worship and instead prayed to lesser gods represented by objects of the natural world around them.

From the book of Genesis in the Torah we learn that Ibrahim (as) crossed the Jordan River onto the plain of Shechem (Nablus), north of Jerusalem. At a holy place there, known as the Terebinth of Moreh, he received a revelation that Allah was giving the surrounding land to him and to his descendants, who at the time he didn't have. This must have been very good news indeed and in consequence he built an altar to Allah in that place out of thankfulness. Altars were stones on which to place a sacrifice. They were not shelves for holy objects. They might, however, have indicated the direction of prayer but then what was the *qibla* of Ibrahim (as)? Moving on he came to Bethel, a town whose name translates as – House of Allah. It was a place of excellent pasture and abundant water. In this place the small community encamped and here Ibrahim (as) built another altar to Allah and there he made another sacrifice of an animal.

From Bethel they moved to Hebron and here, on the land that

would eventually be his final resting place, Ibrahim (as) and his family stayed for almost two years. The rains had been decreasing steadily and the crops that depended on rain failed. Pastoralists have meat and milk but they need bread also. They trade milk products and animals for the agricultural supplies they need. If there is not enough then it is not for sale. Good pasture was harder and harder to find and there was rising pressure over who had rights to it. Newcomers were the first to be excluded. At one point the small group had nothing to eat. Sarah (rah) suggested that Ibrahim (as) go to visit a man of his acquaintance to see if he would perhaps sell them or give them some food. Ibrahim (as) made the long journey but found the man unable to give him what he asked. Traveling home Ibrahim (as) sadly thought of the disappointment on the faces of his family when he arrived. He filled his saddlebags with sand so it would look like he had been successful and then he could tell them the truth later. On reaching home he went to rest and woke up to the delicious smell of fresh baked bread. He knew they had no grain and so immediately arose to ask where the flour had come from. Sarah (rah) laughed and said "Why you know because you brought it with you." When Ibrahim (as) looked in his saddlebags he found them full of the choicest wheat and barley. He thanked Allah who out of compassion had turned sand into grain so that Ibrahim (as) would not have to disappoint his loved ones.

The small group, under God's guidance, moved on again going south. The Torah says they went south to the Negev but the Hadith say they went south all the way to Yemen. Eventually they crossed through the Sinai and entered Egypt, where the mighty Nile, whose source is in Paradise, kept the gardens watered and the crops from failing. This retreat to Egypt when there was famine in Sham was to be repeated by Ibrahim's (as) descendants in the time of Ya'qub (as) and Yusuf (as).

Map of the travels of Ibrahim (as).

Statue of Mentuhotep from the Cairo Museum. He was one of the pharaohs around the time of Ibrahim (as) 2,000 BCE.

CHAPTER TWENTY-THREE
The Third Lie – My Sister

Ibrahim (as) and family arrived in Egypt and asked permission of the officials to enter and pasture their flocks. They were allowed to settle in the area of Goshen which is the eastern side of the Nile Delta and just exactly where the Banu Isra'il lived when they came to Egypt at the time of Yusuf (as). And here is where a very important event occurred in their lives.

Ibrahim (as) was now about seventy-seven or seventy-eight and Sarah (rah) ten years younger, according to the dates given in the Torah. Apparently Sarah (rah) was such a remarkable woman that, even in her old age, she began to attract the attention of the Egyptian authorities. She was the second most beautiful woman ever created. She had a lovely and noble appearance. She was also a believer and the wife of a prophet. She must have radiated a spiritual light that added to her other charms. The Jews say that her husband was so uninterested in the world that he had never noticed how beautiful she was until, arriving in Egypt, he saw her reflection in the clear waters of the Nile. Once his eye fell on her in this way, she was left unprotected and she began to attract the attention of others as well. Up until that time presumably, Ibrahim (as) had simply known and loved her for the fineness of her character and the love they shared for Allah. We will never know. But we do know that she caused a stir in Egypt and Ibrahim (as) began to notice and fear for the worst.

Word reached the tyrant who was the Pharaoh at that time, of the arrival in their country of the most attractive lady anyone had ever set eyes on. And Pharaoh developed a desire to see her and to make her his own. Ibrahim (as) must have known that this was a possibility. When Pharaoh's attendants came to inquire after Sarah (rah) Sayyiduna Ibrahim (as) did not tell them she was his wife. Instead he told them she was his sister. It might have been only a partial lie since there is some possibility that in addition to being his wife, Sarah (rah) was also his stepsister or even, as the Jews say, his half-sister.

According to the hadith of Abu Hurayra (ra), the Prophet Muhammad (sas) said that Ibrahim (as) only made three untrue statements in his whole life. The first was when he told his family that he was sick and could not go to the festival of the gods. The second was when he claimed that the big idol, on whose neck he had hung his axe, was the one who had chopped up the smaller idols out of jealousy. These both were considered to be lies told for the sake of Allah. This third lie was more problematic. Some commentators say that Ibrahim (as) told this third lie because if the Pharaoh found out that Sarah (rah) was already married, it would not have cooled his desire in the slightest. He would simply have ordered her husband killed and then he would have taken what he wanted anyway. With Ibrahim (as) dead, Sarah (rah) would have been alone in the world and in the hands of an unbelieving people without hope of rescue.

According to Abu Hurayra (ra) Sayyiduna Ibrahim (as) told Sarah (rah) that he had lied about her and asked her to support his lie with her own. He said: "O Sarah, there are no believers on the face of the earth except me and you, and this person asked me and I told him you are my sister, so do not contradict me." She always obeyed him so she promised to tell the officials, if they asked, that she was his sister. Ibrahim (as) told her that he feared for his life and for hers because they were the only people on the face of the earth at that time who were worshipping the One God Almighty and if they were gone, there would be nobody. But it still sounds to some commentators like an unconvincing excuse. They have trouble understanding how Sayyiduna Ibrahim (as) could allow his wife to be taken against her will or how he could consent to gain economically from the transaction, taking gifts and a bride price from Pharaoh. As Sayyiduna l-Khidr (as) explained when Musa (as) objected to his seemingly random acts of violence: **'I did not do it of my own accord'** (18:82). Ibrahim (as) also acted as he was directed regardless of what others might think in his time or even in our time. And Allah turned the situation around to bring goodness out of attempted evil.

It is clear in retrospect that Allah had a purpose in bringing Ibrahim (as) and his family to that place and in attracting the eye of Pharaoh. Ibrahim (as) of course was confident of this even if it broke his heart and tried his patience. He was a man of action and had proven himself unafraid to stand up alone against an unjust authority. He could have fought Pharaoh as he fought Namrud but he did not. He was rightly guided and applied the right solution to the right problem. This problem called for no action and perhaps that was a great deal harder for Ibrahim (as) than taking action. He stuck to his prayer carpet and let Allah do the acting. They had come to Egypt as part of Allah's plan. They must be steadfast and let that plan play out.

Camels as they might have looked leaving Egypt for Canaan.

CHAPTER TWENTY-FOUR

Pharaoh's Gift

What Ibrahim (as) feared came to pass. Pharaoh heard about the loveliness of Sarah (rah) and wanted her for his wife. He began to send gifts to Ibrahim (as) as her brother and guardian. He sent animals and silver. These gifts were accepted gratefully by the famine stricken refugees. Finally one day, Pharaoh sent his attendants to collect his bride. As they carried her off, Ibrahim (as) stood up to pray. We don't know the prayer of Ibrahim (as), its forms or its words or its intervals. We know from a Hadith that he prayed at least four *rakat* in the morning. We are sure it included bowing and prostration (*ruku'* and *sajda*) since Allah has said: **And thus did We command Ibrahim and Isma'il: 'purify My House for those who walk around it, those who stay there, and those who bow and prostrate themselves in worship'** (2:125) and **When the signs of the Most Merciful were recited to them, they fell down prostrating and weeping** (19:58). And he continued to pray to Allah for the safety of his wife.

She meanwhile was taken to the women's quarters of the palace and made ready to receive Pharaoh. She also began to pray that Allah protect her from his advances. When he came, he watched her for a while and then at some point reached out to touch her. Immediately his arms were frozen in place. He was paralyzed and could not move. He begged Sarah (rah) to pray for his recovery which she did because she did not want to be accused of killing the king. Allah released him. Sarah (rah) continued to pray for Allah's protection. Whereupon Pharaoh reached for her again. The same thing happened, perhaps even more severely. He started shaking involuntarily and neither his arms nor his legs would obey his command. He promised Sarah (rah) that he would not touch her if she prayed again for his recovery. This she willingly did and he was restored to full power. However, when he broke his promise for the third time and again the same thing happened, he was finally convinced that she could not be his. The God to whom she prayed was stronger than any he had at his disposal and he no longer desired to have her. He considered her instead to be some sort of witch or demon.

Pharaoh immediately had his attendants take her back to Ibrahim (as) with a thousand coins of silver because at that time silver was extremely rare and of more value than gold. He had already given as her dowry many goats and sheep. Now he gave Ibrahim (as) in addition, as a parting gift, two things that would change the world forever. The first was a gift of camels, animals which were still unknown in Palestine but are thought to have been domesticated around that time in Egypt and southern Arabia. Perhaps it was Sayyiduna Ibrahim (as) who introduced the camel to Ash-Sham for the first time. It would have made a huge difference in the lifestyle of the region. Since camels need to be watered much less frequently than other herd animals, it would have made drier areas more habitable. Since camels have greater stamina and can travel days without water or much food, it would have made movement across desert wastes faster and more possible. This would have increased the interaction and trade between previously far distant lands. It would have had an effect on the culture of the area somewhat like the introduction of the horse to the Indians of the American plains. And it would have enabled Ibrahim (as) to travel farther and faster than it had been possible before, even as far as Mecca in the heart of Arabia.

The second gift that Pharaoh gave Sarah (rah) was the true gift and undoubtedly the real reason why this whole trip and trial had been ordained by Allah. Pharaoh gave Sarah (rah) an Egyptian slave girl to serve her, by the name of Hajar (rah), who some say was a granddaughter of the

Arabian prophet Salih (as). It is interesting to note that Allah had given Salih (as) a miraculous mother camel and baby as a sign for his people, the Thamud. She gave such abundant milk that all the poor were fed. The rich complained about how much water she drank and how much pasture she ate and so in disbelief and thanklessness they killed her and brought about their own destruction. It could be that this gift of Allah was the first camel to be docile enough to allow herself to be milked and that it marked the beginning of the domestication of camels. Then his granddaughter, Hajar (rah), was the means by which camels were introduced further north into Canaan and Sham. Only Allah knows.

When Sarah (rah) returned she found her husband in the exact same place she had left him, praying to Allah. She made a sign so that he would know that she had returned safely and he continued to pray, thanking his Lord for her delivery from the tyrant. He had done the only thing he knew that might save his beloved wife from the hands of Pharaoh, he had asked the help of Allah. And if she were not saved then it was Allah's will and he knew for certain that it was out of love and caring, and for the best. So he had stayed in prayer until her return and it is said that Allah showed her to him the whole time she was in Pharaoh's hands so that his heart might be consoled and he would know she was unharmed. Immersed in prayer, concentrating on his Lord was perhaps the only way Ibrahim (as) could endure the passivity required by this test.

It is unlikely that Ibrahim (as) remained totally quiet and inactive during his whole stay in Egypt, however. Egypt, like the rest of the world at this time, was a theocracy. Perhaps more than anywhere else, however, its culture was completely focused on the worship of many gods and on the preparation for the life to come. Pharaoh was one of an extensive pantheon of gods. The religion was obsessed with death and preparing for the afterlife but in a very materialistic way. They buried their dead with all the food and clothes and objects they thought they would need in an afterlife that would be very similar to their worldly life. Even the body of the dead was preserved at great cost and trouble, leaving nothing to chance or to the Creator. The great pyramids had probably already been built as huge tombs and they dominated the horizon of the large cities. Burial and mummification were major concerns. Ibrahim (as) and Lut (as) avoided the religious centers and frequent festivals but they must have discussed religion with the people they met and gently tried to remind them of their Creator who can create with a single word and has no need for pickled bones and skin.

In the end what happened between Sarah (rah) and the Pharaoh must have been whispered around among the people and it confirmed all that Ibrahim (as) had been saying. It was a clear sign to Pharaoh and his people that the God of Ibrahim (as) was more present and more powerful than all their other gods combined. So the terrible test of faith that Sarah (rah) and Ibrahim (as) endured assuredly served to teach those who could see, where the truth lay. Undoubtedly some Egyptians accepted and followed Ibrahim (as) even when he returned to Sham.

The Torah doesn't consider that Ibrahim (as) told a lie because it says that Sarah (rah) was actually his half-sister. So at worst it was only half a lie. However, the story that he told about Sarah (rah) being his sister did not sit well with Ibrahim (as) himself. We know this because it is recorded in the Hadith that at the time of the final Judgment the resurrected souls will ask each of the prophets to intercede for them with their Lord. Each prophet will be too ashamed to face Allah and ask for favors because of something he did while living on earth. Sayyiduna Adam (as) will be ashamed for having disobeyed his Lord and eaten what was forbidden. Sayyiduna Nuh (as) will be ashamed for having asked for the destruction of the people to whom Allah had sent him with prophecy. Sayyiduna Musa (as) will be ashamed for his having killed a man. Sayyiduna Dawud (as) will be ashamed for having taken another man's wife. Sayyiduna Yunus (as) will be ashamed for trying to run away from his mission. Sayyiduna 'Isa (as) will be ashamed that his community has ascribed to him divinity. Sayyiduna Ibrahim (as) will be ashamed for having told a lie. Of all the 124,000 prophets, known and unknown, only the Prophet Muhammad (sas) will be without shame or sin and he will pray for all of us.

CHAPTER TWENTY-FIVE
A Gift for Lut (as)

Pharaoh no longer wanted Ibrahim (as) and his tribe living in Goshen. Official permission to pasture their herds there was rescinded and they were sent back to the Negev desert in what is now southern Israel. But they had acquired so much wealth, livestock, and foodstuffs from their stay in Egypt that they could manage to survive there and since they had spent a few years in Egypt perhaps the famine had passed. So Ibrahim (as) and his companions left Egypt and headed back to Bethel where they had previously built an altar to Allah. They traveled slowly because this time they had vast herds of animals that needed food and water. They thought that Bethel had enough water and pasture land to accommodate their new abundance.

According to the Torah, after a little while trouble developed between the herdsmen of Ibrahim (as) and those of Lut (as). Even the well-watered grasslands there provided insufficient pasture for the numbers of animals the two men now owned. They were competing for pasture. Uncle and nephew recognized that they needed to separate their herds and their families. So they stood on a high hill and, surveying the land

Above is the Oak of Mamre as it looked in a photograph taken in 1900. Below is a drawing of the same tree as it looked much earlier.

below them, each man chose which area would be his. Lut (as) chose the country to his left, the rich agricultural plain which it is believed the Jordan River flooded and fertilized every year just as the Nile continues to do in Egypt. Five fortified city-states were established in this region around the great fresh water lake whose remnants are now the Dead Sea. He would give up the nomadic life to settle and preach in the towns of Sodom, Gomorrah, Adnah, Zeboiim, and Zoar. Ibrahim (as) chose the vast pasture lands of Palestine on his right where he and his family would remain living in tents tending to the needs of their herds. They would stay clear of the cities and their sins. They moved in the vicinity of the place where Ibrahim (as) had set up an altar and a place of prayer on a hill called the Oaks of Mamre near Hebron.

But the Muslim commentators explain the cause of the separation very differently. They say that one morning after the prayer Ibrahim (as) looked into his nephew's face and saw a change and a light that had not been there before. Lut (as) confirmed that during the night the Archangel Jibra'il (as) had visited him and given him a mission and the station of prophet. In those early days before travel became fast and relatively easy, each prophet was sent to a particular people and no other. It was possible, and not uncommon, to have two prophets living near to one another, each with a different mission. Lut (as) had been honored by Allah with the very difficult task of setting a righteous example and of delivering a warning to the people who were reputed to be the most perverse and disobedient people of any on earth until that time. So uncle and nephew divided their wealth and with great sadness parted company in order for each of them to follow the path Allah had laid out before them.

The station of Khidr (as) to one side of the Dome of the Rock on the Temple Mount, Jerusalem, marking the place where he prayed.
Courtesy Akram Reda.

CHAPTER TWENTY-SIX

A Leader of Men

There is a story concerning Ibrahim (as) and Lut (as) that happened some time after they split up their herds and families. The only place this story is told is in the book of Genesis in the Torah. It paints a picture of the living situation of Ibrahim (as) in Sham that is quite different from the picture given up to now. He was hardly the lone believer living in a tent far from human company, perched on a hill with only his wife and his God.

The five cities in the Jordan plain where Lut (as) had been sent to preach had sworn allegiance to the King of Elam, whose name was Chedorlaomer. Some years later the local kings of all five of the cites agreed to unite in rebellion against the Elamites and refuse to pay the obligatory tribute tax. Chedorlaomer gathered a large army and the following year he marched from his capital city of Elam in what is now Iran. The purpose of the expedition was to suppress the rebellion and punish the rebel kings. It was also to strengthen the Elamite hold over all the area and to discourage similar rebellion by plundering and laying waste wherever they went. After months of marching and pillaging they met the army of the five kings in the valley of Siddim which is now thought to be at or under the southern end of the Dead Sea. Chedorlaomer's massive army won a decisive victory. Those they didn't kill they took into slavery. City by city they ransacked and destroyed. Anyone they encountered they took captive including Lut (as), his wife, and two daughters. Then the exultant army turned eastward and began the long march home. Every day they marched but they moved slowly because of the wagons heavy with plunder and the weak captives they were dragging behind them. Every night they celebrated their victories. The soldiers and their commanders were confidant and relaxed. They had devastated all the small kingdoms between there and home. They thought that they had nothing to fear.

Before being captured, Lut (as) had sent one of his servants to find Ibrahim (as) and inform him of what had happened. When the servant finally found the tent of Ibrahim (as) he fell at his feet and related the whole story of the defeat and capture. Sayyiduna Ibrahim (as) immediately went to consult men with whom he had a relationship of support and cooperation. They were three brothers of the Amorite people by the names of Mamre, Eshcol, and Aner. They agreed to join him in pursuing the tyrant Chedorlaomer. Each of the four called on their herdsmen and retainers. It is said that Ibrahim (as) had 318 men who were trained in weapons and each of the others might have had almost as many. United they formed quite a large army although still small compared to that of their enemy. They marched double time in order to quickly overtake the Elamites.

Their hope was to overcome the larger force by stealth. They planned to sneak up and attack at night. They had complete surprise on their side because the army of Chedorlaomer had no idea they were pursuing them or that they even existed. The Elamites, exultant in their victories, were celebrating every night, drinking heavily and carousing. The army of Ibrahim (as) and his allies caught them completely off guard. Out of a drunken sleep they woke to the arrows of Ibrahim (as) and his soldiers. Many were killed and the rest fled in disarray in the direction of home, leaving behind all the booty and all the captives.

Lut (as) and his family were rescued along with all of the other people from the five cities of the plain. When the people of the surrounding country heard of the rout of Chedorlaomer they were joyous for they had suffered greatly when the army had passed through their lands. The king and high priest of Salem (perhaps Jerusalem), by the name of Melchizedek (q) (*Maliki sadiq* in Arabic - truthful king), and his people streamed out of the gates of their city to cheer and welcome the victorious army. They prepared a great feast for the battle-worn soldiers and exhausted captives. Melchizedek (q) is a mysterious saintly figure who appears out of nowhere in the Torah as a believer in Allah the Most High, (*El Elyon* in Hebrew, *Allah al-'Ala* in Arabic) the One God and Creator. He blessed them all in the name of El Elyon, the same blessing that the Torah says Ibrahim (as) would use himself at a later time. Ibrahim (as) showed him the greatest respect and deference and even shared with him a portion of the spoils of war.

The Jews thought that Melchizedek (q) might be Sam (as) the son of Nuh (as) who lived 600 years and might have still been alive. 'Isa (as) is told in the New Testament that he is "a priest forever in the order of Melchizedek" (Hebrews 5:5-11). Some Muslims think that Melchizedek (q) might be Idris (as) (Enoch) who was sent as a prophet between Adam (as) and Nuh (as) and who is accredited with transmitting much of the useful knowledge that distinguishes mankind: writing, weaving and sewing, tools and weapons, and the domestication of animals. Idris (as) died and was restored to life. Since then he has served as the head of the saints who protect and support the world by maintaining firm and continuous worship. **And mention Idris in the Book. He was a man of truth (*sidiq*), a prophet and We raised him to a high (*'aliy*) place** (19:56-7). He is joined now by the other prophets who have yet to die, Ilyas (as), 'Isa (as), and

Painted by Dieric Bouts the Elder in 1464 -67 showing Ibrahim (as) as a warrior on the right and Melchizedek on the left.

Khidr (as) the teacher of Musa (as). At-Tabari says that the father of Khidr (as) was one of those who left his homeland to follow Sayyiduna Ibrahim (as) to Canaan and it was there that his son happened upon the water of life, drank, and became immortal. Some think that Melchizedek (q) could have actually been Khidr (as). Whoever he is, he remains a holy figure representing those eternal hidden servants of whom, Allah in His mercy, has promised to never deprive the world.

After resting, Ibrahim (as) and his allies continued on to their homes by way of the cities of Sodom, Gomorrah, Zoar, Zeboiim, and Admah. It was the custom at the time that the spoils of war were to be distributed among the leaders and the fighters of the victorious army. But Ibrahim (as) relinquished his rights and refused to take even a thread from the spoils. A prophet fights for justice not for wealth. After his allies had taken their share, everything was returned to their original owners and all the captives were set free.

Here we see Ibrahim (as) in a totally different light, as the patriarch, the leader of men. **When his Lord tried Ibrahim with commands, and he fulfilled them, He said, 'I will make you a leader of men'** (2:124). Ibrahim (as) had extensive personal wealth in animals and land for which he required the services of a large number of men. He needed herders to care for the animals and he needed guards to protect them all from both human and animal predators. All of these men probably had families as well. They attached themselves to Ibrahim (as) to be in his service in return for protection and pay. Ibrahim (as) was a shaykh, a chief. His good judgment, wisdom, kindness, and generosity attracted many families to live under his beneficent protection. Certainly they must have accepted his spiritual leadership as well and submitted to Allah and become Muslim. Acting as a leader of a large community, he had alliances with neighboring chieftains who were willing to follow him even to war against a much larger force. He upheld justice, he defended the weak, he rescued his neighbors regardless of their beliefs or practices and refused to profit from his kindness. He was a model of righteous leadership. He was a prophet of God, a warrior, and a political leader in much the same way as the prophets Musa (as), Dawud (as), Sulayman (as) and the Prophet Muhammad (sas). He led his people down the straight road in all aspects of life.

A miniature showing the Green Man, Sayyiduna Khidr (as).

A mosaic from a church in Ravenna Italy built in 540 CE, showing the angelic guests of Ibrahim (as).

CHAPTER TWENTY-SEVEN
Welcome Guests

One of the very special attributes for which Ibrahim (as) is famous, is his hospitality. There is a hadith reported in Malik's *Muwatta* that Ibrahim (as) was the first person on earth to show hospitality. It is unlikely that he was the first in the world to host a guest but he was the first to understand that hospitality is in fact a duty of the believer, an act of worship. He gave hospitality to guests freely without either expecting compensation or incurring obligation. And this has become an almost sacred duty for the Muslims. A visitor has a right to food and shelter for three days without question or obligation. The host expects nothing in return; he hopes only for reward from Allah.

The rewards for hosting a guest are many. It is said that forty days before the arrival of a guest an angel is sent from the Lord with the guest's provision. This provision consists of nine parts. One part is to satisfy the needs of the guest and the other eight are to provide for the host and his family. The angel continues to stay in the house of the hosting family until the guest comes and leaves. During this time the angel prays to his Lord continuously for the benefit of the host. For each bite that the guest takes, the reward of one Hajj and one Umra are written for the host. When the guest leaves all the sins of the host family have been forgiven and they are as clean as if they were newly born.

Ibrahim's (as) home was open to all guests, day or night. It is said that he had a special house or tent just to accommodate guests and it had, not one door but, four doors to receive travelers from whichever direction they came. There would have been bachelor men without their own homes who would be semi-permanent residents. There would have been people in need, looking for help or charity. There would have been people with a dispute or a problem who needed advice or judgment. A shaykh's house is rarely empty but when it was, it is said that Ibrahim (as) would go out before the meal searching for some man to share his table.

His guesthouse must have also served as a place of worship where his retainers and their families gathered for congregational prayers on certain special days or whenever they could. We don't know if he observed a Sabbath and if he did on which day. Allah says in The Qur'an: **And Ibrahim, who fulfilled** [his obligations] (53:37). The Prophet Muhammad (sas) related in a Hadith Qudsi that Allah says: "O Bani Adam, if you pray four *raka'at* for Me at the beginning of the day, I shall supply everything you need until the end of it." (Tirmidhi). And there is another Hadith in which the Prophet (sas) explains that these four *raka'at* were the obligation, mentioned in this verse that Ibrahim (as) fulfilled faithfully every day. So we know that Ibrahim (as) prayed at least these and we also know that he made *sajda*, prostration, since it is mentioned several times in the Torah that he fell on his face in thankfulness to the Lord. We know also that he set up altars to Allah for animal sacrifice.

It was also the custom of Sayyiduna Ibrahim (as) to fast for long periods of time. We know that the fast of the prophet Dawud (as) was on alternate days, one day he fasted and the next day he did not. The fast of the prophet Muhammad (sas) was Mondays and Thursdays. The fast of Ibrahim (as) was to fast and continue fasting unless there was a guest to break fast with him. He would look for a guest but, if there was none, he would drink some water and make intention to fast again the next day without eating. Depending on the narrator, Ibrahim (as) would continue to fast in this way without eating from three to thirty days unless Allah sent him a guest.

At some point the archangels Jibra'il (as), Mika'il (as), 'Azra'il (as), and Israfil (as) were looking down from heaven at Ibrahim Khalil Allah (as), the friend of Allah, and they saw that he had grown very wealthy. His herds of sheep covered the hillsides. His horses and donkeys ran freely through the valleys tearing up the grass. His goats and sheep had twins every six months and his cows twinned once a year. Even the dogs he used for herding numbered in the thousands. They became worried for his sake and sent prayers of concern to their Lord. They thought that Ibrahim (as) had forgotten Allah and must be devoting himself entirely to earthly matters, collecting and hoarding wealth. Allah knew that the heart of His friend was only for Him but He gave the angels permission to take the forms of men and descend to earth to see for themselves.

When Ibrahim (as) saw the four young men from far away he began to prepare a meal for them. He ordered a sheep sacrificed immediately. Its meat was roasting and bread was in the oven baking by the time the travelers arrived at his door. He sat them down before this delicious meal. Angels, since they are beings of light, do not of course eat food. But they asked Ibrahim (as) what he wanted in payment for this meal. Ibrahim (as) was surprised and said that he asked nothing other than that they should pronounce the name of Allah, *BismiLlāh*, before eating.

Jibra'il (as) possesses a deep sonorous voice and he was happy to praise his Lord. He recited, "*subbuhu l-Quddus Rabbuna wa Rabbu l-Mala'ikatu wa r-Ruh*" – "Praise be to the All-Holy One, our Lord and the Lord of the Angels and of the Spirit".

سَبُّوحٌ قُدُّوسٌ رَبُّنَا وَرَبُّ الْمَلَآئِكَةِ وَالرُّوحِ

Ibrahim (as) was speechless with wonder. It was such a beautiful phrase and said with such a sublime voice. He begged the angel in the form of a man to please repeat it. But Jibra'il (as) had come for the purpose of testing the sincerity of Ibrahim (as) and so he said, 'What will you give me if I say it again?" Ibrahim (as) replied "a third of my wealth." The Angel repeated his praise and it was even more beautiful than the first time. Sayyiduna Ibrahim (as) was nearly fainting in ecstasy and pleaded with Jibra'il (as) to say it again and then again. Under the same conditions

Jibra'il (as) recited his praise of the Lord Almighty three times until Ibrahim (as) had given him the entirety of his wealth. And Ibrahim (as) would have loved to ask him to keep repeating it but he had nothing more with which to pay him.

At last the angels were deeply impressed with their host and they revealed to him their true nature and the purpose of their visit. "In truth," they said "you are the friend of God and there is nothing in your heart other than love of Him. O Ibrahim, take your animals and your servants, your tents and your goods, we are angels and have no use for such things. You are truly *Khalil Allah*." But Sayyiduna Ibrahim (as) refused, saying that he could not take back what he had given in the presence of the Lord. He would not take back his wealth and was preparing to set off with only the clothes on his back. The angels were confused and agitated. What were they going to do with all this worldly property they had been gifted? Finally, Allah stepped in to solve their problem. He advised them to tell Ibrahim (as) that Allah had accepted the gift of all his worldly goods but that he must remain as their caretaker. Ibrahim (as) could agree to this arrangement and the four angels returned to their heavenly stations, amazed and much relieved. And Ibrahim (as) continued to watch over the herds of the Lord and praise Him in the words the angels had taught him.

CHAPTER TWENTY-EIGHT

Sarah's (rah) Gift

In the Torah it is said that Allah promised Ibrahim (as) at least five different times a multitude of descendants, as many as the stars in the sky and the grains of sand on the shore. The first time was in Harran and now the last at Hebron. Allah promised him the land from the Nile to the Euphrates for this nation to live. But Sarah (rah) continued to remain childless. So it came to her one day, out of love and duty to her husband and in order to fulfill God's promise, to offer Ibrahim (as) the slave girl given to her by Pharaoh. She said she had found Hajar (rah) to be a good girl, clean and respectful, and she hoped she would have children who would be blood descendants of Ibrahim (as) and who would be a source of love and joy for all of them. This was not unusual among the people of the Torah. The wives of Ya'qub (as), La'iqa (rah) and Rifqa (rah), also gave him their slave girls to be his wives after they already had children of their own. They each had several sons but they considered the sons of their slave girls to be like their own and so they were actually competing with each other in providing children for their husband. Ibrahim (as) accepted Sarah's (rah) selfless offer and he took Hajar (rah) as a second wife. In a short time Hajar (rah) became pregnant.

Sketch by Rembrandt von Rijn of pregnant Hajar (rah) being told by the Angel to return to Ibrahim (as) and Sarah (rah).

The Muslim narrators say that it was also at this point, in Ibrahim's (as) eightieth year, just before the birth of his first son Isma'il (as), that Allah sent the Archangel Jibra'il (as) with the command for Ibrahim (as) to circumcise himself. Circumcision is considered one of the acts of cleanliness that makes a man pure for prayer. Most Islamic jurists regard it as obligatory for every Muslim male. Some of the schools of law have ruled that without it a man cannot pray properly and cannot lead a congregation as *imam*. They also ruled that his testimony is unacceptable in a court of law. There is, however, no mention of it in The Qur'an itself. The Torah tells a different story and draws a different interpretation. It says that circumcision wasn't ordered until Ibrahim (as) was in his ninety-ninth year, just before the birth of his second son Ishaq (as) and it serves as an important symbol of the Covenant between God and the children of Ibrahim (as) through his grandson Ya'qub (as). This Covenant was a promise that God would favor the children of Ya'qub (as) (also named Isra'il) and that they in turn would worship none other than Him. It was only established with people of a particular genetic descent so it makes sense, they say, that it is written on the piece of flesh responsible for producing those descendants. Both Jews and Muslims, however, agree that circumcision is a physical sign of their relationship with their Lord to the exclusion of those who are uncircumcised: it indelibly distinguishes them from the unbelievers. However, even though most Christians do not consider circumcision to be ritually required and do not practice it, they are not considered unbelievers by Muslims.

Ibrahim (as) was working in the field when the angel of the Lord descended with the order. He proceeded to carry it out with the instrument at hand. According to the Jews he was cutting hay with a scythe and so used that tool to circumcise himself. According to the Muslims he was breaking up the earth with a small hoe called an adze and so that is what he used. The angel was surprised at the speed with which the prophet responded to Allah's order and told him that if he had waited only a little bit the angel would have brought him a more appropriate tool from heaven and it would have been far less painful. Ibrahim (as), however, answered the angel that the command of the Lord deserves nothing less than immediate and complete compliance. Probably it never even occurred to him to do otherwise. He then proceeded to circumcise all his male companions and servants, hopefully in a gentler fashion.

According to most accounts it was also at this point that problems arose between the two wives of Ibrahim (as). Although Hajar (rah) was a wife now, she was still under the hand of Sarah (rah) as both her servant and her younger co-wife. The Muslims say that Sarah (rah) began to suffer from jealousy and she started to mistreat Hajar (rah). The Jews and Christians say that Hajar (rah) began to be disrespectful and insolent to her mistress because she was able to conceive her master's child. In those days, the ability or inability to bear children was considered a reflection of a woman's worth. Perhaps both these views are accurate. It was how each of them felt, blaming the other for their own heartache.

There is some truth in the fact that women do not share the attention of their husbands lightly. Even some of the wives of the Prophet Muhammad (sas) admitted to feeling jealous of each other and trying little deceptions in order to get him to spend more time with them and less with their sister wives. However, it never got to the point of causing physical harm or banishment or divorce. So although jealousy seems to be a natural and common consequence of being co-wives, women of the caliber of Sarah (rah) and Hajar (rah) or the wives of the Prophet (sas), were able to handle it in a most righteous manner. And their prophet husbands helped them to overcome their jealousy. It seems definitely demeaning to these very special and chosen women to imagine that they behaved in a petty way or that they momentarily forgot about submission to their Lord. They were much finer than that. Whatever the truth, the story goes that Sarah (rah) began to assert her authority over Hajar (rah) in a physical way.

It it said that Sarah (rah) vowed to cut off the ears and nose and genitalia of her rival in order to disfigure her and make her unattractive to their husband. Before actually carrying it out, however, she repented and told Ibrahim (as). Vows made in the name of Allah are serious promises. They must be carried out or atoned for. They cannot be left undone or ignored. However, if they are unreasonable or wrong, they can be completed in a harmless way. When the prophet Ayyub (as) thought that his faithful wife Rahma (rah) had betrayed him, he vowed to whip her a hundred lashes. When he later realized that she had, in fact, been true to him Allah provided him a way out of his vow by suggesting he hit her once lightly with a hundred stems of grass (38:44). So now Sayyiduna Ibrahim (as) helped Sarah (rah) complete her vow in a relatively harmless way. He told her to pierce Hajar's (rah) ears and nose and to cut a little bit from her private parts. She is said to have done this. Later Allah decreed that Hajar (rah) had the right to retaliate in kind and so Sarah (rah) had to submit to having the same done to her. It is said that this was the origin of these practices among women. They were imposed by women on themselves rather than ordained by God. And the piercing of the ears and nose has become a way to insert ornaments, beautifying rather than causing disfigurement.

As for the ritual radical circumcision of women, there is no evidence that it was ever recommended or condoned by any prophet of Allah. Muslim cultures that practice female circumcision use the story of Sarah (rah) and Hajar (rah) to support their custom. They say that at least some minimal form of circumcision was permitted and maybe even suggested by the prophet Ibrahim (as) and since the prophet Muhammad (sas) has been ordered by Allah in The Qur'an to **follow the way of Ibrahim**, (16:123) then this practice must also be followed in Islam. This is a baseless extrapolation from a story that has no firm hadith to back it up and is not supported by any of the four Islamic legal schools (*madhahib*). In addition, it is not mentioned in the Torah or any existing religious texts of the Jews. The most one could say is that some sort of minimal female circumcision was not forbidden by the Prophet (sas) but neither was it practiced by him on any of his daughters, granddaughters, or wives. The story itself points to the fact that it was a form of punishment meant to harm not to enhance the marital or spiritual life of a woman.

The Torah recounts that as her pregnancy progressed, Hajar (rah) found herself at the end of her ability both to endure the fire of jealousy and the physical abuse. She could take no more. Many months pregnant, Hajar (rah) ran headlong into the wilderness. She headed south, probably for Egypt but perhaps with no destination in mind other than to get as far away as possible. She traveled on foot resting and starting again. She had gone around eighty miles when she reached her limit and collapsed. Tired and thirsty, she prayed to Allah for help and guidance. A well appeared miraculously at her side and she named it Bir-Lahai-Roi - the well of the Living One Who Sees. The scholars have yet to pinpoint the exact location for this well. A place still exists that carries this name but there is no well. Some claim to have found the well in another place and to have drunk its waters (Williams, see bibliography). In this place Hajar (rah) met an angel in the form of a man, who sympathetically asked her where she was going and why. She unburdened herself to this stranger, crying about the heartache and the mistreatment of her mistress. She was willing to give up her home and the father of her unborn child, just to live in peace, just to escape the torment of jealousy.

The angel disclosed his identity and told her that Allah was commanding her to return to Ibrahim (as) to have her child, and to be obedient to Allah's will. The Lord Almighty spoke to Hajar (rah) by the well in the middle of the wilderness. This story either indicates that Allah Almighty miraculously provided two wells for Hajar (rah) on two different occasions, Bir-Lahai-Roi and later Zamzam, or that the well in question is only one but the story of its origin is told differently in the Bible and in The Qur'an.

Hajar (rah) was running away from the only home she had. As a slave she had no one to return to but masters, one a tyrant king and one a jealous woman. In fact, her name, Hajar (rah) in Arabic comes from the same root as *hijra* meaning to flee. In Hebrew it has the same meaning although some say that instead it should be read *Ha'Ajar* – this is the reward. She bowed her head in submission and prepared to return to the tents of Ibrahim (as). Before parting the angel told her that she would bear a son and his name would be Isma'il. He would be a prophet and father nations of believing children. Most likely she was also told that from him would descend the last prophet, the most honored Sayyiduna Muhammad (sas). So, like it or not, she must be patient, endure, and return to her place to await God's guidance. Allah had a plan for her. She must let her destiny play out.

It is not a light or easy thing to be in the presence of a heavenly messenger even when they take the form of a human. The Prophet Muhammad (as) was totally awed and shaken by his first encounter with Jibra'il (as) in his natural form. Not many women have been honored with such a visitation nor have endured it with such calm. Having been spoken to directly by an angel of the Lord, it is not surprising that Hajar (rah) found the strength to return to her home. When she arrived she told Sarah (rah) what had happened and was believed. The two women made every effort to rise above their feelings of fear and anger. They had a long history of friendship and cooperation. They tried to hold on to that reality and to trust in the love of their Lord who had a plan for both of them. Together they prepared for the birth of their son.

Hajar (rah) gave birth to her baby and all were delighted that it was a boy. She had told them that at the time of her encounter with the angel she had been given the baby's name. Ibrahim (as) and Sarah (rah) showed their belief in her by naming the boy Isma'il (as), 'Allah hears'. Allah had heard her cry at the well of Lahai-Roi and comforted her, and Allah had heard the prayer of His servant Ibrahim (as) and given him the much anticipated son and heir. Ibrahim (as) circumcised Isma'il (as) seven days after the day of his birth by Muslim reckoning, or on what would be the eighth day by Jewish reckoning, both being, in fact, different ways to designate the same day. However, the Torah says that Isma'il (as) wasn't circumcised until he was thirteen when the order to circumcise descended at the time of the birth of his half brother Ishaq (as). And it is even said that this became the subject of argument between the brothers. Ishaq (as) claimed that he had been circumcised properly, as a baby, and Isma'il (as) argued that he had been a consenting adult and therefore deserving of more reward. Perhaps this is why the Jews circumcise at eight days and the Muslims often wait until the boy is much older. Perhaps one follows the example of Ishaq (as) and one the example of Isma'il (as). Allah knows best.

Byzantine painting of the birth of Ishaq (as).

CHAPTER TWENTY-NINE
The Good News

The time passed quickly. If we are to accept the ages given in the Torah, it might have been twenty years since the birth of Isma'il (as) but in accordance with the Muslim account it was less than three. In Ibrahim's (as) ninety-ninth year, he saw on the horizon three young men approaching his encampment. He alerted Sarah (rah), who was only eighty-nine at the time, to prepare a meal for guests. He went out to look at the baby calves who were in pens nearby. They were being kept separately in order to allow the herdsmen to milk the mothers. He chose one very fine calf and sacrificed it in Allah's name and his men prepared it for roasting. Sarah (rah) and the women kneaded the dough and the fires were lit for baking. By the time the three men arrived at the tent the aroma of fresh bread and cooked meat was in the air.

Ibrahim (as) looked discretely at the men. They were unlike anyone he had ever seen before. They were tall and elegant, dressed in white. They held themselves a little aloof but without seeming proud. They were definitely noble, maybe princes or kings. He treated them with extra respect and a little bit of awe. They greeted him with salams which put him somewhat at ease because he guessed that these strangers must be believers like himself and that they intended him no harm. But there was something about them that made him wary.

He poured water for his guests to wash and he noticed that their hands, faces, and even their feet were clean and bright. There was no dirt or dust on their spotless white clothing. They smelled sweet and fresh, definitely not like men who had been traveling far distances by horse. He tried to act normally and not stare or ask questions. He seated them in his tent and went to get the tray of food that had been prepared for them. He set it humbly in front of his guests and sat down with them. Sarah (rah) stood nearby behind a curtain, ready in case there was anything they needed or wanted. But the three men just sat unmoving, dignified but distant. They showed absolutely no interest in the food that was steaming before them. No hand reached out to take the first bite.

Ibrahim (as) thought that perhaps they were shy so he encouraged them to begin but they just looked away. Then it occurred to him that perhaps, since they did not know him, they might think the food was poisoned. He broke off a piece of bread and put some meat in his mouth. Still the strangers did not reach out their hands toward the food. Then he became very worried. It is the custom that if two men share a meal together they intend each other no harm. So he began to fear that their disinterest in the food might mean they wished to injure him in some way. And he became afraid of them. He voiced his concern. **But when he saw that their hands did reach towards it, he did not know what to make of them and he conceived a fear of them** (11:70). **'We are afraid of you'** (15:52) he said. **They said, 'Be not afraid'** (15:53).

Then the strangers revealed that they were in fact the three Archangels, Jibra'il (as), Mika'il (as), and Israfil (as). He did not recognize them because they had taken different forms than the last time he had seen them. And of course they did not eat food. But this time they had not come on their own accord to test him or to visit. They had come on the orders of Allah Almighty to deliver His message to Lut (as) and his people and that is why their appearance was solemn and intimidating. They proceded to give Ibrahim (as) the incredibly good news that Sarah (rah) was going to give birth to a son. They said: **'We bring you tidings of a boy possessing wisdom'** (15:53). Ibrahim (as) was incredulous. How could this be? Either he considered himself too old to have children, in which case Isma'il (as) must have been born many years before. Or more likely, he had been asking since he was young for children from Sarah (rah) and was surprised to have his prayer answered after he had given up and grown old. He said: **'Do you bring me good tidings when old age has overtaken me?'** (15:54). The angels answered: **'We bring you good tidings in truth. So be not of the despairing'** (15:55). Ibrahim (as) was stunned but he could not doubt the messengers of Allah and he replied: **'And who despairs of the mercy of his Lord except those who are astray?'** (15:56). But in the Torah Ibrahim (as) laughs just as his wife does at hearing the incredible news and so they are told their son will be named Ishaq (as) – he laughed.

Sarah (rah) on the other hand, hidden behind the curtain, also heard what the angels had to say **and she laughed** (11:71). The Muslim commentators say she laughed with relief to hear that the stern and solemn angels had not come with bad news for her family or community. The Torah says she laughed incredulously at the news she was to bear a child. At eighty-nine she was way past the age of bearing children and she had never even once been pregnant. Were they making fun of her? Were they getting her hopes up again only to have them dashed? **Then his wife came forward with a cry, and she hit her face, and said, "a barren old woman?"** (51:29). The angels reassured her that they were not playing with her but she could not believe that this wonderful news could be true. **"Woe is me. Shall I bear a child when I am an old woman and this my husband is an old man? Surely that would be a very strange thing"** (11:72). **"Do you wonder at Allah's decree?"** (11:73) the angels asked her, probably now themselves incredulous that she would doubt their word or the word of her Lord. And they told Sarah (rah) and Ibrahim (as) that within a year, Sarah (rah) would give birth to a boy named Ishaq (as) and he would be a righteous servant of God. He and his son Ya'qub (as) would both be prophets.

After this wonderful news, the Archangels had other important messages. According to the Torah, it was at this time that Allah asked Ibrahim (as) to circumcise himself and all the other males in his community. According to the Torah this would be a sign of the Covenant, special agreement or relationship between Allah and the descendants of Ibrahim (as). They were His chosen people and He was their Lord. It was not, however, the first time that a human being had been circumcised. There is evidence from mummies preserved in Egypt that it was sometimes practiced as much as two thousand years before Ibrahim (as). But this was the first time that it became an order from Allah to be carried out on all male believers. It was to be an indelible and living reminder that they were different from other men and that their seed was blessed.

Another sign was that, from this point forward, the man known as Abram in Hebrew, would now be known as Abraham (as) and his wife would no longer be called Sarai but her name would be Sarah (rah). Abram is usually translated from Hebrew to mean 'his Father is exalted' or 'Exalted Father'. The name Abraham translates as 'Father of the multitudes' because each of the sons born to him would father many nations of people. Sarai is translated to mean 'my princess' or noble woman, the 'i' being the first person possessive. By changing the ending, her name comes to mean 'the princess'. She no longer belongs just to her family but she has become the noble princess, the mother of nations. In both cases the change of name indicates a new role from personal to universal.

It has been pointed out that the name changes involve simply an addition of an 'h' to both names. It is said that the 'h' (*heh*) in the Hebrew numerological system (Gematria) stands for the divine breath (*Hu* in Arabic). It indicates the presence of God on the breath, the entrance of the divine within the only vessel that can contain it, the beating human heart. Also the Name of God, YHWH, which is sometimes rendered as the equivalent of *Ya Huwa* in Arabic, has two *heh*'s. It is said that one was given to Sarah (rah) and one to Ibrahim (as). Each has the value of 5 so together they make 10, the number of divinity. To change a name is an indication of an inward change that has become so established that it must be acknowledged and honored in an outward way. It indicates a new birth, a new beginning; a new name for a new way of being. And so it is said that the change in names of Sarah (rah) and Ibrahim (as) is a sign of the living presence of Almighty Allah in their awakened hearts, not just a sign that they would produce many biological heirs. Their patience and their faith that Allah would hear and answer their prayers had finally been rewarded. Ibrahim (as) and Sarah (as) were established as the father and mother of faith.

This name change is not usually considered a part of the Muslim tradition because Ibrahim (as) is never called by any other name in The Qur'an and the name of Sarah (rah) is never mentioned at all. It is interesting, however, that in one common style of writing The Qur'an, the first fifteen times that the name Ibrahim appears, it is spelled differently than the following fifty-five times it appears. The name Ibrahim (as) is spelled without its second 'y' in the entire second and longest chapter, *Suratu l-Baqara*h (The Cow). There is no obvious reason it is spelled this way, an accepted exception dating from the earliest days of transcribing The Qur'an. Muslim scholars interpret it as a subtle reference to the name change of Abram to Abraham that is mentioned more explicitly in the Torah.

The 'y' was first only a small vowel sign riding above the rest of the letters but then it became a consonant fully integrated as part of the name. In the *Abjad* system where only consonants are counted, 'y' is 10, the symbol of divinity and completion. When talking about the mysterious initial letters of certain chapters of The Qur'an (*al-Muqatta'at*) Ibn 'Arabi (q) says that this 'y' refers to the Prophet Muhammad (sas) as the recipient of Allah's Word. It is missing when we are first introduced to the prophet Ibrahim (as) and then later it appears. Just as the 'h' of Allah's breath was added in Hebrew, so the 'y' of divinity was added in Arabic. It could therefore be understood to signify the attainment of wholeness, Ibrahim **turned to his Lord with a sound heart** (37:84) or as the beginning of revelation.

At best this is only speculation but the reality still stands that the name of Ibrahim (as), unlike that of any other prophet, is spelled in two different ways in at least one traditional writing of The Qur'an. Nothing in The Qur'an is inconsequential or insignificant, neither is there a mistake nor a triviality. Nothing has been overlooked or forgotten. **There is not a single thing We have neglected in the Book** (6:38). Every letter carries meaning but for some of the meanings Allah remains the only Knower.

Salt formation on the edge of the Dead Sea, Jordan, called the wife of Lut (as). She became a pillar of salt as punishment for the request for salt by which she betrayed her husband.

CHAPTER THIRTY
The Bad News

The mission of the Archangels was far from over. The good news for Ibrahim (as) and Sarah (rah) had been the easy part. As they prepared to leave, they informed Ibrahim (as) about the main purpose of their mission. They had been sent by Allah Almighty to punish the people of Lut (as). This would account for the great fear that Ibrahim (as) and Sarah (rah) had felt on seeing them. They were not just carrying blessings and good news, they were bearing the formidable anger and judgment of Allah to be enacted on earth.

Ibrahim (as) was the most soft hearted and forbearing of men. Even though he knew all about the practices of the people of the towns, he had helped them when their kingdoms had been overrun by the Elamite tyrant. He had hoped that their hearts would open after their near destruction. He had hoped that they would listen to what their prophet Lut (as) had to tell them. Their Creator cared enough about them to have sent a special prophet just to turn them from the wrong way to the way in which they had been made, their fitra. How could a prophet of the Lord feel any less compassion for them? But this is not at all what happened.

They continued in the way they were established and perhaps they became even more obstinate and obdurate. And they hardly tolerated their prophet at all let alone listened to him.

In spite of this, Ibrahim (as) pleaded for the people of Lut (as) in the sight of Allah. According to the Torah, he bargained with Allah. If there were fifty righteous people would Allah destroy them all? he asked. No said his Lord. If there were thirty? If there were twenty? If there were ten? No, Allah answered him, even if there were five righteous people He would not destroy them all. Ibrahim (as) thought that Lut (as), his two daughters and his wife constituted four believers and so they only needed one more. He stopped questioning his Lord, satisfied that no destruction would take place. According to Muslim sources, Ibrahim (as) got Allah to promise that unless Lut (as) himself condemned his own people, not once but four times, there would be no destruction visited on the people of the towns.

Lut (as) had been appointed as the prophet for the people of the five towns on the plain of Jordan. These towns, each with its own king, bordered a large fresh water lake that lay in a central valley. The land was rich and fertile. The people were farmers and merchants. The towns sheltered busy markets as people came from all over the area to buy and sell their produce and merchandise. They also attracted caravans who would rest and get supplies on their journeys to the kingdoms to the north and east. But the inhabitants of these towns were not interested in God or the message of Lut (as). They were not interested in being just or fair. They were not interested in being clean or decent. They were not interested in being either wise or good. These words in their vocabulary meant idiot and chump, fool and weakling. In their understanding, a strong man takes what he can from whoever is weaker. A wise man cheats whoever is less cunning. A just man enacts justice only for himself and a decent man is one who follows his lust. They had all the virtues turned upside down.

The Qur'an says that Lut (as) berated his people over and over: **Do you indeed approach men with desire to the exclusion of women? No but you are a people behaving ignorantly** (27:55). This practice is remembered in English by the word sodomy which is derived from Sodom, the name of the town in which Lut (as) lived. In Arabic it is known as *luwwat* taken from the name of Lut (as) himself. The people of Lut (as) committed homosexual acts not only in private but also in their public gatherings while others watched. In addition, they accosted travelers and took the young men by force and raped them.

Lut (as) condemned them himself: **'You surely perpetrate such vileness as no one among mankind has done before you. Indeed, you approach men and menace the road and commit abomination in your meetings'** (29:28-9). The people cheated in their commercial dealings. They stole from travelers. Some of the more imaginative commentators accuse Lut's (as) people of all kinds of horrible things. Some say that they cut off travelers which meant that they not only prevented them from reaching their destinations but that they employed what is known as a 'procrustean bed', a form of medieval torture. They laid a traveler on this bed. If he was shorter than the bed they stretched him to fit, breaking bones in the process. If he was longer than the bed they cut him down to fit. Some say that the indecencies that they performed in their public meetings were sexual acts. But both Aisha (rah) and Umm Hani (rah) were told by the Prophet Muhammad (sas) that the indecency of which they were accused was breaking wind exultantly. This seems probably more a credit to the delicacy of the Prophet (sas) who avoided the use of bad language and improper or indecent subjects.

Whatever they did, it was beyond what anyone else had ever done. They were not only being false to their true nature but they were also willfully hurting other people. They had been warned and they had not heeded. Allah in His great mercy had sent them their own prophet to warn them and they did not listen at all. Instead they said, as if it were the worst crime they could imagine: **'Drive Lut's family out of your city. Indeed, they are a people who keep themselves pure!'** (27:56).

Lut (as) had been living among them for many, many years. He had married one of their women and had fathered two daughters with her. This means that he had ties of family and kinship with most of the people of Sodom. And still he had not been able to bring a single one of them to Allah. Not even his wife was truly a believer. He had visited his uncle Ibrahim (as) many times since they had separated. He walked the two-day distance in order to pray in the company of believers and to ask advice. He complained about his people and often felt near to giving up. He was both angry at their depravity and depressed about his own inability to reach them. He needed to be recharged and encouraged. Ibrahim (as) consoled him, perhaps recalling his own long years among the people of his birth. He was always understanding and kind but he also always sent Lut (as) back to continue the job Allah had charged him with, hopeful that in the end his people could be saved.

It had gotten so bad that Lut (as) was almost completely confined to his house. He was not allowed to attend gatherings or even to invite guests to his house. He was not allowed to speak to strangers or to discuss religion. He continued to pray for his people and to provide a righteous example by his words and his behavior but that was all that was left for him to do. And no one took notice.

It was the custom of the Arabs, even before Islam, to honor the word of one of their community. When Abu Talib (ra) gave protection to the Prophet Muhammad (sas) for instance, his promise of safety was binding on all, even though the rest of his tribe wanted to kill or expel Muhammad (sas). Lut (as) was not afforded even this degree of respect. If they didn't respect his word why would they respect his life? It seemed that he was no longer safe among them. Perhaps it was only for the sake of his wife and daughters, their blood relatives, that Lut (as) had not been done away with already.

CHAPTER THIRTY-ONE
Allah's Wrath

The three Archangels arrived at the gates of Sodom in the evening just before dark. They met one of Lut's (as) daughters cutting hay for her animals outside the city. They asked her to host them for the night since they were strangers and had nowhere to go. She had never seen more handsome youths and she knew they were in danger. So although it was forbidden, she told them to come with her to her father's house, hoping that the encroaching darkness would hide them. When they reached home, her father pulled them inside quickly. He was risking his life in taking them in but they were guests, so for the sake of Allah he accepted them. He settled them comfortably, offering them the best of what he had and asked his wife to prepare food for them.

It is said that his wife went to her neighbor to borrow salt or perhaps some risen dough to make extra bread, and in so doing she revealed knowingly that she and Lut (as) had guests. Word spread. A crowd gathered and made their way to Lut's (as) house and banged on the door. Lut (as) opened for them and saw their angry faces and heard their curses. He was not allowed to harbor guests they said. He must hand

Salt formation of the previous photograph turned into an engraving of Lut (as) and his daughters fleeing Sodom and his wife turning to look behind her. Russia, 1913.

them over to the crowd. He had no right to protect them or keep them out of the hands of those who wanted to take advantage of them. Lut (as) begged them to grant him the honor of respecting those to whom he had given protection but the crowd became even more insolent and rowdy. Lut (as) tried to reason with them. He even offered them his 'daughters' if they would leave his guests alone. **'O my people, these are my daughters; they are purer for you. So fear Allah and do not disgrace me concerning my guests. Is there not a right-minded man among you?'** (11:78). They answered him: **'You certainly know that we have no claim on your daughters, and indeed you know what we want'** (11:79).

Lut (as) was not really offering his daughters to those vile men. Some of the commentators have said that, by daughters, Lut (as) meant the women of Sodom in general, those who would have been his spiritual daughters since he was their prophet. And certainly, if he was offering anyone's daughters, it was not an invitation to rape them. He was telling the men to marry good girls, such as his daughters, and have marital relations with them. He knew both that the offer was not at all what the men had in mind and also that it was not possible for them to accept. His daughters were their kinswomen, their cousins, or nieces. Marriage requires negotiations with the parents and a dowry. It doesn't happen over night and it lasts forever. They were not interested in this kind of sexual encounter. Their lewd activities were reserved for strangers and men without money or family to protect them. At the same time, this crowd was probably hypocritically protective of their own women, reserving them solely for bearing and raising their children.

He shouted at the crowd: **'You surely perpetrate such vileness as no one among mankind has done before you. Indeed, you approach men and cut off the road and commit abomination in your meetings'** (29:28-9). And they replied, unaware that what they said would serve as judgment on themselves: **'Bring us Allah's punishment, if you are among the truthful'** (29:29). Lut (as) answered them with the prayer: **'My Lord, support me against the corrupt people'** (29:30).

Then he shut the door and bolted it. He was ashamed before his guests and afraid for their safety. At that point the angels revealed their true identities and told him not to fear. They had heard him judge his people four times and they had not found in the cities **other than a single**

house of Muslims (51:36). Ibrahim's (as) calculations were in vain since Lut's (as) wife could not be counted among the believers. All attempts at averting Allah's wrath had failed.

The men of Sodom broke through the door of Sayyiduna Lut's (as) house and pushed their way into the room looking for the handsome guests. Jibra'il (as) waved one of his wings at the men and took away their sight. They groped blindly along the walls unable to see anything, confused and terrified. They accused Lut (as) of witchcraft and as soon as they found the broken door they stumbled into the street yelling and calling for help.

The Archangels told Lut (as) to get ready to leave before dawn because as the sun rose the punishment of the towns would descend. The Archangels spoke these chilling words: **'Therefore, set out with your family during a part of the night and let not any of you look back – except your wife; she will surely be struck by whatever strikes them. Indeed, their appointed time is morning. Is not the morning near?'** (11:81). The family set out together climbing up the plateau towards Hebron and the welcoming tents of Ibrahim (as). As they climbed the sun began to dawn. They heard a terrible noise behind them. If they had looked they would have seen a horrible sight. Jibra'il (as) in his true form, an enormous being of light with six hundred powerful wings, used just one of his mighty wings to scoop up the five towns and turned them over upside down into the earth. It was an appropriate punishment for people who turned God's laws upside down. This is why they are called *mu'tafikat*, the overturned. Only Lut's (as) wife turned to look in sympathy with her people. Coals rained down from the sky, each with the name of its intended victim written on it. Lut's (as) wife fell where she was struck. The Torah says she was changed to a pillar of salt, perhaps because it was by means of a little salt that she betrayed her husband. All the inhabitants of the five sinful cities were each struck by their appointed stone and fell lifeless to the ground. By the time the sun was fully risen, it was finished. Everything was gone, the houses, the people, their pride and their cruelty, gone. **Then We made its highest part its lowest and rained upon them stones of hard clay** (15:74). **In that is surely a sign for the believers** (15:77).

The Qur'an says: **Your Lord has prescribed for Himself mercy.** (6:54). Al-Qashani explains that this means that Allah's mercy extends to all of His creation, always, continuously, unrelentingly, forever. His wrath is not the absence of His mercy because there is no place or time where His mercy is absent. Wrath is simply understood as the inability or unwillingness of the creation to receive or absorb the ceaseless shower of His mercy.

The valley, in which the cities lay, runs along a large tectonic fault line that continues all the way to Africa. Some say that a massive earthquake shook the area and widened the rift producing volcanic activity. After the quake, the area sank down below sea level and submerged the towns in water and ash. The drainage of water from the lake was cut off and now it collects in the resulting basin, evaporating in the sun and leaving a salty waste. Today it is called the Dead Sea because nothing can grow in its toxic environment. In Arabic it is called the Sea of Lut (as). It was thought that around it and within it, lie the ruins of the once prosperous cities. However, in recent years, new theories have been proposed based on the discovery of the remains of ancient towns just to the north and others just to the south of the Dead Sea. Around the beginning of the second millennium BCE they appear to have been destroyed by a cataclysmic event that incinerated at extremely high temperatures everything within a radius of 25 km. Since then their broken walls and empty towers have stood as clear signs for all to see and be reminded.

Ruins of a 5th century Byzantine church in Jordan built around the cave in which the Biblical event is supposed to have taken place.

CHAPTER THIRTY-TWO
God Forbid!

At this point the account in the Torah diverges sharply from The Qur'an. It states that Lut (as) got drunk and slept with his daughters. Or alternatively, that Lut's (as) daughters, thinking that the whole world had been destroyed and they were the only survivors, got their father drunk and slept with him in order to keep the human race alive. God forbid. This story has troubled the scholars of the Jews and Christians for centuries. Some explain it by saying that in order to establish the laws of incest one of the patriarchs had to present an example so that it could be condemned. In other words, they say that Ibrahim (as) married his sister and Lut (as) slept with his daughters in order that the command against incest could be expressed. They say that the two daughters became pregnant and from one was born the tribe of Moabites from whom the prophet Dawud's (as) mother Ruth (rah) descended. From the other daughter came the tribe of Ammonites, one of whom became a wife of the prophet Sulayman (as) and mother of his successor Rehoboam.

The Christians contend that this act of incest was necessary in order to bring about the birth of Maryam (rah) the mother of the prophet

'Isa (as), who was a descendant of Sayyiduna Sulayman (as). In Jordan they have uncovered the remains of the Byzantine monastery of Saint Lot which is built around the cave in which the family hid out after the destruction of the cities and in which this less than holy deed is supposed to have occurred.

The Muslims simply reject this fable and do not repeat it. For a prophet of God to perform such an unspeakable act is impossible. A man of God is in harmony with his fitra, the perfect form in which he was created and he is in every way true to God's laws whether or not they have been revealed as scripture. Certainly Lut (as), having just escaped from the punishment Allah laid on the towns for their violent sexual depravity, would hardly have immediately turned around and committed an act even more reprehensible. It is more likely that this was added to the Book in order to vilify the tribes who are supposed to have descended from this act, the Moabites and Ammonites who had become the political rivals of the Banu Isra'il and with whom, in fact, intermarriage was strictly forbidden although not strictly obeyed.

Lut (as) and his daughters reached the haven of Ibrahim's (as) encampment, tired and stunned. They were greeted with open arms by loving family and a community of believers. Ibrahim (as) was saddened by the news of the destruction of all those people but relieved that Lut (as) had escaped safely. Lut's (as) daughters are said to have married there and stayed to raise their families. Lut (as) himself eventually traveled to Mecca to live near Isma'il (as) and Allah's Holy House. He is said to have died there at the age of 140 and is buried in an area near to the Ka'ba.

CHAPTER THIRTY-THREE
Planting The Seed

According to the hadith of Ka'b al-Ahbar (ra), the prophet Ishaq (as) was conceived on the very day Lut's (as) people were destroyed. In spite of Sarah's (rah) doubt, she got pregnant and carried the child safely for nine months. As he came into the world, Ishaq (as) fell to the ground in *sajda* and raised his little hands to proclaim the unity of God. This was on the night that preceded the day of 'Ashura, the eve. When he was born his parents were beside themselves with joy. His father, Ibrahim (as) prepared a banquet and called all the people to come celebrate. The Jews say this was on the eighth day, the day of his circumcision.

Ibrahim (as) was told to name their son Is-haq (as) which means he laughed, for surely his birth brought joy. Sarah (rah) laughed when his birth was announced and of course she laughed with happiness when it actually came about. Sarah (rah) and Ibrahim (as) raised Ishaq (as) with the best of what they had. He was loving and good natured, intelligent, handsome and pious – everything for which his parents had hoped and prayed for over forty years. Although he had an older half brother, he was the only child of his mother. He was her pride and joy and she no doubt

One rose made up of the Names of Allah and one made of the names of the Prophet (sas). Abdullah Buhari, Ottoman 18th century.

expected everyone else to treat him that way also.

Their neighbors, however, had trouble believing the story of the miraculous birth and they began to talk as people will. They said what a stupid old woman to invent such a story when it was clear that they just adopted a foundling and were pretending he was their own. In order to disprove the rumors, Allah created Ishaq (as) as he grew to look exactly like his father. In fact, he resembled his father Ibrahim (as) to such an extant that people could not tell them apart. Ibrahim (as), although one hundred years old, still looked like a young man. And this made problems. People would tell something to the father and then get upset when the son knew nothing about it. The son would ask for something and it would to given to the father and so on. One night, Ibrahim (as) prayed to his Lord to give him some mark that would enable people to distinguish him from his son. When he woke in the morning he noticed that some of the hairs in his beard had turned white. Surprised, he asked his Lord the meaning of this. Allah replied that this was a mark of honor and distinction to help people identify the father from the son. Ibrahim (as) was very pleased with this and asked his Lord to increase him in honor. The next morning, he woke up and his whole beard and all the hair on his head had also turned as white as snow. This was the first sign of aging in the sons of Adam (as).

After the birth of Ishaq (as), the family lived together in peace for only a short while. Some say that from the very first when Sarah (rah) received the news that she too would have a son she felt there was no longer any need to raise Isma'il (as) or put up with his mother. Some say that it was after her son Ishaq (as) was born that jealousy arose again because of childish competition between the boys. Sarah (rah) couldn't bear to see her baby treated roughly or teased by the older Isma'il (as). Perhaps it was the preference that Ibrahim (as) seemed to show for his older son that Sarah (rah) found so difficult to bear. It began even as early as the eighth day at his circumcision ceremony and then on the celebration of his weaning when it is said that Ibrahim (as) sat Isma'il (as) on his right during the feast.

The Muslim accounts are quite clear that Isma'il (as) was still a nursing toddler when Sarah (rah) insisted that Hajar (rah) and her son be removed to a distant place. The Torah is less clear because, although it says that Hajar (rah) picked up her son and carried him, it also contends he was a grown teenager. The ancient Hebrews are said to have nursed for a period of three years. The Qur'an states that a child has a right to be nursed for two years but doesn't explicitly forbid nursing for a longer period. Therefore, we don't know the exact age difference between the two boys and we don't know at what age they were separated. Al-Kisai even says that, although Hajar (rah) conceived first, Sarah (rah) conceived soon after and they were pregnant and delivered their sons on the same day. It could be that Hajar (rah) parted company with Sarah (rah) even before Ishaq (as) was born. However, after leaving his wife and son in Mecca, Ibrahim (as) prays for their safety and well-being and at the same time thanks Allah for giving him both sons (14:39). It is most likely that Ishaq (as) was already born when Hajar (rah) and Isma'il (as) were banished.

Once Sarah (rah) gave birth to her own son, according to the Torah, he became the natural heir to his father to the exclusion of any other sons. The right of the firstborn son to inherit was a law only delivered a thousand years later to Musa (as). It is unclear that this was the custom at the time of Ibrahim (as). Although Isma'il (as) was older, his mother was the second wife or concubine and not a freeborn woman. Sarah (rah) was both first wife and noble. Therefore, her son took precedence over his older brother. Sarah (rah) was not slow to remind Ibrahim (as) of this fact. Perhaps for this reason, Ibrahim (as) separated the family and gave each son his own inheritance. The Torah states that although God promised both sons that they would be fathers of great nations, that they would have many descendants, it was only with Ishaq (as) that He made His covenant, His pledge to keep the religion of Ibrahim (as) alive through him.

Whenever the separation happened, it is said that it was a result of the jealousy between these two remarkable women. Sarah (rah) is said to have insisted that Ibrahim (as) take Hajar (rah) as far away as possible so that she never had to see her again. Sayyiduna Ibrahim (as) must have tried to reason with her. As much as it seems unlikely that these women behaved in this way, as much it seems out of character that this most gentle and compassionate of prophets would allow cruelty between two of the people he loved. For certain, what happened was not due to either the pettiness of the women or the weakness of their husband. These extraordinary individuals were none of these things. The Torah says that it was in fact Allah Himself who stepped in and insisted that Ibrahim (as) listen to the wisdom of Sarah (rah) and do as she asked. It was Allah's wish for reasons which at the time were unknown but which would play out clearly two and a half millennia later with the birth of the Prophet Muhammad (sas). This was simply the way it had to be. They were only ordered to plant the seed. It was Allah who knew when it would swell with life and flower. **Verily, Allah is the one who splits the kernel and the date stone and brings the living out from the dead...** (6:95).

Etching by Rembrandt von Rijn of Ibrahim (as) sending away his wife Hajar (rah) and their son Isma'il (as).

Photograph giving some idea of what the Valley of Becca must have looked like when Hajar (rah) first arrived.

CHAPTER THIRTY-FOUR

The Hijra of Hajar (rah)

In the Torah Ibrahim (as), in an uncharacteristically cruel fashion, sends Hajar (as) and Isma'il (as) away from his tent into the desert alone. In the Muslim accounts, however, he mounts his wife and his baby son together on a donkey or camel and leads them in the direction Allah would indicate, south into the barren wastes of the Negev and beyond. Ibrahim (as) would stop at a town or a well and ask, "Is this the place?" The guiding angel would say "No, not yet. Keep moving." And so the small family moved farther and farther away from the land that they knew, past the cutoff to Egypt and on into the southern deserts until they were approximately 1,200 km from where they had started - a journey of many weeks. Finally, they were told to look for a narrow valley enclosed by walls of craggy peaks, accessible through only four narrow passes. This was the valley called Becca, whose meaning is exactly a narrow valley devoid of vegetation. Here in this desolate and uninhabited spot, under a lone thorn tree or acacia, Ibrahim (as) was ordered to settle his wife and child. **The first sanctuary appointed for mankind was that at Becca, a blessed place, a guidance for the people** (3:96).

Although researchers are still in dispute as to whether there were riding camels at this time in Mesopotamia, they concede that it is possible that Ibrahim (as), being so wealthy and well traveled, had some. There is no solid evidence that camels were being herded for other than their meat and milk but it seems logical that if the herder could get close enough to milk such a large and independently minded animal that he might also be able to tame her to carry burdens or even be ridden in spite of the fact that they had not yet developed the proper saddles. A camel would have cut the travel time in half and made the waterless deserts passable. This would explain how and why Ibrahim (as) was able to take Hajar (rah) and Isma'il (as) so far and still be able to visit them regularly.

Ibrahim (as) pulled at the nose ring of the camel to get her to kneel and helped Hajar (rah) and Isma'il (as) dismount. He set their few belongings beside them in the thin shade of the little tree - a small sack of dates, an old goat skin (*qirba*) full of water, some mats, sheep skins and a cooking pot. He may even have built them a small house or shelter of branches and skins. Soon after, he collected the camels, mounted one and led the other with a rope. There was not enough vegetation in the area for the animals to forage so he couldn't spend much time there. As Ibn Abbas (ra) has told us, Hajar (rah) searched her husband's face intently and asked, "Is this what your Lord has asked you to do?" He looked back down at her and her beloved baby and at the waterless, desolate place that surrounded them and he answered her sadly but confidently, "Yes". Then she sat back down and said "Then we are in good hands. Allah will care for us." As Ibrahim (as) began to ride away Hajar (rah) got up and followed him for a little way, as a host follows a guest to the door, hoping to hold on to the last sight of a beloved, hoping for a bit more reassurance. "O Ibrahim, to whom are you leaving us?" she called after him. "To Allah" he said without turning. And she answered with the beautiful words, "I am pleased with Allah." And she too turned her back and sat down under the tree to nurse her child. It must have been a heart wrenching experience for both of them. No way out but blind obedience in a situation that was beyond understanding.

Ibrahim (as) set off, without turning back to look at his little family alone there in that inhospitable valley. When he reached a place where they could no longer see him, he turned and prayed: **'Our Lord, I have settled some of my offspring in an uncultivable valley near Your Holy**

House, our Lord, that they may keep up prayer. Make people's hearts turn to them and provide them with fruits in order that they may be thankful'** (14:37). Ibrahim (as) knew that this barren desolate spot was in fact the spiritual center of the earth. It was the place where Allah had sent down His holy House, the *Baytu l-Ma'mur*, for Adam (as) and his children to worship there. The house had been raised at the time of the flood of Nuh (as) into, some say the fourth and others say, the seventh heaven but there remained a small mound where it had sat and the emanations of its holiness vibrated in the air around. This was to be Mecca, the place of the holy Ka'ba, the city in which the last Prophet (sas) was to be born. And Ibrahim (as) knew that their purpose in being there was to establish the worship of Allah in preparation for that.

However, in order to relieve the great sadness that he was feeling at the separation from Isma'il (as) and Hajar (rah) but so as not to complain or object, he said: **"Our Lord, You know well what we conceal and what we reveal: nothing at all is hidden from Allah, on earth or in heaven"** (14:38). He knew that the Almighty was intimately aware of everything that was in his heart without being told and he knew that what He commanded was for the best. Some say that this was the first sacrifice of a son by which Ibrahim (as) would be tested, a preparation for the even heavier test that was to come. Then he said **"Praise be to Allah, who has granted me Isma'il and Ishaq in my old age: my Lord surely hears all requests!** (14:39). This points to the fact that Ishaq (as) had already been born. **Lord, grant that I may keep up prayer, and so may my offspring. Our Lord, accept my request. Our Lord, forgive me, my parents, and the believers on the Day of Reckoning"** (14:40-41). His last request in this verse included his parents. The word *walidayn* means those who gave birth to him, birth parents. So it could be that he was praying for Abu Ibrahim (ra), who did not raise him but who was, along with his mother, a believer. Or it could be that he knew that at this time his parents, Azar and Usha (rah) were still alive and he prayed that they come to the truth before they died in disbelief. Allah knows best.

And then he turned his face north and continued to ride until he had returned to his tent in the place where he had left Sarah (rah) and Ishaq (as).

Mark on the marble floor of the Haramu sh-Sharif indicating the original spot of the well of Zamzam. Neither the mark nor the well are to be found there anymore.

CHAPTER THIRTY-FIVE

The Well That Suffices

Meanwhile mother and child sat in the sparse shade of the single tree, seeking protection from the blazing Arabian sun, waiting for whatever might happen next. Hajar (rah) was still nursing Isma'il (as). She was careful with the little water they had. Day by day the water and food decreased and there was still no sign of people or help. Finally, the *qirba* was dry. Hajar (rah) had been drinking as little as she could, although the valley was exceedingly hot. Her milk finished and Isma'il (as) was hungry and starting to cry. There was nothing she could think of to do but wait patiently. After a few days the boy was whimpering constantly and she also felt weak with hunger and thirst. She could not believe that they were actually going to die, alone and forgotten in this unknown place.

At first she was relaxed, sure that Allah would respond to her prayer and that of Ibrahim (as). She waited patiently, expectantly, for whoever or whatever Allah would send. Little by little as the food ran out and the water disappeared and there was still no sign, she began to feel anxious although not despairing. She knew that Allah was watching but she could not know what He was planning. Finally, unwilling to sit and do nothing, she ran to the only high ground nearby, the rocky outcrop of as-Safa. She looked out over the dry valley for some sign of life. She saw only the waves of heat radiating off the stony ground. There was another smaller outcrop, al-Marwa, nearby. She climbed up to see if there was something different from that vantage point. She ran between these two hills seven times in a final attempt to find help. The seventh time, on the hill of al-Marwa, she heard a voice. She cried out, "I hear your voice, do you have help for us?" When she looked down she saw the imposing figure of Jibra'il (as) in his angelic form, standing where she had left Isma'il (as) scuffing at the ground with his heel in distress. In alarm she hurried to the place where this enormous being hovered over her dying child.

To her great surprise and relief, she found that water was gushing up out of the depression that Isma'il (as) had made with his foot, or alternatively, that the Archangel had gouged out of the ground with the tip of his mighty wing. Water was welling up and filling the hollow. She pulled Isma'il (as) out of the way as the water began to seep around him. She scooped away at the sand where the water bubbled up and she made a mud wall to contain it, like a pool. She drank and gave her child to drink and filled her *qirba* and hung it from a branch of the tree. The angel consoled Hajar (rah) and told her not to fear, Allah would take care of her. He said that this hidden dry valley was the site of Allah's Holy House which her son and his father would one day rebuild. From this information Hajar (rah) was assured that her son would live and grow to manhood and she lay in the shade of the tree, with Zamzam by her side, content and at peace. By means of this miraculous water Hajar (rah) and Isma'il (as) were able to live in health and satisfaction alone in this isolated place for some time, although Hajar (rah) missed the company of others.

The water of Zamzam is not like other water. It fulfills the intention of the one drinking it. If one drinks for thirst, it quenches. If one drinks for hunger, it satisfies. If one drinks for health, it heals. If one drinks for wisdom, it enlightens. According to some sources the well has been called by sixty different names of honor. The Prophet (sas) called it, *Birra* – blessed, *Tayyiba* – good, *Sayyida* – noble. Other names for it are: *'Afiya* – wellness, *Bushra* – good news, *Kafiya* – sufficient, *'Awna* – help, *Safiya* – pure. The Prophet Muhammad (sas) would always take some back with him when he returned to Medina, to drink and give to the sick. He said it is better than any other water on earth. It is even mentioned in the Zabur

(Psalms): "Blessed is the man whose strength is in Thee; in whose heart are the ways of them who passing through the valley of Baca make it a well." (Psalms 84:5-6)

The water of Zamzam gushing between the stones.

The name Zamzam comes from a root *za-ma* that means water that flows so abundantly that it makes a gurgling sound as it rushes out. It also refers to water with a slightly brackish taste. Both of these are accurate descriptions of Zamzam. However, Zamzam is not a spring, it is a well. Close to the surface, below a layer of sand and stone lies a layer of porous bedrock that channels rain water from distant mountains to this sacred spot near Allah's Ancient House. In this exceptionally arid and hot place, the well miraculously continues to fill and supply water for all who visit there to this very day. Its water is absolutely pure but it has a salty taste from the nourishing minerals it contains. There is also another meaning of the root *za-ma*. It means to gather, collect together, or dam up. The Prophet (sas) is related by Ibn Abbas (ra) to have said: "May Allah have mercy on the mother of Isma'il (as) if she had not been so hasty (in damming it up), Zamzam would have been a free flowing river." (Bukhari). The original Zamzam was a hole about five meters in diameter, lined with stones. The water visibly and audibly welled up from the bottom and poured out of the sides between the stones.

One day a group of Arabs of the tribe of Jurhum, traveling near this arid valley, saw a bird circling in the sky. This indicated that there must be some source of water near by. The men had passed by this area many times before and had never seen any trace of water so they crossed through an opening in the mountains to see what had attracted the bird. There they found Hajar (rah) and her son living by a pool of fresh water. They asked permission to drink. She was happy to have company and readily gave permission.

Pilgrims drawing water from the open well of Zamzam near the Ka'ba.

People at that time did not think that God's land could be owned in the same way as we do today, to buy and to sell. However, people could possess the rights to use the land or its wealth and to deny its use to others as long as they were not in dire need. A well, which was dug by someone, belonged to him and his family. It was only proper for strangers to ask permission to either use it or to camp for some time beside it. Hajar (rah) was the guardian of Zamzam and she had the right to grant or deny access.

The Jurhum stayed for a while and Hajar (rah) enjoyed their company. So when they asked permission to settle there and to bring their families, she was only too happy to accept as long as they continued to respect her rights over the water. But first she had to ask permission of her husband Ibrahim (as). When he came to visit soon afterwards, he was surprised and happy to see his family supported by a community and he gave his consent to their settlement.

They agreed to her terms and went back to southern Arabia to inform their kinsmen and to return with them to settle in Becca. Then Becca, because it had abundant water, became an important stop on the trade route that ran from Yemen to Sham and beyond. Today we know it, of course, as Mecca. And Allah has so obviously and generously answered Ibrahim's (as) prayer by inclining the hearts of people in its direction and by bringing its provision from all around the world. In a very similar manner the Prophet Muhammad (sas) prayed for Medina. He asked, "O Allah! Make the land between its (Medina's) two mountains a sanctuary. O Allah! Bless them (the people of Medina) in their *mudd* and their *sa'* (two units of measurement)." (Bukhari). And both prayers have been clearly answered.

The Jurhum were a tribe originating in Southeastern Arabia. They are thought to be a different branch of the descendants of Sam (as) the son of Nuh (as). So they were distant cousins of Ibrahim (as) and Isma'il (as). They spoke an early form of Arabic which most probably Hajar (rah) learned and Isma'il (as) grew up speaking. Ibrahim (as) visited his son and wife frequently although it was a very long journey. The camel was domesticated originally in southern Arabia and the Jurhum might have brought their animals with them and given some to Ibrahim (as) if he did not already have them. He could then have had swift camels to carry him quickly from Hebron to Mecca. By some accounts Allah provided a Buraq, the heavenly flying steed that carried the Prophet (sas) on his Night Journey from Mecca to Jerusalem. This would have reduced the travel time to minutes. Only four visits from this time until Isma'il (as) was grown are recorded in the Torah, The Qur'an, or Hadith because on each of these visits something very significant happened. However, he might have visited many more times than that. One narrator assumes that Ibrahim (as) visited once a year to make the pilgrimage. What is clear from the events that are recorded, is that Ibrahim (as) and Isma'il (as) were not strangers to each other. Father and son were familiar with each other and trusted each other. Distance had no effect on the bond or connection between them.

After a few hundred years the tribesmen of Jurhum forgot the worship of the One God. They began to desecrate the Holy House by setting up statues and altars to many gods. The direct descendants of Isma'il (as) stood up against them and were able in the end to evict them from the vicinity of Mecca. In revenge, the Jurhum filled in the well of Zamzam before they left and buried within it most of the treasure of gold and silver implements and ornaments that pilgrims had left as gifts in the holy sanctuary. They planned no doubt to return when it was safe at some later date to retrieve what they had stolen. The Khuza'a tribe, also descendants of Isma'il (as), eventually migrated to Mecca and took their place. However, they knew nothing of the lost well and knowledge of its whereabouts somehow was lost. The residents of Mecca, in order to continue to live there, were reduced to carrying water in skins or jars on their backs or the backs of donkeys from other wells dug far from the Ka'ba in order to relieve the thirst of themselves and the pilgrims.

One day when Abdu l-Muttalib (ra), the grandfather of the Prophet Muhammad (sas), was a young man asleep near the Ka'ba he had a dream. In the dream a voice told him to dig *Birra*. He asked, what is *Birra*? The next night he was told to dig *Tayyiba*. He asked, what is *Tayyiba*? The third night he was told to dig *Sayyida*. Again he asked what is *Sayyida*? This time he was shown where to dig. He started to dig so close to the walls of the sacred House that the residents of Mecca threatened to stop him by force. They almost succeeded because he had only one son to protect him while he dug. He uncovered the well of Zamzam and the golden treasure that had been buried with it. Like Hajar (rah) before him, the well came under his authority. He thanked Allah for this wonderful gift and prayed for ten strong sons who would help defend him the next time he might need it. He vowed that if Allah gave him what he asked for he would offer one of those sons as a sacrifice in gratitude.

This story is understood by some to indicate that the early Arabs practiced human sacrifice. However, it is clear from the outcome of the story that the rest of the people of Mecca were horrified by his vow. It is unlikely that Abdu l-Muttalib (ra) himself ever really expected to actually be given ten grown sons and so have to redeem his promise. To the Arabs and later to the Muslims, a man's word is sacred. A vow must be taken seriously and fulfilled even if it is wrong. In Islam a vow that is unlawful or impossible must still be compensated for either monetarily or by fasting. The Prophet (sas) warned against making promises in Allah's name because once made, they must be fulfilled. Neither do they disappear nor are they forgotten. The Qur'an, on the other hand, praises those who are faithful to their oaths and Allah promises to reward them with Paradise (17:34). Therefore, when his sons were grown he expressed his intention to fulfill his vow. The sons drew lots and the choice fell on Abdullah the youngest and the one who would later father the Prophet Muhammad (sas). The rest of his tribe, in particular the maternal relatives of the boy, rose in opposition and found a way for Abdu l-Muttalib (ra) to redeem his vow by substituting one hundred camels. This he did happily and to everyone's satisfaction.

If all your water were to disappear into the earth, who then could bring you pure flowing water? (67:30). As Allah uses water as a metaphor in The Qur'an for His blessing and His grace, so the story of Zamzam serves as a metaphor for the legacy of Isma'il (as). When Ibrahim (as) and his descendants brought Islam, belief flourished and Zamzam flowed above ground. As the way of Ibrahim (as) was forgotten so was the well. Zamzam, although always there, was buried and forgotten. The religion of Ibrahim (as) remained among a few true believers but for the most part it sank out of sight into the depths of polytheism. Two thousand years later the water and the religion both miraculously welled to the surface of a dry and thirsty earth with the coming of the last Prophet, Muhammad Mustafa (sas).

An illustration from a Timurid Anthology of the sacrifice of Isma'il (as). Shiraz, 1410.

CHAPTER THIRTY-SIX
The Sacrifice of Isma'il (as)

When Isma'il (as) was around fourteen, **when he had reached the age of walking with him** (37:102), meaning when he was old enough to join in his father's work or to travel with him, Ibrahim (as) had a vision. He saw himself sacrificing his son as one would sacrifice a lamb, by laying him on the ground and cutting his throat. It is said that the dreams of prophets are akin to prophecy, their dreams are true visions and a form of revelation. The grandson of Sayyiduna Ibrahim (as), the prophet Yusuf (as), is known for having been given a special ability to understand or interpret dreams. Yusuf (as) thanked his Lord saying: **O my Lord, You have given me something of power and taught me the interpretation of dreams** (12:101). There were many instances where the Prophet Muhammad (sas) also foresaw in a dream the events that would actually take place at a future time. There is a hadith explaining that the good dreams of believers are one forty-sixth of prophecy and all of it that remains (Bukhari). At the time of Ibrahim (as) and the prophets of the Banu Isra'il, true dreams are said to have been more common and an accepted vehicle for the delivery of divine messages.

Ibrahim (as) believed in the inner absolute truth of his dream but perhaps he was not so sure of how he was supposed to act on it. The Lord he knew was Ar-Rahman, the Most Merciful. He was the Lord who forbid killing, especially the killing of children whether before birth as in an abortion (6:140), or after birth as was the pre-Islamic practice of killing girl children, or the killing of children in war as the Prophet (sas) prohibited his soldiers many times (Muslim). So Ibrahim (as) tried first to sacrifice animals from his vast herds. First he tried sheep, then camels, and then finally horses in large numbers. The sacrifices were accepted but the debt was not paid and the vision was not fulfilled. Others say that he tried to ignore the dream but, in the way of true dreams, it repeated itself seventy times until he had no alternative but to submit to the inconceivable thing that was being asked of him. Every night he saw the same terrifying dream. Finally, he had to accept that the dream was literal and the sacrifice that was being asked of him was that of his dearly beloved son.

Having reached the point of understanding, he acted in the way he had acted for every other trial in his long and difficult life, with complete certainty and unwavering determination. But he continued to show concern and consideration for those around him. He did not act without first discussing the contents of his vision with his son and asking his opinion. **'O my son, indeed, I have seen in a vision that I am sacrificing you, so see what you think'** (37:102). And Isma'il (as), after all a prophet in his own right and the son of a prophet, replied in the way that his father must have anticipated: **'O my father, do what you are commanded. You will find me, Allah willing, among the patient'** (37:102).

Together they left Hajar (rah) without telling her the purpose of their journey. Shaytan seeing an opening, came to her and told her where they were going and why. She would listen to none of his deceitful whispering and she chased him away with stones, confident that whatever her husband did was what Allah wanted. So shaytan hurried to catch up with Ibrahim (as) and he whispered in his ear, trying to make him doubt that his vision was from God. But Ibrahim (as) recognized him right away and chased him off with stones. Then shaytan figured he had one more chance to prevent these righteous servants from following the command of their Lord. He lingered behind and began to whisper to Isma'il (as) that his father just wanted to be rid of him. But Isma'il (ra) was sure of his father's love and sure of his father's goodness and confident that what happens is only by Allah's will. He also chased shaytan away with stones. And these three incidents of stoning are reenacted by every pilgrim up to today at the *Jamarat* during Hajj.

They passed through the valley of Mina about 4 miles outside of Mecca. They climbed a little way up the slope of Mount Thabir, which overlooks both Mina and Muzdalifah. It was finally here that Ibrahim (as) was told that they had reached their destination. Isma'il (as) knelt down on the ground and Ibrahim (as) took out the knife he had carefully sharpened at Isma'il's (as) request, so as not to cause unnecessary pain. Isma'il (as) asked his father to remove his shirt so it would not get stained with blood and could be taken to his mother to dry her tears and be of some consolation for her. Isma'il (as) was no doubt afraid, but he was mostly afraid that he might unwillingly struggle against his father and against death, so he asked his father to tie his hands. Ibrahim (as) complied with his son's requests slowly in a silence heavy with grief. But even then he could not do what he knew he must. So Isma'il (as) offered to turn over so that his father no longer had to look him in the face while he did what his Lord had ordered.

The normal position for sacrifice is the same as that of the corpse in the grave, lying on the right side facing *qibla*. In this position Ibrahim (as) had to look into the face of his beloved son while he took his life. He was unable to do this so he consented for Isma'il (as) to put his forehead on the ground. Essentially in the position of *sajda*, Isma'il (as) awaited the sharpened blade. It is said that in the battle of Siffin, Sayyiduna 'Ali (ra) was pierced in the leg by an arrow. In order to avoid hurting him while removing it, his son Hasan (ra) recommended that they wait until he was absorbed in prayer. Then they extracted the arrow painlessly without Sayyiduna 'Ali (ra) even noticing, such was the depth of his immersion in prayer. Perhaps it was the same for Isma'il (as) and another reason why he asked to be laid in *sajda*.

It is said that father and son, obedient to the command of their Lord could not, however, prevent the signs of the grief, which filled their hearts, from overflowing. As they continued to dutifully go through the motions of preparing for sacrifice, the ground around them became soaked with their tears. **Then when they had both surrendered and he had put him down on his forehead** (37:103), Ibrahim (as) tried again to cut the throat of his beloved son. This time he prayed to God, *"Allahu Akbar"* the prayer of sacrifice, and swept the knife across his son's tender throat. Nothing happened - at least nothing visible in the apparent world. But with each stroke it is said that a veil fell from the hearts of the two prophets, removing some trace of love for the world, cutting out of their hearts anything that might be there other than Allah.

Seventy times Ibrahim (as) picked up the knife and swiped. Seventy times the knife did not cut. Finally driven to desperation Ibrahim (as) hurled the knife away as hard as he could. In its trajectory it sliced through the adjacent boulders as though they were butter. "What is wrong with you?" Ibrahim (as) addressed the knife. "You prolong our agony and prevent our obedience." Allah gave the knife a voice and it said, "Why did the fire not burn you?" "Because the Lord ordered it to be cool and peace for me" replied Ibrahim (as). And the knife said, "The Lord of the fire ordered it only once not to consume you but He has ordered me now seventy times not to cut even one hair from the body of Isma'il (as)."

Ibrahim (as) retrieved the knife, determined to keep trying. As he lifted his arm he heard a voice, **"O Ibrahim, you have fulfilled the vision. Thus do We reward the doers of good"** (37:105). It was Allah Himself speaking to Ibrahim (as) and his son - the reward of absolute faith. And **He** [Allah] **ransomed him with a mighty sacrificial victim** (37:107). Ibrahim (as) had not backed down from his certainty either in the goodness of Allah or in His promise of eternal life. Looking up, father and son saw the Archangel Jibra'il (as) descending carrying a fat ram with a woolly coat mottled white and black or maybe pure glistening white. It had black eyes and large curling horns. Some say that it was the sacrificed sheep of Habil (as) that had been accepted and raised to browse on the pastures of Paradise until this day when it was brought back to earth to be the ransom for Isma'il (as). Some say that instead they heard a bleating sound and turning, they saw a ram or a wild mountain sheep with its horns caught in the bushes nearby.

Ibrahim (as) unbound Isma'il (as) and both men stood shoulder to shoulder before their Lord in prayer, their hearts full of His love and beyond thankful that the test had been successfully passed. Together they took hold of the ram and prepared it for sacrifice. This time the knife did the bidding of Ibrahim (as) and the ram gave up its life easily for the prophets. Father and son carried the animal back down the mountain and distributed its meat among the hungry. They used every part of the sheep, letting nothing go to waste. Animal sacrifice among the Muslims is to provide meat for family and the needy and to make people thankful. At the time of the Prophet Muhammad (sas) the curled horns of that heavenly ram were still to be seen hanging from the roof of the Ka'ba.

An Arab illustration of the sacrifice of Isma'il (as) from the 18th century.

A painting of Ibrahim (as) with family by Jozsef Molnar, 1850.

CHAPTER THIRTY-SEVEN

Ibrahim (as) Had Two Sons

From the earliest days of Islam there has been disagreement about which son Sayyiduna Ibrahim (as) was ordered to sacrifice. There are identical hadith that originate with two of the most respected companions, Ibn Abbas (ra) and Ka'b al-Ahbar (ra), but are transmitted through different chains of people (*isnad*). Some identify Isma'il (as) as the *dhabih* (sacrifice) and some Ishaq (as). Most of the early historians and scholars, al-Tabari (ninth century), al-Tha'labi (eleventh century), al-Kisai (thirteenth century), either say it was Ishaq (as) or present both possibilities. Ibn Taymiyya (also known as al-Harrani because he was born in the prophet Ibrahim's (as) city of Harran in the thirteenth century) and then Ibn Kathir in the fourteenth century, came down decisively on the side of Isma'il (as) and it might be their influence that put the dispute to rest. Most Muslims today do not even seem to know that there could be a legitimate difference of opinion.

The first Muslims accepted the stories of the Jews of Medina, many of whom had become Muslim. They brought with them knowledge of the Torah which they were asked to share and which was accepted by the Prophet (sas) and his companions as long as it did not contradict The Qur'an. Recent generations have dismissed much of this, calling it *Isra'iliyat,* explaining it away by saying the early generations of Muslims were still trying to placate the Jews in the hopes that they would eventually enter into Islam. But it could also be said that the early generations of Muslims were far less likely to make political accommodations to their religion when at the time they were sacrificing their lives to protect it and keep it pure. The later generations, on the other hand, did have political motives because they had regimes and empires to legitimize.

We have, however, been cautioned by the Prophet (sas) in regard to accepting the earlier scriptures. The Jews used to recite and translate the Torah to the Muslims of Medina and the Prophet (sas) advised his companions: "Do not believe the People of the Book or disbelieve them but say: **We believe in Allah and that which is revealed to us and that which was revealed to Ibrahim, and Isma'il, and Ishaq, and the Tribes, and that which was given to Musa and 'Isa and that which was given to all the Prophets by their Lord. We make no distinction between any of them and unto Him we have surrendered"** (2:136). (Bukhari). The proper understanding of this has of course been the subject of much debate. Most scholars accept that the original Torah and Gospel have been corrupted; they are not the same books that were revealed to the prophets mentioned in the verse above. Some say that the actual text has been changed: parts of it hidden or erased such as the passages that predicted the coming of the Prophet Muhammad (sas), while other parts of it have been fabricated and inserted. As a result, some of the book is the unaltered word of God and some is not. To untangle the two is dangerous because you might unwittingly either reject something of divine origin or accept something of human invention and in so doing be misled or worse, incur the anger of Allah.

Others say that the text is preserved intact but it is translated or interpreted incorrectly. For instance, the Torah describes the prophet Isma'il (as) as "a wild donkey of a man. His hand will be against everyone, and everyone's hand will be against him. He will live in conflict with all his relatives." (Genesis 16:12). Many of the Jews and Christians agree that this passage is hard to attribute to the Lord Almighty who chose Isma'il (as) to be His prophet. That Isma'il (as) was a prophet is a fact that nobody disputes. Some commentators try to say that the original understanding was that he and his descendants were nomads, moving freely about the land like the herds of wild donkeys, outside the rule of governments and settled authorities. But Isma'il (as) himself was a hunter who lived in a town and it is unlikely that being compared to a donkey was ever considered a particularly good thing. Others say that this is a deliberate misinterpretation of the original unvoweled Hebrew word for wild (donkey) which with different vowels can instead mean, fruitful. This fits the text better since in Genesis 17 it goes on to say that Isma'il (as) would father the twelve tribes of Arabs, just as his brother would father the twelve tribes of Jews. The phrase "his hand will be against everyone" should accurately be translated as "his hand is with everyone". Instead of meaning rebellious it could mean peacemaker. In any case the Banu Isra'il were no better at getting along with each other or their neighbors according to the Torah itself. The description does not characterize the descendants of Isma'il (as) in particular. There are many scholars who believe passages such as this were purposefully adjusted in order to reflect the political situation several millennia later when the Torah, as we know it today, was written down and the vowel signs were added.

The Torah says definitively it was Ishaq (as), the son of Sarah (rah), whom Ibrahim (as) was commanded to sacrifice. However, the passage in Genesis in which the sacrifice is mentioned calls Ishaq (as) the only son, which by universal agreement he never was. Nobody disputes that Isma'il (as) was the first to be born and consequently the only son who was ever an only son. Even as the son of a slave he still counts as a son. Four out of the twelve sons of Ya'qub (as) were born to slaves and the tribes they engendered were treated equally as part of the Banu Isra'il although they are not the two tribes from which the priests or kings were chosen. According to the law sent down to Musa (as) in the Torah (Deuteronomy), the firstborn son receives double the inheritance of the other sons and inherits the position of the father as head of the household even if he is not the favorite. There is no preference for the firstborn in Islamic law. Interestingly enough, none of the patriarchs of the Banu Isra'il, neither Ibrahim (as) himself, nor Ishaq (as), nor Ya'qub (as), nor Yusuf (as) were firstborn sons. And most of the prophets who followed after them including Musa (as) himself, Dawud (as), and Sulayman (as) were also not the firstborn and were still chosen to inherit in preference to an older brother.

However that might be, according to the Torah, with the birth of Ishaq (as), Isma'il (as) did not just fall into second place by virtue of the status of his mother, he seems to have fallen out of the family tree altogether. He lost both his material and his spiritual inheritance. Certainly this was the case in the eyes of the Banu Isra'il but clearly not in the eyes of either his father or more importantly, of Allah. What we do know for certain is that the Prophet Muhammad (sas) was a descendant of Isma'il (as) and that he came from a long unbroken line of pure believers.

The Muslims derive most of their differing opinions from the same thirteen verses of The Qur'an. These are as follows: When Ibrahim (as) was forced to leave his father and and brothers in Harran, he set out with this prayer: **'Verily I am going to my Lord. He will guide me** (37:99). **Grant me offspring from the righteous'** (37:100). And Allah answered him: **So We gave him tidings of a patient boy** (37:101). And He continues: **And when he** (the son) **was old enough to walk with him, he said 'O my son, I have seen in a dream that I am slaughtering you. So look what do you think?'** The son answered: **'O my father, do what you are commanded. You will find me, Allah willing, among the patient'** (37:102). **Then when they had both surrendered and he had put him down on his forehead,** (37:103) **We called to him, 'O Ibrahim, you have fulfilled the vision.' Thus do We surely reward the doers of good** (37:104-5). **Indeed this was a clear trial** (37:106). **And We ransomed him with a great sacrifice,** (37:107) **and We left for him among the later generations: Peace be upon Ibrahim** (37:108-9). **Thus do we reward the doers of good** (37:110). **Indeed, he was among Our believing servants** (37:111) **and We gave him the good tidings of Ishaq, a prophet from among the righteous** (37:112).

The pro Ishaq (as) people say that there is only one son whose birth is ever foretold in The Qur'an. Ibrahim (as), in the quote above, prays for a righteous son when setting off from his homeland after having been without children for twenty years. He has only one wife Sarah (rah). He has no idea that Hajar (rah) is even in his future. When he makes this request of Allah his intent could only be for a child from Sarah (rah). And Allah's immediate answer could only refer to this request, a son from Sarah (rah). In this understanding, the only son who is mentioned in The Qur'an passage quoted above is Ishaq (as). First Ibrahim (as) asks for him, then Allah answers that he will be born, then when he is grown his sacrifice is described and after it the good news of his birth is mentioned again out of sequence.

The ones who disagree say that the passage above must be chronological. Sayyiduna Ibrahim (as) asks for a righteous son and is given news instead of a patient son. When the angels announce the birth of Ishaq (as) they call him the **wise boy** (15:53) (51:28) and **righteous** (21:72) (37:112). When The Qur'an talks about Isma'il (as) he is called the **patient boy** (37:100) (37:102) (21:85-6) although he is also called righteous once (21:85-86) in conjunction with two other prophets. So it would seem that in the passage quoted above, Isma'il (as) is the patient son who is announced first and Ishaq (as) is the righteous, wise son who is announced last. The sacrifice mentioned after the announcement of the birth of Ismail (as) therefore refers to him. At the end of the passage, Allah grants Ibrahim's (as) original request by announcing the birth of Ishaq (as), the wise son. Once this has been pointed out it seems very logical. The only problem is that The Qur'an does not always conform to human logic and in a very many cases it does not relate stories in a chronological way.

There is a hadith cited by At-Tabari, in which the Prophet (sas) was addressed by a bedouin as the son of the two sacrifices. When his companions asked the meaning, he replied that two of his ancestors were the ransomed sacrifices of their father. The first was the Prophet's (sas) father 'Abdullah (ra) who was chosen to be sacrificed before the Prophet's (sas) birth in order to fulfill a vow of Abdu l-Muttalib (ra). The second was his forefather Isma'il (as). This would seem to be conclusive proof that the *dhabih* was Isma'il (as). However, this hadith is uncorroborated and has a problem with one link in its chain of narration (*isnad*) and is, therefore, judged to be weak.

There is a tradition that comes from a Jewish convert during the reign of the *Khalif* 'Umar ibn 'Abdu l-'Aziz. This man had been a scholar among the Jews prior to his conversion. He said that Isma'il (as) was the son whom Ibrahim (as) was asked by Allah to sacrifice and that the Jews know this but out of envy they deny it. The implication is that they had changed the wording in the Torah and there are many contemporary scholars of all denominations who take this view. That could explain why the Genesis passage so strangely states "Take your only son, who you love, Isaac." (Genesis 22:2). It seems curiously redundant and overly emphatic when Ishaq (as) was not an only son, nor was he the only beloved son.

It adds credence to the possibility that the name of Ishaq (as) was added later to the original description. Only Allah knows.

Probably the strongest statement than can be made in the end, is that The Qur'an seems to indirectly imply that the son Sayyiduna Ibrahim (as) was asked to sacrifice as an offering to his Lord was his patient first born son, Isma'il (as). However, if Allah had wanted to make the name of the sacrificed son clearly known He could have easily inserted the name of Isma'il (as) into the text. The ambiguity must be intentional. It allows for two truths. One that was held true for the millennia of Hebrew prophets and one that is true now for the era of Muhammad (sas). The Qur'an cannot be taken as a history book. Its subject is eternal truth, that rises above or dwells within the apparent events of this world. But again, Allah knows best.

The people on either side of the question, however, are eminently trustworthy and authoritative. Al-Tha'labi states that among those of the opinion that Ishaq (as) was the sacrifice were: 'Umar ibn al-Khattab (ra), 'Ali ibn Abi Talib (ra), and Ibn Ishaq. Among those who felt that Isma'il (as) was the intended sacrifice were: 'Abdullah ibn 'Umar (ra) and 'Abdullah ibn Abbas (ra), Mu'awiya (ra) and al-Hasan al-Basri (ra). Ibn 'Arabi (q) and Jalaluddin Rumi (q) at different times call both Isma'il (as) and Ishaq (as) the intended sacrifice as if for the purpose of spiritual teaching it makes no difference. It is out of respect for all of them that we will follow in their footsteps and present both possibilities.

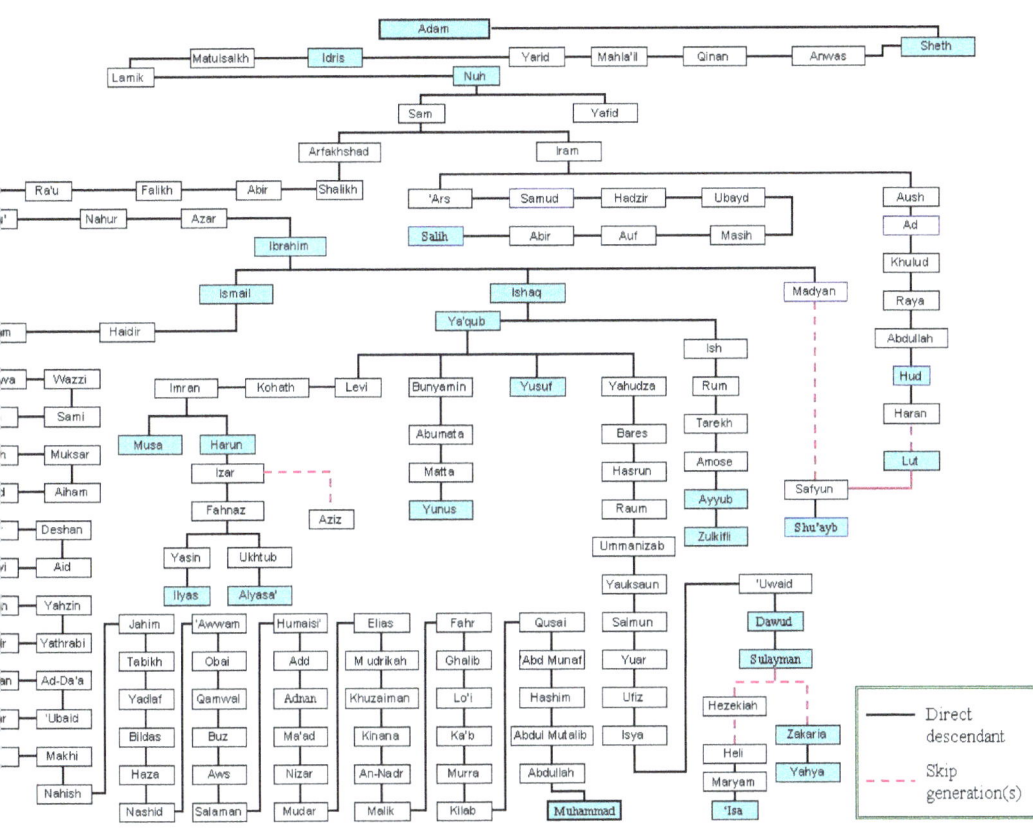

A genealogical chart of the prophets.

A Jewish miniature of the sacrifice of Ishaq (as) painted on the back of a wooden door panel.

CHAPTER THIRTY-EIGHT

The Sacrifice of Ishaq (as)

The Muslims who believe that the son Ibrahim (as) was asked to sacrifice was Ishaq (as) tell the same story as the one related before about Isma'il (as) but with one very major difference. Since Ishaq (as) and his mother lived in Canaan, the sacrifice itself most likely took place in the vicinity of Jerusalem rather than of Mecca. Otherwise the details of the story are the same, taken from The Qur'an and Hadith.

The story as it is told in the Torah, however, differs in a number of other ways. Ibrahim (as) does not receive the order to sacrifice Ishaq (as) in a dream. He is spoken to directly by Allah so there is no possibility of misunderstanding. He does not wait to have the order confirmed. He does not try to substitute sheep or cows. He rises early in the morning of the next day, intent on carrying out the command of his Lord, perhaps afraid to spend too much time considering the horror of its content. He neither seeks the counsel of his son nor that of his wife. He rouses Ishaq (as) telling him only that they have been commanded to make a burnt offering. He says goodbye to Sarah (rah) and leaves. He takes with him two servants, a donkey, a knife, a live coal with which to start a fire, a rope, and some firewood. They set off together in the direction their Lord would guide them.

The land to which they were directed is called Moriah in the Torah. It is the mysterious Land of Moriah because there are different theories about where it is, none of them certain or universally accepted. Today it is usually identified as the Temple Mount, the rock under the Dome of the Rock in Jerusalem near where the Temple of Solomon was supposed to have been built, holy to the Muslims also because of the Night Journey of the Prophet (sas). The Christians accept this location but consider it part of the mountain range that includes the Mount of Golgotha where 'Isa (as) was said to be crucified. Many others including the Samaritans, an ancient Jewish sect, believe, however, that Mount Moriah is Mount Gerizim near Nablus (Biblical Shechem) where they built a temple and place of sacrifice.

Some Muslims interpret it as being Mina in the Hejaz rather than a location near Jerusalem. It is said that after the redemption of Ishaq, (as) Ibrahim (as) renamed the mountain *Jeru-el*, meaning 'Allah will provide' (Genesis 22:8). Mina is the area outside of Mecca where the sacrifice is supposed to have taken place and in Arabic it means a gift freely given. *Minat Allah* would then translate also as 'Allah provided'. This adds some inconclusive linguistic support to the possibility that Ibrahim (as) took his son Ishaq (as) from their home in Hebron and journeyed with him all the way to Mecca in order to carry out the orders of his Lord and to enact the events which would come to be associated with the rites of Hajj. However, the Torah says it took Ibrahim (as) and Ishaq (as) only three days to reach Moriah by donkey which, if accurate, would make the Hejaz a good deal too far unless by donkey was meant the heavenly winged creature called a *buraq* or by days was meant weeks.

In the Torah, Ibrahim (as) does not confide the divine command to his son. He tells him only that the purpose of their journey is to make a burnt offering to Allah. Ishaq (as) was not given the opportunity to agree and submit willingly or to advise his father on how to perform the sacrifice in the least painful way for both of them. There is, however, a story in the Midrash (commentary on the Torah) that is very similar to the Qur'anic one in which Ishaq (as) is told the purpose of their journey and submits himself willingly. However, we don't know the date this commentary was written and it is not part of the Christian tradition. In fact, none of the early life of Ibrahim (as) is found in the Torah. Rather it derives from the Midrash and Talmud and so is not accepted by Christians.

As in the Muslim account, on the way to Mount Moriah the devil tried to prevent the prophets from obeying their Lord. First he went to Sarah (rah), who had remained at home, and told her that her husband was going to sacrifice her beloved only son. She did not believe him but still she panicked and ran after them looking for where they had gone. She ended up in Hebron and there she died from the shock. Ibrahim (as) heard the news of Sarah's (rah) death on his way back and came to mourn and bury her. There in the cave called Machpelah he buried Sarah (rah). It would become the place of burial for all the family except Hajar (rah), Isma'il (as), and Rahila (rah) the beloved wife of Ya'qub (as). Today Hebron, also called Khalil, is in Israel just over the border from Jordan. The Jews consider the cave to be one of the entrances to Paradise and say that both Adam (as) and Hawwa (rah) were the first to be buried there.

Then the devil began to whisper in Ishaq's (as) ear that his father was taking him to slaughter. He tried to make Ishaq (as) afraid but Ishaq (as) knew that his father would only do what his Lord commanded and that was goodness. Ibrahim (as) recognized the devil and helped Ishaq (as) chase him away. Finally, the devil, in a last ditch effort tried to shake the resolve of Ibrahim (as) himself by making him doubt that the order had come from Allah. But for the third time he failed and in rage he fled.

They continued to walk alongside the donkey carrying their things three days to the vicinity of the Land of Moriah where the Lord told them to stop. The day fell on the first day of the new year, Rosh Hashanah or Muharram. They left the donkey and the servants at the foot of one of the mountains and told them to wait there. Father and son climbed until they were commanded to stop, presumably in a place where there was a large rock to serve as an altar. Ibrahim (as) carried the coals, the rope, and the knife. Ishaq (as) carried the firewood. The need to carry their own firewood perhaps points to a more desert location. The area around Jerusalem has adequate rainfall to maintain hills covered in trees and brush, certainly capable of providing what was needed locally.

A burnt offering is a technical Biblical term for a sacrifice presented to God that is completely burned to ash on an altar constructed specifically for that purpose. The term burnt offering in Hebrew is *qorban olah* (Arabic *qurban 'ala*) - an offering that goes up, as smoke. In the Greek Bible it is called a *holocaust* meaning that it is completely consumed by fire. The most important thing was that it was given in its entirely to God; there should be nothing left of the offering, not meat nor skin nor bone was to be used by man. Later the skin was given to the priest but at this time, before the Torah was revealed, this was not the law and there were no priests. To qualify as a *qorban olah* the offering must be in perfect condition and the very best of what the owner possesses; if animal, it has to be male, young, and healthy, the best of the herd. Perhaps this explains why it was Ishaq (as) who was chosen for sacrifice, the son of the freeborn noble mother. The sacrifice must be made on an altar of some kind. Later Allah prescribed for Musa (as) on Mount Sinai the nature of this altar (Leviticus). It must be made of acacia wood covered with bronze, a five-cubit cube. It should have horned projections on the corners and rings through which poles could be inserted for transport because the early Banu Isra'il were a nomadic people. Although the shape and form of these altars was not revealed until a thousand years later, still some sort of altar is said to have been prepared for this sacrifice.

Adam (as) was the first to present a burnt offering to God in thanks for his being forgiven. Adam's (as) sons, Habil (as) and Qabil, were the next who were recorded making a burnt offering. Qabil, a farmer, offered the first fruits from his garden and Habil (as), a shepherd, offered a lamb. A flame descended from heaven and consumed Habil's (as) offering completely which indicated that Allah found it acceptable. Qabil's offering, however, was left untouched indicating its rejection. The Muslims say that whereas Habil (as) offered the best of his flock, Qabil offered the poorest of his crop. This rejection contributed to the enmity that eventually led Qabil to kill his brother and commit the first murder. The next prophet to to be recorded making a burnt offering was Nuh (as) in order to thank Allah for bringing the Ark safely to rest (Genesis 8:20). Ibrahim (as) then was the next prophet for whom a burnt offering is mentioned and it is said that all these offerings were made somehow on the very same altar.

Ishaq (as) innocently accompanied his father, unaware of the true purpose of their journey but he did notice that they had all the things necessary for a sacrifice except the sacrifice itself. He asked about it and Ibrahim (as) answered that Allah would provide, "*Jehovah-jireh*" (Genesis 22:14) an indication of the future name of the mountain, *Jeru-el*. There

Ibrahim (as) prepared an altar to the Lord following His instructions: "Take your only son, who you love, Isaac, and go to the land of Moriah and offer him there as a burnt offering on one of the mountains of which I will tell you." (Genesis 22:2). If this rock altar was on the Temple Mount then perhaps it explains why it was already a holy place when much later the Prophet Muhammad (sas) tethered the *buraq* there, led all the past prophets in prayer, and ascended into Heaven on the Night Journey. When he began his ascent, the rock, not wanting to lose the touch of his foot, began to rise with him until it received a divine order to stop. That is why it is said today to be hanging unsupported above the mountain. It is, in consequence, a place sacred to all the People of the Book.

According to the Torah, Ibrahim (as) without explanation trussed up the startled Ishaq (as) with the rope like a sheep and laid him on the pile of wood they had prepared on the altar so he could not struggle. The incident is referred to in Hebrew as the *akeda*, or the binding of Ishaq (as) thereby putting emphasis on the innocent victim rather than on the faithful father. Ibrahim (as) could have had no other intention than to cut the throat of his son and then set him on fire as instructed by the divine decree, a highly more detailed and disturbing image than that provided by The Qur'an. The famous old master paintings of Christian themes usually show Ishaq (as) going to the sacrifice terrified and unwilling, bound hand and foot by his determined and undeterrable father, a lamb to the slaughter. At this point a voice from heaven commanded Ibrahim (as) to stop. But his determination and focus were so intense that he did not hear at first. An angel had to be sent to physically grab his arm and prevent him from cutting with the knife. To his relief he looked up and saw a ram whose horns were tangled in the thorn bushes nearby. He untied his son and together they sacrificed the ram instead. Some of the Midrash accounts (all of them transcribed after the second or third century CE) say that Ishaq (as) was cut and wounded before the angel could stop his father and he was taken to Paradise for three days to be healed. Some say that he was actually slaughtered and taken to Paradise for three years before he was resurrected and returned to Ibrahim (as). This would explain why in the Torah it is only Ibrahim (as) who is said to return from the mountain. It also prefigures the resurrection of 'Isa (as) three days after he was taken from the cross and laid in his tomb.

The Christian theologians tend to interpret the Old Testament by means of the New. They see each story as a sign of what would later manifest in the ministry of 'Isa (as). This was especially true of what is referred to as the binding of Ishaq (as). They connect Mount Moriah with the Temple Mount and with Golgotha, the mount on which they believe 'Isa (as) was crucified, in order to complete the metaphor between 'Isa (as) and Ishaq (as). One is the only son of Ibrahim (as), the other is the only son of God. Both carried the wood for their own sacrifice up the mountain: the one, wood for burning, and the other, timbers of the cross. But whereas Ishaq (as) was redeemed by a sheep, 'Isa (as) himself became the Redeemer and the sacrificial lamb and he died in order to absolve all of mankind of sin. The ram represents the bodily sacrifice of 'Isa (as) and the thicket in which it was caught is his crown of thorns. Ishaq (as) himself represents the spiritual reality of 'Isa (as) which will never die.

In the Midrash it is said that the ram Allah provided was no ordinary sheep. It had been created on Friday the sixth day of Creation specifically for the ransom of Ishaq (as) and no part of its blessed body was wasted after its sacrifice. Its horns were made into two *shofar*, trumpet horns. One of these was blown on the day Musa (as) received the Torah on Mount Sinai and the other will be blown on the Day of Judgment. The ashes were used to fill the inside of the Temple altar. The sinews were used to string the harp of the prophet Dawud (as). The skin was used to make a waist wrap for the prophet Elijah (as). However, the definition of an *olah* sacrifice is that everything, skin, horns, bone, is reduced to smoke that ascends to God and only some ash remains. Nothing is for human use.

Then the Lord made a promise to Ibrahim (as): "The angel of the Lord called to Abraham from heaven a second time and said 'I swear by Myself, declares the Lord, that because you have done this and have not withheld your son, your only son, I will surely bless and make your descendants as numerous as the stars in the sky and as the sand on the seashore. Your descendants will take possession of the cities of their enemies, and through your offspring all nations on earth will be blessed, because you have obeyed Me.'" (Genesis 22:15-18). The Jews understand this promise literally as the emergence of the Banu Isra'il and they speak of Ibrahim (as) with familial affection as *Abraham Abinu*, Ibrahim (as) our Father. The Christians, however, interpret the promise of a multitude of descendants as foretelling the spread of the church and its many adherents.

The Prophet Muhammad (sas) also referred to Ibrahim (as) as his father and Allah calls him his father in The Qur'an, and the father of the Muslims (22:78). The closeness that the early Muslims felt for Ibrahim (as) is illustrated by the story of the Prophet's (sas) great granddaughter Sayyidatuna Nafisa (rah) who grew up in Medina and eventually died in Cairo. As a young woman she prayed every day to be able to visit the grave of Ibrahim (as) in Hebron. She knew that her grandfather Muhammad (sas) was the answer to the prayer of Ibrahim (as) when after building the Ka'ba he said: **Our Lord, raise up a Messenger from among them who will recite to them Your signs and teach them the Book and wisdom and purify them.** (2:129). When she finally arrived at his graveside, she saw with her waking eyes the figure of Ibrahim (as) standing clearly before her and she addressed him with love as *Jiddi*, my grandfather. And like a kindly grandfather, he showed concern for her wellbeing and advised her not to spend all her time in prayer but to also take better care of her health.

An 18th century Byzantine fresco of the sacrifice of Ishaq (as) from a church in Raduil Bulgaria.

Aerial view of the rock under the Dome in Jerusalem where the Prophet Muhammad (sas) stood and where the sacrifice of Ishaq (as) might have taken place.

CHAPTER THIRTY-NINE

What Difference Would It Make?

Covenant

In the Torah there is something called a Covenant, *berit* in Hebrew, between the Banu Isra'il and God. The Children of Isra'il (as) promised to worship Allah and only Allah. In return Allah promised to favor them. They believe that this Covenant was made on behalf of the Banu Isra'il by their ancestor Ibrahim (as). Starting from the time he left Harran, before he had any children, there are at least four occasions in the Torah where God promises Ibrahim (as) many descendants, the land of Canaan to live in forever, and blessings for himself and for the whole world by means of him. However, twenty-five years later, after the birth of Isma'il (as), when Sarah's (rah) pregnancy was announced by the angelic messengers, God appears to have narrowed the scope of His promise to include only Ishaq (as) and his descendants. Ibrahim (as), out of love and concern, asked that Isma'il (as), his firstborn, and at the time his only son, be included. Allah promised to make him fruitful but repeated that His Covenant was with Ishaq (as) alone. This Covenant was written in the flesh and sealed with blood by the act of circumcision. Even though Isma'il (as) was circumcised first, only the children of Ishaq (as) would "walk with God" (Genesis 17:18). Later the Torah claims that because of two deceptions on the part of Ishaq's (as) son Ya'qub (as), the children of his older brother 'As (as) (Esau) were also excluded. They continued to increase in number but were not part of the divine pact. They allied themselves by marriage with the children of Isma'il (as) and so together they became the unchosen people.

Now, three thousand years later, we can see that the divine promise has been fulfilled but not quite in the way it was projected. All the children of Ibrahim (as) became fruitful, the children of Isma'il (as) even more so than the children of Ishaq (as), as the Arabs greatly outnumber the Jews. The children of Isma'il (as) have kept possession of the land of Canaan without interruption since the time of Ibrahim (as) as they were promised, the children of Ishaq (as) have to a lesser extent. So unless God's word is false, at least these two parts of the Covenant were clearly shared by all the children of Ibrahim (as). As for the third part, certainly the Banu Isra'il have blessed the world with a multitude of beautiful, wise, inspired men and women, the prophets, their families and followers. The whole world continues to be blessed by their words and their example. But there were at least two prophets that we know of who are descended from Ibrahim (as) through some of his other sons. The prophet Shuayb (as) is said to have descended through one of the sons of Katurah (rah) named Madyan (ra) and the Prophet of the End of Times, the Seal of Prophethood, Sayyiduna Muhammad (sas) descended through Isma'il (as). So it can be truthfully said that, in the light of current evidence, the descendants of Isma'il (as) and even the other sons of Ibrahim (as) were neither ejected from God's favor nor excluded from the Covenant. Rather it extended to all the children of Ibrahim (as) regardless of mother or of who was the sacrifice at either Moriah or Mina. **Abraham was neither a Jew nor a Christian, but was one who turned away from all that is false (*hanif*): having surrendered himself unto Allah (*muslim*); and he was not of those who ascribe divinity to aught beside Him. (3:67)**

To the Christians the covenant of Ibrahim (as) was superseded by a new covenant established between God and 'Isa (as). The proof of this is that they discarded circumcision as a required ritual practice. They explain that the first covenant between Ibrahim (as) and God was made before the order to circumcise. This is proof that God made His pact with an uncircumcised man and that circumcision is not necessary. Their new covenant is symbolized by baptism. But the sacrifice of Ishaq (as) rather than Isma'il (as) is important to them for two reasons. The first is that

'Isa (as) is a descendant of Ishaq (as) and as such a member of the chosen people, carrying the authority of the prophets who preceded him. The second is that portions of their theology rest on 'Isa's (as) sacrifice being a consummation of the sacrifice of Ishaq (as). As the 'lamb of God' 'Isa (as) was the true fulfillment of Allah's order to Ibrahim (as). The aborted sacrifice of Ishaq (as) was merely a hint of the required sacrifice that was to come, that of Christ (as) who they claim actually did die to save mankind.

Muslims, however, do not believe either that 'Isa (as) died for the sins of man or that he died at all. Nor do they have the same definition of a covenant with Allah. All souls, without exception, made a covenant with their Lord on the day called the Day of Promises when Allah addressed the seed of Adam (as), all the souls which had been created, long before they were given bodies and a life on this earth. He said: **'Am I not your Lord?' They said, 'Yes, indeed we bear witness to this.'** (7:172) This is a promise that most human beings forget, including Adam (as) and his wife, and of which they need to be constantly reminded. It is the main duty of the prophets to remind them and to this end Allah also **took a covenant from the prophets** (33:7). Remembrance of this pact is the essence of what makes a man a human being. If he remembers then he is in accordance with his *fitra*, the perfect way in which he was made.

Muslims also regard male circumcision differently. It is required in Islam but it is not as a symbol or seal of a covenant. It is thought of as an act of necessary cleanliness, to be pure for prayer and should be performed on a male child before the age of puberty when he becomes responsible for keeping his religious duties and eligible for marriage. Ibrahim (as) is considered the first recipient of the rules of cleanliness, *tahara*. In addition to circumcision, there is also the removal of body hair and making ablution with water (*wudu'*). The true sign of a covenant for Muslims would be the five pillars: to declare the unity of God and the prophethood of Muhammad (sas), to perform the five daily prayers, to fast the month of Ramadan, to give *zakat* (tithe), and to make the Hajj if possible.

The only aspects of Islam that might be affected if Ishaq (as) were the sacrifice would be one or two of the rites of Hajj and then only if the event of the sacrifice took place somewhere in Palestine. However, the pilgrimage with all its rituals began with Adam (as). Not just the encircling of the Holy House, but all the rites of pilgrimage from the *sa'i*, to the standing on 'Arafah, to the stop at Mina - all of them were taught by Jibra'il (as) to Adam (as) and Hawwa (rah) after their descent to earth. And the Hajj has been a duty performed by every prophet since. It is through Ibrahim (as) and his son Isma'il (as), however, that the rites of Hajj have been relayed to us. And it is Allah's invitation, conveyed by Ibrahim's (as) call, to which all the Hajjis respond. Those facts remain unchanged. The stoning of the shaytan and the animal sacrifice, however, would become powerful symbolic reenactments of actions that took place elsewhere. The only thing that Muslims might gain by the acceptance of Isma'il (as) as the sacrifice would be to reintroduce him more solidly into the Ibrahimic family to take his rightful place among the covenanted people rather than being reduced to a rejected or irrelevant aside.

If Ishaq (as) was indeed the sacrifice, we see that Ibrahim (as) had to give up both sons. First Allah required him to leave Isma'il (as) and his mother in an inhospitable place without any means of support. He had to set them down in what would be to ordinary humans only a place to die. He had to turn his back and leave them to Allah. Then when the desire of his heart was answered and Sarah (rah) gave birth to a beautiful righteous son, again Ibrahim (as) had to give him up to his Lord; to sacrifice him on a stone, bound like a lamb, in the fierceness and intensity of his love for God. So it might be in actuality that Ibrahim (as) was asked to sacrifice both boys, and both sons were in fact *dhabih*.

Diversity

The difference of opinion does not seem to have been a matter of much concern at the time of the Prophet Muhammad (sas) or someone would presumably have asked a direct question. It did not have much spiritual importance but rather it seems to have gathered political importance as the Muslim state developed. The early Muslims clearly adhered to the verses in The Qur'an that order the believers to respect all the the prophets equally. This doesn't mean that prophets do not have ranks and degrees which distinguish one from the other, but that they all stem equally from the same sacred source. **Say: 'We believe in Allah, and in that which has been bestowed from on high upon us, and that which** has been bestowed upon Ibrahim and Isma'il and Ishaq and Ya'qub and their descendants, and that which had been vouchsafed by their Lord unto Musa and 'Isa and all the prophets: we make no distinction between any of them. And unto Him do we surrender ourselves.' (3:84)

Perhaps the reason that the name of the son who was chosen for sacrifice is not mentioned in The Qur'an is simply that it is beside the point. The point is that the religion of Ibrahim (as) is for those who follow his teaching. It is not a covenant with any single blood line. The Qur'an, unlike the Bible, cannot be read as a tribal history. The stories it relates are rarely sequential or detailed enough to be called a history at all. Their sole purpose is rather to illuminate spiritual truths. Islam is intended by God as the last and universal religion, a restatement of the religion of Ibrahim the *Hanif* (as). The message of the Prophet Muhammad (sas) was to abolish tribalism and its monster son, nationalism. All believers in the One God, the Creator, are brothers regardless of origin, language, race, or history. So Muslims do not, and should not, consider themselves the Banu Isma'il (as). They are an amalgam of many ancestors all tracing their genetic inheritance back to Nuh (as) and to Adam (as) and their spiritual inheritance to Ibrahim (as).

Islam is established in such a way that there is not a single proper way to do anything. Each *Madhhab*, school of law, supports different options for most ritual observances, all based on The Qur'an and Hadith. There are now four main schools of law but there used to be hundreds of accepted schools each one derived from certain companions of the Prophet (sas) and scholars among their followers; each one based on the actions and words of the Prophet (sas) and on an informed interpretation of The Qur'an. Some of the differences between the schools could, of course, be due to error on the part of the observer or interpreter but most of it can be traced back to the Prophet (sas) himself. He did things differently at different times, all of them proper, all of them correct.

A story is related in *Riyad As-Salihin*, about two companions of the Prophet (sas) who were upset to the point that they felt their faith was at risk by the fact that they each recited a portion of The Qur'an differently and they each had been taught by the Prophet (sas) himself. They approached the Prophet (sas) wanting to know which of them recited correctly. The Prophet (sas) calmly told them that they were both right. He said: "Jibra'il (as) and Mika'il (as) came to me, and Jibra'il (as) sat on my right and Mika'il (as) sat on my left. Jibra'il (as) said 'Recite The Qur'an with one way of recitation.' Mika'il (as) said 'Teach him more, teach him more.' Until there were seven modes of recitation (*ahruf*), each of which is good and sound." The Prophet (sas) considered this as a mercy for his nation.

They say that Islam is a coat that should fit comfortably. It must come then in all shapes and sizes. From the way the worshipper holds her hands in prayer, to how and when she makes ablution, to what can be eaten and how to be clean, there are multiples of permissible differences. This variation, rather than causing conflict and accusation, was traditionally a source of immeasurable interest and discussion among Muslims. The intention must have been to avoid division by acceptance of difference. The only thing that is One, is Allah. Everything human must include room for diversity. However, saying that there is not one right way is not the same as saying that all ways are right. Some ways are crooked and some are straight, some are right and some are clearly wrong. But just because your way is right does not mean that you can judge everybody else as wrong. And this is important to remember in the world and time in which we live. Only at the very end of times, when the Messiah, 'Isa son of Maryam (as), returns as a member of the nation of Muhammad (sas) will we all be united under one law.

No one can say that the *dhabih* was Ishaq (as) or the *dhabih* was Isma'il (as), that one is true and the other false. Such a judgment rests on one weak hadith and opinions formed by choosing between contradicting strong hadith. Even if one point of view is more reasonable than the other, it can never be stated as fact because it wasn't revealed by Allah. There is always the less reasonable but equally possible truth of its opposite. And we must accept that this too can be Allah's plan and His will and that there is important wisdom to be gained within the murky depths of a purposeful ambiguity.

The early Muslims did not dispute that Allah had made a covenant with Ibrahim (as) and Ishaq (as). That was only the beginning of the story of which they were the ending. Ishaq (as) was the righteous son and from one of his sons descend all the later known prophets except four, Shu'ayb (as), Dhul Qarnain (as), Luqman (as), and Muhammad (sas). When that epoch was over Allah uncovered the treasure that He had kept hidden and protected in the desert, like Zamzam under the sand. Described as patient and forbearing, Isma'il (as) carefully transmitted the light of the Prophet of the Last Days, Sayyiduna Muhammad (sas), inherited from his father Ibrahim (as) and it passed from pure parents to pure parents. Waiting patiently, this heritage came to light in the sixth century CE. Then what was hidden was made manifest. It became clear that the covenant and the favor had not been taken from Isma'il (as) the elder son and given to Ishaq (as) the younger son, but rather had been given to each in their own time. **Indeed, the most worthy people in relation to Ibrahim are those who followed him, and this prophet** [Muhammad] **and those who believe. And Allah is the protector of the believers** (3:68).

The Mount of Mercy, Arafat, Saudi Arabia near where the sacrifice of Isma'il (as) might have taken place and where Adam (as) and Hawwa (rah) prayed together for forgiveness.

Qur'an (65:4) "Allah makes things easy for those who are mindful of Him (*taqwa*)." Or "For who has *taqwa*, Allah makes it easy to obey His commands."

CHAPTER FORTY
A Clear Test

Life on earth is a test. It is full of pain and difficulty. After Allah Almighty finished molding the shape of Adam (as) from the clay of the earth, He set the lifeless form out in the wind and the rain for forty years. During this time, it seemed that Adam (as) was cast out and forgotten (76:1). The angels looked down at him in dismay. Iblis mocked him, kicking the clay to make it ring with emptiness. And so the rain fell on Adam (as) as a rain of separation and sorrow. But to cure clay properly it must be kept moist. If it dries too quickly it will crack and break. Perhaps in much the same way, if man enjoys too much ease he will not grow strong. After forty years of lying as a thing unremembered under the showers of sorrow, Allah turned towards him once more and Adam (as) basked in the light of his Lord's gaze for a full year. So it is said that in the life of this world there are forty sorrows for every joy, forty troubles for every comfort. This is built into who we are and is the only way to become what we are meant to be.

Allah ends the account of the near sacrifice of the son of Ibrahim (as) by saying: **Indeed, this was a clear test** (37:106). In the Torah the story of the sacrifice of Ishaq (as) is introduced by saying: "God tested

Abraham." (Genesis 22:1). So clearly this was a test but who is being tested and what is the test? This has challenged the creativity of the Peoples of the Book since it was first revealed. Explanations, imaginations, and even apologies abound. Philosophers, psychologists, religious men and lay, saints and sinners, have all tried to accommodate God's word within the bounds of the human mind. How could a loving God, a God who at all times has forbidden killing, command a father to kill his innocent child? And how could a prophet of God, the embodiment of all that is good, obey Him? There are probably as many understandings as there are souls to witness.

Some (Tafsir Ibn Abbas) say that before Isma'il (as) was born Ibrahim (as) had made a vow that if Allah should give him a son he would in return sacrifice what was most dear to him. **You will not attain to piety (birra) until you spend of that which you love** (3:92). Allah was now reminding Ibrahim (as) of his debt which is another way to interpret the verse, **Ibrahim, who to his trust was true (waffa)** (53:37), since *waffa* can also mean paid a debt, fulfilled a duty, or kept a promise. This was apparently not an uncommon form of vow. It recalls the sacrifice of the daughter of Jephthah in the Torah and of Iphigenia by Agamemnon in Greek mythology, as well as the already mentioned vow of Abdu l-Muttalib (ra).

Others (Tafsir As-Suyuti) say that when Ibrahim (as) requested that Allah show him how He could bring the dead back to life with the example of the birds, Allah had told him that in return for showing him this miracle, one day He would also ask something of Ibrahim (as). Allah was saying now that He had given the heart of Ibrahim (as) certainty about resurrection would Ibrahim (as) trust Allah to bring his son back from the dead? His willingness to perform this sacrifice attests to his complete assurance that there is indeed another eternal life waiting and that the word of his Lord is true.

Ibn 'Arabi (q) says that Ibrahim (as) misunderstood the significance of his vision, that he took literally what was meant to be symbolic. He was a very decisive prophet who acted immediately once Allah's command was communicated, as evidenced by his rejection of the gods of his people and by his circumcision. Even though he was a prophet, he had to be taught how to properly interpret the signs that were shown him just as the prophet Yusuf (as) had been taught (12:101). Although in his dream he saw himself sacrificing his son, in fact the meaning was to symbolically cut out of his heart that which he loved other than Allah. In actuality he was meant to sacrifice a sheep. Ibrahim (as) should have used his reason to know that Allah would never ask for the murder of a child. **Lost indeed are those who kill their children** (6:140). Then Allah substituted the heavenly ram because that was actually what was being asked for. This then absolves the Creator of having commanded a sin and teaches something to His creation about commitment, understanding, and the use of the divine gift of reason.

Mawlana Jalaluddin Rumi (q) introduces the story of Musa (as) and Khidr (as) to explain the sacrifice of Ishaq (as). Khidr (as) shocked Musa (as) by the seemingly arbitrary killing of a child (18:74). But Khidr (as) later explained that he was obeying divine instruction and that the child, although innocent at the time of his death, was destined to be evil and endanger his believing parents (18:80). Allah was protecting the parents from unbelief and corruption and he was taking the child in his innocence before he committed a sin. In this way He was actually safeguarding the eternity of all of them. There is no fault, however, ascribed to the son of Ibrahim (as) for which his death could be counted a mercy. The lesson to be learned concerns instead the majestic enigma that is our Lord. He is greater than anything we see, wiser than anything we know, beyond imagination or investigation. We must beware trying to judge His actions as we judge our own. The Sufis say, "Glory be to Allah, who is known only by the fact that He is unknown." We should also not presume to judge the motivation of a prophet of Allah. For Ibrahim (as) the highest moral action was simply to accept and immediately act upon the orders of his Lord, whatever they might be. That was the highest form of goodness.

The test was also not to prove to Allah that Ibrahim (as) was His submitted servant, for Allah, being his Creator and omniscient, knew that already. Some actually say that it was Ibrahim's (as) test of Allah to see if He would stop the sacrifice in order to keep His promise to bring generations of believers from Ibrahim's (as) descendants. But there is no way Ibrahim (as) would have had the audacity to put his Lord to the test.

Others say the purpose was to paint a clear picture, in the most dramatic of colors, of what complete submission to the will of Allah, true

Islam, looks like for all following generations to witness. Allah commanded the Prophet Muhammad (sas) to **Say, "surely my prayer and my sacrifice and my living and my dying are for Allah, the Sustainer (Rabb) of the worlds."** (6:162). And again to **Say: if it be that your fathers, your sons, your brothers, your mates, or your kindred; the wealth that you have gained; the commerce in which you fear a decline; or the dwellings in which you delight – are dearer to you than Allah or His Messenger, or the striving in His cause – then wait until Allah brings about His decision, and Allah guides not the rebellious.** (9:24).

Without doubt, as we too become involved in the story, each one of us also enters among those being tested. And the fact that on Hajj the Muslim *Ummah* every year repeats the steps of Ibrahim (as) and his son is clear evidence that our Creator wishes us to bodily and spiritually re-enact the movements of this sacrifice and make it our own. Allah asked His prophet to do possibly the hardest thing imaginable and he obeyed. Could we obey even the lightest of orders? Can we stop what we are doing and pray on time? Can we get up on a dark night to remember our Lord? Can we leave something we like because our Creator asks us to? Even these small, mundane requests are simple to say but not simple for most of us to do.

The higher the spiritual rank, the greater the tests and trials that are sent. This we learn from The Qur'an and the Hadith of our Prophet (sas). All men are tested according to their capacity and not beyond it. (2:286). The saints are given harder tests than the average man. The prophets are tested harder than the saints. And of all the prophets, the Prophet Muhammad (sas) said that he was tested the most intensely, no doubt because his capacity was greatest. This might mean that the capacity of the prophets to endure suffering was greater so they were given more burdens to carry. But more likely it means that because of their enormous generosity of spirit, their intimate grasp of right and wrong, their unwavering love of Allah and His creation, their foresight and knowledge, their dignity and refinement, these perfect human beings felt sad for so many things that most of us glide over without a twinge of either remorse or shame. It means firstly that they were exquisitely more sensitive to their own shortcomings and weaknesses as they stood always in the light of their Lord. In addition, these most open-hearted and compassionate of men had to watch the pain of others, knowing a cure was available but not being able to convince them to take it. Seeing the reality clearly, how difficult it must be to carry the blindness and ignorance of others. They held in their hands the key to happiness, but could not convince their people to take it no matter how hard they pleaded or what miracles Allah permitted them to show.

Most definitely the death of Isma'il (as) was never the intention or the goal of this test. Allah could have accomplished that by Himself with a lot less trouble. In the Old and New Testaments and in The Qur'an it is said that the taking of one innocent life is as the taking of all life and the saving of one life is as the saving of all life. **if anyone kills a person – unless in retribution for murder or spreading corruption in the land – it is as if he kills all mankind, while if any saves a life it is as if he saves the lives of all mankind** (5:32). Secondly, Allah has said about sacrifice in general: **Neither does their flesh nor their blood reach Allah; it is only your *taqwa* (God-fearing) that reaches Him** (22:37). This would clearly define the test as being the willingness to make the sacrifice rather than the sacrifice itself.

Taqwa is a word difficult to translate into English. It means fear of God but it is a fear arising out of intense love; fear to displease the One you love as a child fears the displeasure of his parents. It means also consciousness of God: to be aware of His presence at all times and at the same time to know for a certainty that it is not possible to be truly conscious of God for He is beyond mind and consciousness. The Prophet (sas) said: "The head (beginning) of wisdom is fear of Allah." It was also one of the proverbs of the Prophet Sulayman (as) in the book that was revealed to him: "Fear of the Lord is the beginning of wisdom." (Proverbs 1:7). To please Allah is the guideline for each action and the ultimate goal.

To sacrifice is to give up something you love, something you care about, for someone or something else that you care about more. Simply put, Allah is asking us to care about Him more; more than those things that we imagine have benefit for us: our property, our posterity, our purpose. He is the Creator, He made all we have out of love for us. How can we hold those things more dear then we hold Him? Allah is not asking us to kill our children, or even to burn our property, or to abandon our purpose. They are His gifts to us. He has no need of any of them. He is only asking for what is His right, our thanks and our love. In fact, the word in both

Arabic and Hebrew for sacrifice, *qurban*, is derived from the root, meaning to draw near. To sacrifice is simply a way to come closer to Allah. There was one last idol that Ibrahim (as) had left standing between him and his Lord, and on it he had hung his axe. The time had come to finish the job.

The Prophet Muhammad said: "No one of you truly believes until I am dearer to him than his father, his son, his own self, and all the people." (Bukhari). And in The Qur'an, Allah tells the Prophet (sas) to tell us, **'If you love Allah, follow me; Allah will love you.'** (3:31). This is the description of true faith. The story of Ibrahim (as) was sent to illustrate how it looks when it is lived. This story is not really about sacrifice. It is about love.

CHAPTER FORTY-ONE
The Great Sheep

And We ransomed him with a great sacrificial victim (*dhabhin 'adhim*) (37:107). One cannot help but wonder just what kind of sheep could possibly be described as magnificent or great. As Ibn 'Arabi (q) says in the *Bezels of Wisdom*: "Would that I knew how a mere ram came to be a substitute for the Vicegerent (*khalif*) of the Merciful."

Some say that his greatness came from the fact he had been the sacrifice of Habil (as) that had been raised to pasture in Paradise and so become both fat, honored, and not in the least ordinary – a truly transcendent ram. To be acceptable as a burnt offering the sheep must be the very best of the herd and this sheep was in fact the very best in all the world; a perfect model of a sheep that would be the pride and joy of any shepherd. As far as we know, no more beautiful or perfect a sheep has ever existed.

There are many hadith detailing the superior nature of sheep in general. Their qualities are admirable and desirable in humans as well - mildness, submission, humility, and usefulness. They give their milk, their meat, and their wool. They are clean and pure and full of goodness

A most dignified portrait of an ancient breed of sheep.

and they are devoid of harm. It is permitted to pray in the sheep pen – their leavings are not impure and do not void ablution. The water of their noses brings blessing in contrast to that of a dog which causes impurity and must be cleansed seven times with water and once with soil. Their wool is the chosen fabric of all prophets. In fact, Ibn Abbas (ra) relates that the Prophet (sas) said that the Archangel Jibra'il (as) was dressed in garments of wool. When the Prophet (sas) remarked on this, Jibra'il (as) answered that even the pedestal of the Throne is wrapped in wool. Wool was the clothing that Allah sent to Adam (as) after he had been evicted from Paradise, when the leaves he had grabbed to cover his nakedness had withered and fallen away. It was the favored cloth of the Prophet (sas) who wore a linen shirt beneath it. It is said to bring the sweetness of faith to the heart. Abu Hurayra (ra) related that the Prophet (sas) said: "Treat your sheep well, wipe the mucus running from their noses, clean their resting places, and pray in their vicinity for they are animals of Paradise."

But why is this simple sheep, even if he was a special Paradise sheep termed **a mighty sacrificial victim** (37:107)? There may be another explanation that will sound even stranger to modern ears. It has been confirmed that at the time of Sayyiduna Ibrahim (as) the rites of the idol worshippers were not merely licentious, crude and purposeless, they were also unbelievably cruel. It is a fact established by archaeologists that both the Sumerians and the Akkadians practiced forms of human sacrifice. They can't say how or why or even who were the chosen victims but there is irrefutable evidence in the cemeteries of Ur that up to seventy people were sometimes killed to accompany the royal dead. And according to their deciphered writings and temple drawings, there were some gods that required the sacrifice of babies and children. In several places, the Torah condemns the ritual sacrifice of human beings practiced by the idol worshippers who surrounded the believers (Leviticus 18:21, Deuteronomy 18:9-12). But it also recounts the sacrifice of a child among the Banu Isra'il (Judges 11:30-40). Certainly we know that in ancient times, people around the world killed other people for the purpose of pleasing or appeasing their deity. It was a ritual belief of any number of cultures, from Peru to Greece to China, that by the sacrifice of an innocent human life, the society at large would prosper. And it has been said that the Christian story of the crucifixtion of Isa (as) is an echo of this ancient belief.

Even at the time of the Prophet Muhammad (sas) some sort of

human sacrifice was known and possibly practiced. These were people after all who found it acceptable to kill their girl children essentially because they didn't want to waste resources feeding them. The Prophet's (sas) grandfather Abdu l-Muttalib (ra) made a vow that if Allah granted him ten sons he would sacrifice one. That one turned out to be the Prophet's (sas) father Abdullah (ra). It is unlikely that Abdu l-Muttalib came up with the idea all on his own. His vow must have been derived from some sort of known practice. Even though the boy was his favorite, it is recorded that it took a lot of persuasion on the part of the boy's maternal relatives to get Abdu l-Muttalib (ra), a man of honor, to back down from his vow and accept the sacrifice of one hundred camels instead.

In the light of this terrible reality the test of Ibrahim (as) and the ransom of his son constitutes Allah's absolute irrefutable prohibition against this practice. If anyone ever thought that this was a way to please God, they should think again. And an animal has taken the place of a human victim until the end of time. If this sheep represents the replacement of murder with sacrifice, then surely it can be described as great.

But even if the order to sacrifice a son was revoked, the need for blood sacrifice was not. We are still commanded to sacrifice something, to bring death to something living, to actively, irrevocably, with our hands and hearts acknowledge that the difference between life and death is as thin as the blade of a knife, that one leads inevitably into the other. Even though we are afraid, we must stand witness to the truth that **to Allah we belong and to Him we will return** (2:156). Our Creator has the ultimate right to take us back however, wherever, and whenever He pleases. We belong to Him.

A Muslim begins, or should begin, every activity in life in the name of his Creator, Allah the Merciful, the Most Merciful – *Bismi Llahi r-Rahmani r-Rahim*. There are, however, a few important exceptions: when he enters the ritual prayer and for every change of position within the prayer; when he prepares to sacrifice an animal; when he faces the enemy in battle. In these three instances he begins by saying *Allahu Akbar* – Allah is Greater, indicating that whatever he is facing or leaving behind, Allah is far, far greater. In prayer it serves to remind that, whatever else is happening, when he steps on the prayer carpet he leaves it all behind because Allah is greater. And as he moves through the various positions of prayer, he moves closer to Him, giving up one station for the next, not holding on to any of them. It signals a relinquishing of the world and of our power to control it. It is a rehearsal for dying. Allah is Greater, greater than the life of this world and He is greater than death. In fact, the Arabic and Hebrew word for sacrifice, *qurban*, comes from the root that means to be near. It is a way to approach Allah, to come closer to the Creator.

Part of an Ottoman miniature from the 16th century with the angels bringing the ransom for Isma'il (as).

The Qur'an speaks about animal sacrifice as a duty Allah has imposed on mankind that also brings benefit. **It is neither their meat nor their blood that reaches Allah but your piety (*taqwa*). He has subjected them to you in this way so that you may glorify Allah for having guided you.** (22:37). It is not a simple thing to kill an animal. Allah put these gentle animals under the hand of man as a favor. There is a proper way to raise them and a proper way to take their lives and in this there is blessing for both. Every hair of a properly sacrificed animal sends blessings on behalf of the one who sacrificed it until the Day of Judgment, whereas even the meat of an animal sacrificed improperly is not permissible food for believers. Animal sacrifice is not an act to be taken lightly. But to refuse to do it, to refuse to take a life when it is called for, means that you hold the life of this world more dear than obedience to your Creator. **It may well be that you hate a thing the while it is good for you, and it may well be that you love a thing the while it is bad for you: and Allah knows, whereas you do not know.** (2:216). The act and purpose of sacrifice is to bring you closer to Allah.

Allah made man to be His deputy on earth and He established the prophet Sulayman (as) as an example of what it means to rule in His name. All things were put under the command of Sulayman (as), even the wind. However, the relationship of master to servant entails duties on both sides. The master must also be responsible for and responsive to those in his charge. So Sulayman (as) heard and understood the ant's cry of alarm as his troops approached. He ordered his entire army to make a detour around the ant hills so as not to crush them. (27:18-19). This is what it means to be a deputy of God (*khalifatu Llah*).

Ibn 'Arabi (q) says that rather than animals being dependent on or in need of man, men are dependant on and in need of animals - for food, for transport, for labor. Men spend their time and energy protecting, watering, feeding animals, not the other way around. Animals know who they are and who is their Lord. They also know the nature of people and instinctively they know to be wary of them. It is mankind who does not know who he is or how to worship his Creator. So man must understand that, far from being set above animals, he is actually indebted to them and he should remember this fact and not be proud.

To call the sacrifice '*adhim*', great or tremendous, is not an exaggeration or inappropriate for a mere sheep. It is never merely a sheep. It is always a recipient of Allah's caring and love, His manifest creation. Its sacrifice should never be taken lightly but rather executed heedfully in the name of the One who is the Lord of us all.

A design of the face of a ram in which the curling horns have been made into mirror images of the Arabic letter 'Qaf', abjad value 100, representing the hidden 100th name of Allah.

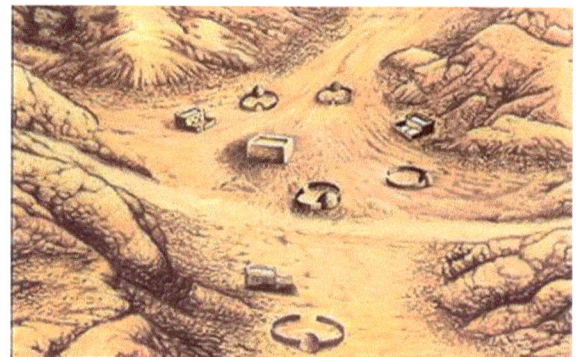

The development over time of the Ka'ba and Haram Sharif. Top: how it was at the time Ibrahim (as) settled Hajar (rah). Middle: how it was after he rebuilt the Ka'ba and the Jurhum came. Bottom: how it was rebuilt by the Quraysh at the time of the Prophet (sas).

CHAPTER FORTY-TWO

The Qibla of Ibrahim (as)

At some point after the birth of Ishaq (as), Sayyiduna Ibrahim (as) was commanded by the Lord to go to the valley of Becca and rebuild the House of God as it had been from the time of Adam (as) until the onset of the flood of Nuh (as). It is said that after Adam (as) left Paradise, he became sad with longing for the nearness of Allah and the sound of the angels praying to which he had become accustomed. Allah in His mercy sent down from heaven the spiritual center around which all the angels make *tawaf*, called the *Baytu l-Ma'mur* whose location is directly under the Throne (*'Arsh*). Its heavenly fragrance would help to soothe Adam's (as) heart and it would serve Adam (as) and his descendants as a reminder and a place of worship and pilgrimage.

Allah Almighty chose for its location the valley of Becca and made it a holy land for the people of earth for all time. The building was in the shape of a rectangular prism or cuboid and it was made from the rubies of Paradise. It had two doors which were fashioned of cut emerald. One door faced northeast and one southeast and they were at ground level. The House was like a jewelry box containing the most precious stone of all, a white stone which was set in its eastern corner. This stone was actually a resident of Paradise and is an angel. On the day called the Day of Promises Allah Almighty assigned this angel to record the covenant between the children of Adam (as) and their Lord. The unborn souls of all human beings acknowledged their Creator and promised to remember Him, to be thankful to Him, and to worship Him and only Him. Then Allah ordered this angel to swallow what he had written. Allah changed his appearance into a white shining jewel and set him into the corner of the Holy House. This jewel shone with such a strong light that it illuminated an area approximately 11 km in every direction. This circle of light constitutes and defines the borders of the *Haram*, the boundary at which the pilgrim enters into the sanctified state for Hajj (*ihram*). And even though today this white jewel has turned black from being touched by the sinful hands of man, he still has a light visible to those who can see.

As the pilgrims circle the Ka'ba in the ritual called *tawaf*, on each round they touch or kiss the stone if they are able, just as the Prophet (sas) did. If they cannot get close enough to do this, they stop to face the stone and give their salaams. The angel returns the salaam for he knows each pilgrim by name. On the Judgment Day this angel, of what is now called the Black Stone (*al-Hajar al-Aswad*), will testify against all of us who did not live up to our promise to give our thanks and our worship to Allah our Creator. And he will testify to the sincerity with which we greeted him at Allah's Holy House.

However, it is said by some that the House was never the actual heavenly house but was an exact copy built by Adam (as) from regular earthly stones like the one that exists now. But everyone agrees that the pilgrimage as we know it today began with Adam (as). In The Qur'an it is also called **al-Baytu l-'Atiq** (22:29), the most ancient House, because it dates from the very beginning of life on Earth. Adam (as) and his faithful descendants used to go every year from all corners of the globe. Every place he rested or prayed became a place where people later settled. Where he stopped became a village or a hamlet. Where he rested became a town and where he spent the night became a big city. And Mecca is called the Mother of Towns, **Ummu l-Qura**, (42:7) because it was the first place in which Adam lived with his wife and established prayer. Wherever you find people living today you can be sure was a spot where sometime in his 930 years Adam (as) stopped and prayed.

When water covered the earth in the time of the prophet Nuh (as), Allah raised the Heavenly House back up to the seventh heaven. The Ark of Nuh (as) sailed carefully between the mountain peaks of Mecca. There on the restless waters it made seven circles, high above the spot where the House had stood, before heading north to its final mooring on Mount Judi. The white stone in the eastern corner that had come from heaven, however, did not return there. It is the only part of the heavenly house that remained on earth. The mountain of Abu Qubays, one of the peaks that looks directly down on the sacred spot, offered to conceal and protect this precious stone from being washed away or damaged in the flood waters. After the water receded, all that remained of the Holy House was a mound of red earth in the center of the valley and the vibration of sacredness that continued to charge the air around it.

Sayyiduna Ibrahim (as) responded to this divine order, as he had responded to all the previous commands of his Lord. Saying goodbye to Sarah (rah) and Ishaq (as), he immediately set out from Hebron for the Hejaz. On arriving in Becca he found Isma'il (as) sitting near the same tree, near the well of Zamzam, where he had left him as an infant many years before. Isma'il (as) had grown into a handsome young man. He was sitting in the shade of his house, trimming and fletching his arrows. Ibrahim (as) and Isma'il (as) greeted each other warmly. Then Ibrahim (as) said to his son: "O Isma'il, Allah has commanded me to do something." Isma'il (as) replied firmly: "Then you must do what your Lord has commanded." Ibrahim (as) asked: "Will you help me?" "Yes," said his son. Even though the last command from Allah had involved his own sacrifice, he answered without hesitation: "I will help you." Then Ibrahim (as) explained that Allah had instructed him to build His Holy House near the very spot where Isma'il (as) was sitting.

Some say that there remained a small domed area of red earth indicating where the House had originally stood. Some say, however, that Allah sent the Archangel Jibra'il (as) to show Ibrahim (as) where to build by tracing the outline of the foundation on the ground with the tip of his mighty wing. Others say that Allah sent a cloud which made a shadow on the ground exactly in the shape and spot where they should build the House and the cloud hung there without moving until the job was finished. It is also reported from Sayyiduna 'Ali (ra) that it was the sakina that Allah sent. He described the *sakina* as something like a wind but with a woman's face. It is felt as a state of serenity that fills the heart, the personal experience of the presence of God. It kept company with Ibrahim (as) all the way from Hebron until it reached Mecca and there it formed itself into a small whirlwind that blew until it had cleared the exact area for the House. In whichever way it was done, Allah directed the placement, as He says in The Qur'an: **We chose the site of the House for Ibrahim** (22:26).

The House is called the Ka'ba which is usually translated as the cube, but since it is not and never was a cube, it probably means cuboid - four of its sides being rectangles and two of them being squares. The first meaning of the Arabic root k-'ayn-b, is a prominent join, like the ankle bone or the knotty joints on a piece of bamboo. The second common meaning is glorious or elevated. Either of these meanings could be applied to the Ka'ba. It is certainly built on a slightly elevated mound and is a place of glory and distinction. It is also the place where the world of materiality meets the world of spirituality and so in reality a join between them.

Today the Ka'ba gives the appearance of being a cube measuring between eleven and thirteen meters on all sides. But it was not always like this. The area to the northwest that is now enclosed by a low wall is called the *Hateem*. The area within the *Hateem*, three meters from the Ka'ba wall, is called the *Hijr Isma'il*. It was given this name because it is said that it is the spot where Ibrahim (as) built Hajar (rah) and Isma'il (as) a small house and where they lived until the Ka'ba was built. It is within the *Hateem* now but it used to be within the walls of the Ka'ba itself. The Prophet Muhammad (sas) told Sayyida 'Aisha (rah) that if she prayed in the *Hijr* it was as if she was praying inside the walls of the Ka'ba. The Prophet (sas) is recorded as having said that he would have rebuilt the House to its original dimensions, on the foundations of Ibrahim (as) which included the *Hijr*, but that he felt the residents of Mecca, who had just entered Islam, would not accept this change. That is why the pilgrims today still make their *tawaf* around the House and outside of the *Hateem*. There were others who wanted to change it back but were advised not to set a precedent for fear that every subsequent king would want the honor of restyling and rebuilding Allah's Holy House.

The reason that the cuboid Ka'ba was reduced to a cube is that at the time the Quraysh rebuilt it, when the Prophet Muhammad (sas) was still a young man, they did not have the money to rebuild the whole thing.

They had agreed that their budget would be restricted to what was halal, money obtained cleanly and legally, neither from cheating, nor from theft, nor from usury. And of this, the very prosperous merchants of Mecca did not have enough. So they made it smaller, approximately in the shape of a cube and enclosed the rest by building a low wall that sits on top of some of the original foundation stones. They took down all the walls planning to rebuild the whole from the ground up but when they got to the bottom, they found red, or some say green, stones like the humps of camels. Whenever a man tried to remove one of these stones the whole ground of Mecca would shake like in an earthquake. So in the end it seemed best to leave the foundation set by Ibrahim (as) as it was and put new stones on top of the old foundation.

Wind reveals second door of the Ka'ba, Hajj 2018.

The House is oriented with its corners pointing in the four cardinal directions. The Black Stone is in the eastern corner. The single door is in the northeastern wall. But there used to be two doors, the second in the southwestern wall opposite the other - one door to enter and one door to exit. In fact, the outline of the second door and its lintel can still be seen in the wall of the Ka'ba today. The doors were at ground level and could be entered easily without stairs or a ramp. At that time the Ka'ba was a rectangle approximately 18 meters long (including the *hijr*) by 11 meters wide by 11 meters tall. It is interesting that the Torah instructs Musa (as) to build a box to hold the tablets of the Torah and some other sacred objects including perhaps, the *sakina* (2:248). This box is called the Ark of the Covenant in English or *Tabut* in Arabic. Its dimensions, as ordered by Allah in the Torah, were 2.5 cubits by 1.5 by 1.5 cubits in height. This is almost exactly the same relative dimensions as the original Ka'ba rectangle – 5x3x3. It is also possible according to Wahb ibn Munabbih (ra) that the *Tabut* of Musa (as) itself spent some time in Mecca after it was smuggled out of Jersalem before the destruction of the temple of Sulayman (as). In many ways the Ka'ba is a *Tabut* itself, a chest to hold holiness. In fact, it is said that on every stone that was laid to make up its inner walls was inscribed the name of one of the 124,000 of Allah's prophets just like the Ark of Adam (as) and that of Nuh (as).

Footprints of Ibrahim (as) imbedded in the stone on which he stood to build the walls of the Ka'ba.

Ibrahim (as) and Isma'il (as) started building the house. Isma'il (as) would go to the mountains surrounding Becca to collect and bring stones. In one account the first row of stones came from Mount Hira where the Prophet Muhammad (sas) would later stay in seclusion, praying and fasting, and where the Archangel Jibra'il (as) would deliver the first revelation of The Qur'an. Others say that Jibra'il (as) brought the stones used for the walls from four other mountains as well: Mount Sinai - the mountain where Musa (as) received the Torah, the Mount of Olives where 'Isa (as) performed the miracle of feeding the multitudes, Mount Lebanon whose cedar forests were used to build the temple in Jerusalem, and Mount Judi where the Ark of Nuh (as) came to rest.

Isma'il (as) would chip the stone to size and hand it to his father. Ibrahim (as) would put it in place with mortar mixed from the water of Zamzam. The trough in which they mixed the mortar still exists as a large depression now covered in marble along the wall to right side of the door. It is called the *Mi'jan*. In the Ottoman guild system Sayyiduna Ibrahim (as) was the patron of stonemasons and Isma'il (as) of the apprentices. Ibrahim (as) and Isma'il (as) built the walls until they were as tall as Ibrahim (as) could reach. Then Isma'il (as) brought him a rock on which he stood to reach the higher levels. It is said that this rock moved around the House and when he finished laying that round of stones the rock would lift off the ground just the right amount to let him set the next row. The footprints of Sayyiduna Ibrahim (as) became indented in this remarkable stone which still exits inside the little pagoda called the *Maqam Ibrahim* just to the side of the Ka'ba today. It is an order in The Qur'an to **take the *Maqam* of Ibrahim as a place of prayer** (2:125). The stone used to rest right beside the Ka'ba wall where it was left after Ibrahim (as) was finished using it. Sayyiduna 'Umar (ra) had it moved to where it is today so that those who pray there do not interfere with those who are making *tawaf*.

Ibrahim (as) asked for a beautiful stone to set in the corner, a stone to be a sign for mankind of the connection between the earth and the heavens. Isma'il (as) went out to look for a suitable stone. Just then he heard Mount Abu Qubays speaking with its angelic voice, because every member of the creation has its own angel. The mountain was telling him about the Black Stone which had lain hidden in the depths of the mountain since the flood. The Prophet (sas) said that this stone was originally as white as milk until it was blackened by the sinful hands of man. So if sin can turn a stone of Paradise black, imagine what it can do to the human heart. By another account, Jibra'il (as) had to be sent by Allah to pry the stone out of the body of the mountain because Abu Qubays found it too difficult to let go of its treasure. Now the time had come to return the stone to its proper place in Allah's House. Isma'il (as) took this stone and and gave it to his father to set in place in the eastern corner.

And all the while they were building, for every stone they set and for every step they took, father and son kept repeating the prayer:

"Our Lord, accept this from us. Indeed, You are the Hearing and the Knowing" (2:127).

They roofed the building with rafters made of the slender trunks of trees and covered them with woven mats and mud, although it is sometimes said that the first Ka'ba was not roofed at all but open to the sky. Inside this sacred house they put neither rock nor statue, neither picture nor sign, but it was not empty. Like the *Bayt al-Ma'mur*, which means the Frequented House, the Inhabited House, it is visited by a continuous stream of worshippers both earthly and otherwise, and it is always filled with the Divine Presence.

When they had finished they stood back to look at what they had done. They had not yet cleaned up the mess from the construction. Chips of stone, mud, and straw lay all around the site. A strong wind blew up and lifted all the debris into the air and spun it around, scattering bits of it all over the world. Wherever the wind deposited some of the debris, a mosque would later be built; a small amount made for a small praying place, *musallah*, a big amount made for a Friday Mosque.

The Ka'ba was the first place ever built on earth solely for the worship of our Creator, Allah Almighty. **Indeed, the first House** [of God] **established for mankind was that at Becca, a blessed place and a guidance for the worlds** (3:96). The second place was the Temple in Jerusalem. The Ka'ba is truly the spiritual center of the earth. The opening to Heaven is situated just above it and the Heavenly House, the *Baytu l-Ma'mur*, which is the *qibla* of the angels lies directly above that in the seventh heaven. Somewhere directly above that, in the highest reaches of the spiritual realms, lies the Divine Throne and a direct connection to Allah Almighty. Symbolically and actually, the Ka'ba is the point at which the material realms and the spiritual realms conjoin. It is the join between the worlds. Some call it metaphorically the navel of the world. It is the spot on the Earth that was created first and then the globe was stretched out on all sides around it like pulling dough into a ball. It is the connection to the Creator like the umbilical cord is the connection to the mother. Some prefer to call it the heart of the world, the organ that pumps life to the rest of creation. Like the mystical human heart, it can somehow contain the majesty of its Creator because "Neither My Heaven nor My Earth contain Me but the heart of My believing servant contains Me" (Hadith Qudsi, Al-

Ghazali).

It is said that before his move to Medina, the Prophet (sas) used to pray northeast in the direction of Jerusalem but facing the southwest wall of the Ka'ba so that, in fact, he was praying directly to the Holy House. For the first sixteen months after he emigrated to Medina, he turned his back on Mecca and faced North to Jerusalem in prayer. Then one night in the month of Sha'ban it was revealed: **So from wherever you may come, turn your face towards the Sacred House; and wherever you may be, turn your faces toward it** (2:150). Therefore, except for a short period of sixteen months, the Ka'ba was always the *qibla* of the Prophet (sas). All supplications made there, are heard. All requests made there, are answered. The Prophet (sas) said that one prayer offered at the Ka'ba is equal to one hundred thousand prayers offered anywhere else.

The Prophet Muhammad (sas) addressed Mecca saying: "By God, you are the most excellent spot on Allah's earth and the dearest spot to Him. If I had not been driven out, I would never have left you" (Bukhari).

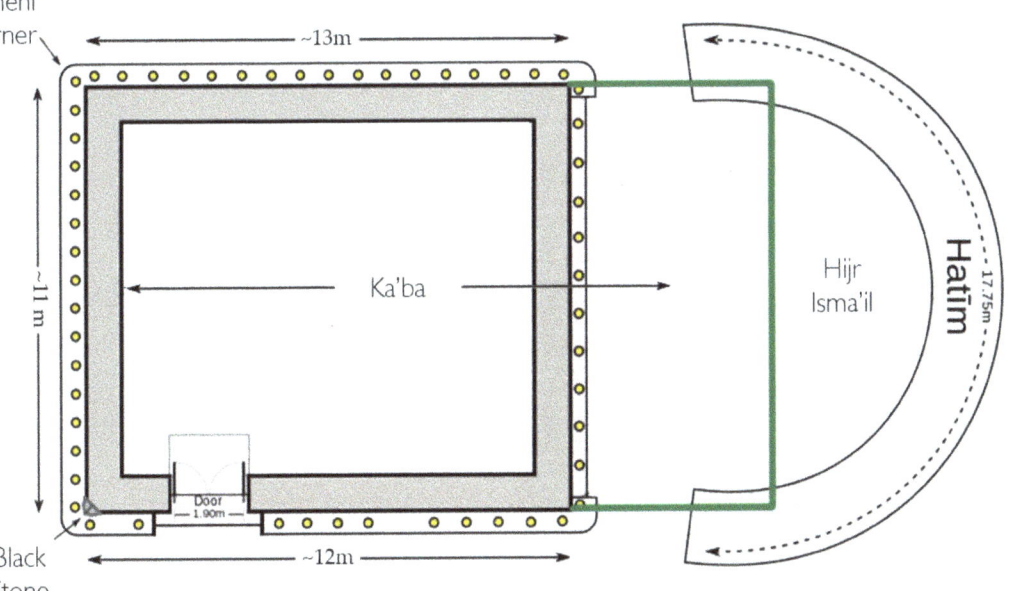

Diagram of the Ka'ba with its approximate dimensions before and after is was reduced in size.

An old photograph of a caravan of pilgrims leaving Damascus for Hajj. Above a calligraphy of the pilgrim chant, *Labbayk Allahuma Labbayk*.

CHAPTER FORTY-THREE

Ibrahim's (as) Call

After the House was completed Allah Almighty commanded Ibrahim (as) to call the people of the world **and proclaim the Hajj to mankind** (22:27). Ibrahim (as) asked, "But how will my voice reach them?" And Allah replied, "You are only responsible for calling. I am responsible for making it reach." And so Ibrahim (as) mounted a high place, maybe it was the stone that had lifted him up to be able to finish the high walls of the House and that now rests in the Maqam Ibrahim. Maybe it was from the top of as-Safa or maybe the summit of Abu Qubays or even, some say, from the Mount of 'Arafah. He called out as loudly as he could, first to the South, then to the East, then to the North and finally to the West – to every direction in the approximate order in which they would eventually come to Islam. "Come to the House of the Lord. Come to make the pilgrimage." And Allah carried his voice across the whole earth and all souls heard, even those that had not yet been born, the men and women of the future. All of them heard and some of them responded: *Labbayk Allahuma Labbayk* – "Here I am at Your service, O Lord, here I am." Those that responded on that day will make the Hajj in their lifetime. Who answered twice will make the pilgrimage twice. Who answered twenty times will make it twenty times. Who did not answer at all will not make the pilgrimage at all.

And all the animals heard also and even the stones and the trees. All living things heard and stopped what they were doing. The wind lay still and the waterfall paused. They replied with their angelic voices *labbayk Allahuma labbayk* – "we are at Your service, O Lord and we are coming." And although the rocks could not grow wings and the trees could not grow feet, their angels flew as fast as they could to obey the call. And the wind picked up its skirts and blew there and the water thinned itself into clouds and flew there. And the birds continue to make *tawaf* in the sky, circling with spread wings above the Holy House. **They will come to you on foot and on every kind of thin riding animal, from every faraway place (22:27).** And they are still coming today, answering the call of Sayyiduna Ibrahim (as), and saying *Labbayk Allahuma Labbayk*.

When Ibrahim called, he heard a multitude of voices answering him. Altogether they sounded like the loud humming or buzzing of a billion bees. He became concerned and he expressed his concern to his Lord. He was the most generous of hosts and he feared that he would never be able to care for or feed such a large number of guests. But Jibra'il (as) gave him a container of water and told him that Allah was instructing him to scatter the water into the wind. So Ibrahim (as) whirled around with the bucket. The water blew in droplets all over the world. Where it fell it became salt. When it fell in water it became salt water. When it fell on the land it became rock salt. Whoever eats of any salt, is eating the provision of Ibrahim (as) and accepting his hospitality.

On the eighth day of the month of *Dhul-Hijj*, the last month of the Muslim lunar calendar, the Archangel Jibra'il (as) came to lead Sayyiduna Ibrahim (as) and Isma'il (as) and Sayyidatuna Hajar (rah) through the rites of the pilgrimage, showing them how they should worship Allah in the presence of His Holy House. Jibra'il (as) led them counter clockwise in seven full circuits around the Ka'ba while they praised Allah, the Creator of the Worlds and asked for His favor and forgiveness: **let them make *tawaf* around the Ancient House (22:29).** The circling began and ended at the Black Stone. Each time they passed it, they kissed it if they could, or greeted with their hand from near or far because it is an angelic being. And although Sayyiduna 'Umar (ra) said that he felt it was only a stone without the power to help or to hurt, he kissed it because he had seen the Prophet (sas) kiss it. However, the Prophet (sas) said that the Black Stone has eyes with which to see and on the Day of Judgment it will be given a voice and will testify on behalf of those who have greeted it with sincerity. And when he greeted it the tears rolled down his cheeks and he said "It is here that tears must be shed" (Bukhari).

The Prophet Muhammad (sas) also used to kiss or reach out to touch the large vertical stone that comprises the Yemeni or Southern corner just as he greeted the Black Stone in the adjacent corner. The Sunni Muslims say this is in respect for the fact that this stone rests on, or actually is, one of the original stones of the Ka'ba built by Ibrahim (as). It has a crack or hole in it that has been filled and mended with metal spikes many times because it keeps breaking. The Shi'a Muslims say that it was through this hole that Fatima bint Asad (rah) exited after giving birth to Sayyiduna 'Ali ibn Abi Talib (ra) inside the Ka'ba. Allah knows best.

Then they drank from the well of Zamzam which was about 20 meters east of the Ka'ba to the side of where the Maqam Ibrahim (as) now sits. Then Jibra'il (as) took them to As-Safa and Al-Marwah to perform the *sa'i*. He reminded them how Hajar (rah) had, in her anxiety, walked seven times between these hills looking desperately for help. **Behold, as-Safa and al-Marwah are among the rites set up by Allah** (2:158). He reminded them how she had left Isma'il (as) dying of thirst under the tree. And Jibra'il (as), recalled how he had come to save them by Allah's command; how he had scooped the sand with his wing and Allah had made the healing water of Zamzam well out of the ground.

Then he took them walking to revisit other holy places. On the ninth day they entered the plain of 'Arafah and climbed the rocky outcrop that lies in the center. This was the place where our father Adam (as) reunited with our mother Hawwa (rah). They had been sent down from Paradise in different locations thousands of miles apart. Hawwa (rah) had been set in Arabia at the place where Jeddah (which means grandmother) now stands. Adam (as) had been set on a mountain in Serendip (Sri Lanka). After spending three hundred years standing on one leg and crying to Allah to forgive him for his moment of forgetfulness, Adam (as) was told to seek his wife and forgiveness on the other side of the world. It was here that they finally met, first at the Ka'ba and then on the arid plain called

'Arafah meaning 'to know' - the place where they came together and were forgiven. And it is here also, on this arid plain that all the pilgrims gather together in one place at one time and recognize that they are all brothers, children of one father and one mother; all of them dressed the same, without the worldly trappings that make them appear different. Here they send their love to their Maker and know their frailty and His Mightiness, and know their multitudes and His Oneness, and know their smallness and His Greatness. It is a small taste of the conditions they will meet on the Day of Judgment when all human souls will be resurrected in the sight of their Lord. All the people who have ever lived will gather on the plain of Canaan (al-Mahshar – the gathering) that will probably have to extend as far as 'Arafah and include all of the holy land known as As-Sham. And it will be here that all people will surely know the truth of what they have been told.

Ibrahim (as) and Hajar (rah) and Isma'il (as) stayed on 'Arafah all afternoon, immersed in their prayers and their memories, asking forgiveness. At sunset they moved to the valley of Muzdalifah to pray and to sleep under the mountain where they had been tested many years before. They remembered Allah's order to them and their submission to His command. They remembered the knife that would not cut and the beautiful ram of Allah's Mercy. In the morning on their way back to Mecca they passed the places where shaytan the deceiver had tried to make them doubt; where he had tried to shake their certainty and make them question their conviction of Allah's love. And so lastly they also remembered shaytan and how he had tried to get them to disobey Allah just as he had done. And in memory of that they threw stones at him once more, cursing him again and for all time.

After this Jibra'il (as) took them to sacrifice an animal in remembrance of that Paradise ram which Allah had sent as Isma'il's (as) ransom so very many years before. And these special animals that have been chosen for the 'Id sacrifice will pasture in Paradise and the ones who have given them in sacrifice will be blessed for every woolly hair on their bodies.

The next year Ibrahim (as) returned with his wife Sarah (rah) and their son Ishaq (as). Together with Hajar (rah) and Isma'il (as) they all made the Hajj together. And it is said that Isma'il (as) and his wife were so gracious in their welcome and hospitality that they won over the heart of Sarah (rah) and she made peace with them and gave them her blessing. At the end of this Hajj the united family of Ibrahim (as) prayed together at the Ka'ba for the nation of the prophet who would come at the end of days to re-establish the religion of Ibrahim (as) the Hanif. They prayed for the *Ummah* (Nation) of Muhammad (sas). Ibrahim (as) prayed for the old people, Isma'il (as) prayed for the middle aged, Ishaq (as) prayed for the young, Sarah (rah) prayed for the free, and Hajar (rah) prayed for those who are not free.

Two thousand and five hundred years later when the walls of the Ka'ba were starting to crumble, the people of Mecca determined to rebuild it. It was by the hand of the last prophet in the line of Ibrahim (as), the Prophet Muhammad (sas), that the Black Stone was set back in its place in the eastern corner as it exists to this day. The people of Mecca still remembered that the House was holy and that it was built by the Prophet Ibrahim (as) and his son Isma'il (as) but they believed that Allah had many children or lesser gods under His control. These they worshipped. They had put three hundred and sixty idols inside and around the Ka'bah itself and they worshipped them in all kinds of unclean ways, including making *tawaf* naked.

Persian miniature of the Prophet (sas) placing the Black Stone back into place in the corner of the Ka'ba. Jami' al Tawarikh, 1307.

How was it that these descendants of prophets forgot the ways of their righteous ancestors? Ibn Ishaq says that it happened little by little over time. When the Jurhum were expelled from Mecca they missed the Ka'ba. So they took with them some stones and they built a replica Ka'ba in their new home. They began to make *tawaf* around that replica and over generations it became holy to them. Other people also, when they moved to another area or even if they just came to visit the Holy House, took back home with them some pieces of its walls or some stones. And gradually they began to forget what it was that the stones represented and instead attributed power and holiness to the stones themselves. This is why Islam is so strict in forbidding images, or statues, or stones set up. It seems that stones have a special allure for mankind and are easily turned into objects of worship. It is important to keep the religion purely for Allah.

In 630 BCE, in the month of Ramadan, twenty-five years after the Ka'ba was rebuilt, Sayyiduna Muhammad (sas) returned to Mecca in peace and was finally able to take possession of the House and to clean it of all the statues, paintings, and ritual objects that had been set up in and around it, and to forbid the pagan practices. On the day of the victory he rode slowly around the Holy House on his camel Qaswa and, some say with his staff and others say with the tip of his bow, he pointed at each of the three hundred and sixty statues that encircled Allah's House and declared: **The truth has now come, and falsehood has withered away: for, behold, all falsehood is bound to wither away** (17:81). As he did so, each idol fell over on its face before him. Then he called for Sayyiduna 'Uthman (ra) to unlock the door of the Ka'ba. When they entered they found the walls covered in paintings and talismans. He ordered them all to be cleaned away except for three: the first was an icon of Sayyidatuna Maryam (rah) and her son 'Isa (as), the second was a picture of an old man that was said to be Sayyiduna Ibrahim (as), and the third were the horns of the heavenly ram that hung on the wall. These he left but they ended up being destroyed later when the Ka'ba was burned in 683 CE. Then the Prophet (sas) showed the people how to perform a visit to the House, the *'umra*, just as Jibra'il (as) had taught Ibrahim (as) so many years before.

So not only does the Ka'ba sit at the center of the circles of people bowing and prostrating in the holy city of Mecca but, as when you throw a stone into a lake it makes rings in the water that continue to move outward from the center, so the rings of people extend outward around the earth just as the skin of the earth was pulled from that spot to cover the globe. All hearts are turned to their Lord, all faces turned to His Holy House – the place whereon Ibrahim once stood; and whoever enters it finds inner peace. Hence, **the pilgrimage unto the House is a duty owed to Allah by all people who are able to undertake it. And as for those who deny the truth – verily, Allah does not stand in need of anything in all the worlds** (3:97).

20th century map of the waves of the Ka'ba radiating around the world by Nusret Çolpan.

The *sabil* or fountain for making ablution outside the Masjidu l-Aqsa in Jerusalem.
Courtesy Akram Reda.

CHAPTER FORTY-FOUR

The Book of Ibrahim (as)

There were 124,000 Prophets that Allah Almighty sent to the peoples of Earth. Of these only 313 were Messengers, those who came with Books or pages of revelation. Sayyiduna Ibrahim (as) was one of those most honored, both *nabi* (prophet) and *rasul* (messenger). Two verses in The Qur'an mention his book: **Or was he not informed of what was in the scriptures of Musa and Ibrahim?** (53:36-37). **Indeed, this is in the former scriptures, the scriptures of Ibrahim and Musa** (87:18-19).

A companion of the Prophet Muhammad (sas), Abu Dharr al-Ghifari (ra), once asked him about the number of Books that Allah had revealed. The Prophet (sas) answered that there had been one hundred individual pages revealed and four Books. Sayyiduna Adam (as) received ten pages. His son Seth (as) received fifty pages. Sayyiduna Idris (as) received thirty pages and Sayyiduna Ibrahim (as) received ten. The four Books were the Torah to Sayyiduna Musa (as), the Zabur (Psalms) to Sayyiduna Dawud (as), the Injil (Gospels) to Sayyiduna 'Isa (as) and lastly The Qur'an to Sayyiduna Muhammad (sas).

The Books still exist, although perhaps not in their original form, but of the individual pages we have little or no information. They are either lost or they have been incorporated into the other scriptures without being specifically identified. However, we know that the message has always been the same since the first revelation. Allah's word is unchanging so nothing, God willing, can have been totally lost.

Abu Dharr (ra) continued to ask in particular about the pages belonging to Ibrahim (as). The Prophet Muhammad (sas) said that they consisted of wise sayings and warnings. Here are some of the examples he gave:

"O ruler I did not send you to heap up the riches of this world on top of each other, but I sent you to keep away from Me the prayers of the oppressed. For how shall I turn down those requests even if they arise from a nonbeliever?"

"As long as he is in possession of his faculties, the wise man ought to devote four hours in the day in this fashion: one hour which he spends with his Lord; one hour which he spends contemplating His creation; one hour in secret examination of his own conscience; and one hour eating and drinking permissible things."

"The wise man ought to seek for three things:

1. to supply himself with provision for the journey to the next world.

2. to find his provision for this world.

3. to find enjoyment that is not haram."

"The wise man must have insight about the events of his time. He must devote himself to his own affairs. He must keep guard on his tongue."

"The man who recognizes that his words cause greater harm than his actions will rarely speak on a matter that does not concern him, and God will help him in times of danger."

The Prophet (sas) then advised Abu Dharr (ra) to read *Suratu l-A'la* (The Most High) in The Qur'an where it says: **He who purifies himself and mentions the name of his Lord and prays, has certainly succeeded. But you prefer the life of this world, while the Hereafter is better and more lasting. Indeed, this is in the former scriptures, the scriptures of Ibrahim and Musa.** (87:14-19).

Suratu l-Najm, the Chapter of the Star, also lists some of the things that were in both the Book of Musa (as) and of Ibrahim (as):

that no soul shall bear the burden of another;
that man will only have what he has worked towards;
that his labor will be seen
and that in the end he will be repaid in full for it;
that the final goal is your Lord;
that it is He who makes people laugh and weep;
that it is He who gives death and life;
that He Himself created the two sexes, male and female,
from an ejected drop of sperm;
that He will undertake the second Creation;
that it is He who gives wealth and possessions;
that He is the Lord of Sirius; (53:38-49)

Many of the ritual practices that we still perform today according to the Prophet Muhammad (sas) date from the time of Ibrahim (as), in particular the rules of cleanliness. Ibn Abbas (ra) said that there were ten rules that were given to Ibrahim (as), five for the body and five for the head. The ones for the body were: trimming the nails, shaving the pubic hair, circumcision, removing the hair under the arm, and washing with water after using the toilet. The five for the head were: trimming the mustache so it does not hang over the mouth, rinsing the mouth, rinsing the inside of the nose, brushing the teeth with a tooth stick, and showering on the day of *Juma'*, Friday.

In addition, there were six rites related to the Hajj, pilgrimage, that have come down to us from Sayyiduna Ibrahim (as) all of them transmitted by means of the Sunnah, the example of the Prophet Muhammad (as). The first is the counter clockwise circling (*tawaf*) of the Ka'ba seven times. The second is the *sa'i* running seven times between the hills of al-Safa and al-Marwa. The third is the stoning of the pillars, and the fourth is the quick departure from 'Arafah on the last day of the pilgrimage. Some say the sacrifice of an animal is also in memory of the near sacrifice of Isma'il (as) but others do not link the two sacrifices.

In addition, we know that among the practices of Ibrahim (as) that he passed down to his people with his Book were prayer and *zakat*. He prayed at least one daily prayer in the morning and it included a *sajda*, prostration. And he paid a percentage of his wealth, given each year as a tithe or tax, to be used to take care of those in need. **And We made them** [Ibrahim and his descendants] **leaders in the land, guiding by Our command. And We inspired to them the doing of good deeds and the establishment of prayer and the giving of** *zakat*, **and they were worshippers of Us** [alone]. (21:73).

CHAPTER FORTY-FIVE
Isma'il (as): The Rest of the Story

There was no agriculture in the area of Mecca and even the pasture was scarce so when Ismail (as) grew up he became a hunter of wild game with bow and arrow and he was very proficient in this art. We know this because once the Prophet Muhammad (sas) came upon some young men in Medina competing in an archery contest. He was pleased with them and encouraged them by saying: "Shoot O sons of Isma'il, for indeed your father [meaning Isma'il (as)] was an archer." Isma'il (as) grew up with the people of Jurhum who had moved to be near Zamzam. And when he was old enough he married the daughter of their chief.

One day Ibrahim (as) felt a strong desire to see his son Isma'il (as). Sarah (rah) made him promise that he would not stay long, in fact she made him promise that he would not dismount from his riding animal. He traveled all that long way and stopped for a while with Hajar (rah) and then proceeded to the house where Isma'il (as) lived with his wife. Ibrahim (as) halted at the door and called for his son but Isma'il (as) was out hunting. His wife came to the door and looked suspiciously at the stranger. Ibrahim (as) asked her how she was and how her husband

Painting of Isma'il (as) the *dhabih* of Allah. 19th century Moghul India.

was and in general how life was for them. To every question the girl answered negatively, complaining about the conditions and the food and the hardship. Ibrahim (as) was polite and asked her to relay a message to Isma'il (as). He said, cryptically, to tell Isma'il (as) that his house was very good but that the threshold needed replacing. Then Ibrahim (as) turned his animal around and he left.

Isma'il (as) up in the mountains saw the light of his father from a distance and rushed back to Mecca but he arrived too late. Ibrahim (as) had left. He asked his wife and she told him that a dusty old man with white hair and beard had stopped by and asked for him. Isma'il (as) knew that must be his father. She then repeated the odd message that he had left. Isma'il (as) understood immediately that the threshold of his house was his wife and that Ibrahim (as) was advising him to replace her. He let her go in kindness and she was happy to leave. Because Isma'il (as) was carrying the light of the Prophet Muhammad (sas) it was very important that his wife be the right one to receive it and pass it on.

Isma'il (as) married another girl from the Jurhum, whose name was Sayyida or Hala (rah). Again Ibrahim (as) longed to see his son and with the same restrictions as the last time Sarah (rah) agreed to his visit. He entered Mecca and found his son's house and called his name. A lovely young girl came out and begged him to dismount and offered him what refreshment she had. He asked her what she had to eat and drink and she answered that they were blessed with meat and water, both of which she would be happy to serve him. When he asked how she was and how her life was in this barren valley, she had nothing but positive things to say. She was happy with her husband and with her life. She was thankful for all God had given her and content with what she had. He ate from the food she brought him without dismounting. After he finished, he blessed her and her family and the valley of Mecca: "Bless Mecca in its meat and in its water" he said. If Hala (rah) had had some bread he would have blessed that too, the Prophet Muhammad (sas) said, and then Mecca would have been overflowing with grain. And he (sas) also said, according to Ibn Kathir, that any other place where they only have two kinds of food, they suffer from poor health, except in Mecca because of this prayer of Ibrahim (as).

Ibrahim (as) again could not wait for his son to return so he left him a message. He asked the girl to tell her husband that his house was very good and that his threshold was even better. Then he turned his face north and left. Isma'il (as) came running from the mountain, this time hoping to catch his father, but again he was too late. Hala (rah) told him that a stranger had come looking for him, a dignified old man with light on his face and she told him the odd message he had left. Isma'il (as) was very happy and told her that the old man was his father and that he had blessed her and approved of her.

They rejoiced in each other and went on to have thirteen children. They had twelve sons, six sets of twins: Qaydar and Nebaioth, Adbeel and Mibsam, Mishma and Dumah, Massa and Hadad, Tema and Jetur, Naphish and Kedemah. He also had one daughter named Basima. As the twelve sons of Ya'qub (as) fathered the twelve tribes of the Banu Isra'il, so the twelve sons of Isma'il (as) fathered the twelve tribes of Bedouin Arabs. His first born son Qaydar is the ancestor of the tribe of Quraysh into which the Prophet Muhammad (sas) was born. Nabaioth is the ancestor of the Nabateans. Basima went on to marry 'As (Esau) (as) the son of Ishaq (as) and twin brother of Ya'qub (as). Their children became the Arab tribes of the North. So when Qur'an says: **Verily Ibrahim was an *Ummah* (a nation)** (16:120) it means not only that he was a leader of men but that he actually was the progenitor of nations. Ibrahim (as) was sent as a prophet to the people in the area in which he lived but also Allah had made him a model for all coming generations and for the believers of all nations.

Shortly after this Hajar (rah) died and Isma'il (as) prayed for her and placed her in her grave somewhere near the Ka'ba. Many other prophets were later also buried there including Isma'il (as) and Lut (as). Some say that Hajar (rah) was buried in the area called the *Hijr* and that explains its name. However, that would have been unlikely if at that time it was included inside the Ka'ba wall and more unlikely that people would be encouraged to pray on top of their graves because the Prophet Muhammad (sas) said: "Do not turn graves into places of prayer." The Prophet (sas) also said that prophets are buried in the places they die. Maybe Hajar (rah) and Isma'il (as) were buried near where their houses had been moved after the Ka'ba was built. The next time Ibrahim (as) came he heard the sad news of Hajar's (rah) death and he stood for a long time at her grave and prayed for her blessed soul. She had also been tested severely and had remained faithful and true to both her husband and her

God.

One day Jibra'il (as) came to Isma'il (as) and announced to him that Allah was making him His prophet and His messenger. Isma'il (as) was in awe at the news but when he finally found his voice he asked to which people he was being sent and what was his message. He was told that his people were his family and the tribes living in the area of Mecca and those who came for pilgrimage. His message was that of his father Ibrahim (as). All his people believed him and accepted Islam. It is said that of all the prophets ever sent, the mission of Sayyiduna Isma'il (as) was the easiest. The only place he encountered opposition was when he was invited to the Yemen. Some of the people there argued against him and rejected his message just as they had rejected the prophet Hud (as) who had come to them a few generations before.

The Qur'an says of him: **And remember Isma'il in the Book, verily he was always true to his promise and was a messenger, a prophet, who commanded his people to pray and give alms, and his Lord was well pleased with him** (19:54-55). Isma'il (as) was not just a prophet (*nabi*) but he was also a messenger (*rasul*). According to one hadith there were 124,000 prophets sent but only 313 of these were also messengers. To be a messenger prophet is a much rarer and more honored position. All prophets were sent as a reminder and warner to a particular group of people, except the prophet Muhammad (sas) who was sent for all people. However, a messenger prophet brings a new book to a people who have either never received one or whose book was forgotten or corrupted. There is no new book that is ascribed to Isma'il (as). However, As-Suyuti says that Isma'il (as) was the first to be inspired with, and to have fully developed a written Arabic script. He relates a hadith from Ibn Abbas (ra) that Isma'il (as) wrote the book of his father Ibrahim (as) in his own native language which was the Arabic of the Jurhum. The form of his writing is described as being conjoined letters, with no spaces between them, each letter forming part of the one that follows it. He delivered this book to his own descendants who were not members of the original tribes of Arabs to whom the prophets Hud (as) and Salih (as) had been previously sent. His mission was to bring the book of Ibrahim (as) to the new tribes of Arab speakers who had had no messenger sent to them before and to try and reach out to the original tribes who had rejected their earlier prophets.

More importantly Isma'il (as) inherited from his father the Light of Muhammad which continued to pass from child to child among his descendants. It was visible on the forehead of Abdullah (ra) the son of Abdu l-Muttalib (ra) and it passed to his wife Aminah (ra) on their wedding night. It radiated so brightly from her that it lit far distances enabling her to see the palaces of the Persians. Then it became wholly manifest in this world, shining from the brow of Allah's Beloved, Muhammad Mustafa the last Prophet (sas).

Altogether Isma'il (as) served as a prophet to his people for sixty years. It is said that he died at the age of 137 or 160 and he was buried next to his mother. Before Ibrahim (as) died he took a solemn promise from all his sons that they would keep to the way that Allah had chosen for them, that they would not die except as Muslims (2:132). This might have been the promise that Allah is commending Isma'il (as) for being true to or it could be the more general promise that was the taken of all the prophets on the Day of Promises. Isma'il (as) died submitted to Allah and he left his children, and their children after them, bound to the same promise to follow in the footsteps of their father Ibrahim (as) and to carefully carry the light that was entrusted to them.

An Aerial photograph of the *Hijr Isma'il* (as), the place where Isma'il (as) had his house and where some say he and his mother are buried. Mecca.

A fresco of Ishaq (as), Ibrahim (as) and Ya'qub (as) from the ceiling of the Abuna Yemata Church in Ethiopia from the 15th century.

CHAPTER FORTY-SIX
Ishaq (as): The Rest of the Story

Sarah (rah) died at the age of 127 or 137 in Hebron in Palestine. When she died Ibrahim (as) purchased a plot of land from his neighbor with the cave of Machpelah as part of it. He and Ishaq (as) prayed over Sarah (rah) and laid her to rest inside that cave as her mausoleum. When Ishaq (as) was around forty years old, he still had not married. Allah commanded Ibrahim (as) that the time had come to find his son a suitable wife.

According to the Torah, Ibrahim (as) did not want his son to marry a local woman so he sent his servant back to the place where his father had lived, Harran, to see if there was any girl from among his relatives who would be a good bride for Ishaq (as). The servant promised to do his best and carried with him the gold, silver, and cloth for the bride price. He arrived at a well in Harran and there he prayed to Allah to make known to him which girl was the best. He was inspired with the idea to ask each girl, who came to draw water from the well, to give him something to drink. If she agreed and if she offered also to water his donkey he would know she was the right girl. The first girl to come along gave him to drink from her water jar and offered to water his donkey for him as well. Then she invited him to her father's house to stay the night. When he arrived at the house he found that the girl's father was none other than the son of Ibrahim's (as) brother Nahor. Everyone was overjoyed to receive news of their relatives and they agreed to send their daughter Rifqa (Rebecca) (rah) to be the wife of Ishaq (as). After only a few days they packed her things and sent her along with her own servant and Ibrahim's (as) servant to join her husband far to the south.

They arrived first at the tents of Ibrahim (as) and he was pleased with Allah's choice. So Rifqa (rah) continued on to the tents of Ishaq (as). They met each other and were pleased. In a very simple ceremony Ishaq (as) took her into the tent which had belonged to his mother Sarah (rah) and Rifqa (rah) became his wife.

Ishaq (as) was notified of his prophethood while his father was still alive. He was sent to the people living near Bir-Lahai-Roi, the place where Hajar (rah) had been consoled by her Lord and told to return to Sarah (rah) to have her child. He is not a messenger prophet probably because his mission was to continue the work his father had begun among the same people and following the unchanged book that had been already revealed.

Ishaq (as) and Rifqa (rah), like Ibrahim (as) and Sarah (rah) before them, did not immediately have children. It was twenty years before Ishaq (as) raised his hands and implored Allah for righteous offspring. It is said that the purpose of this infertility among the family of the prophets was meant to highlight the fact that their children were not simply the product of their parents' procreative activites but rather miraculous gifts from Allah. Rifqa (rah) found herself pregnant finally, with twins. According to the Torah, the twins fought inside her. People around her could hear them arguing all day and all night and kicking each other. This made her pregnancy very difficult and she cried out to her Lord in pain. Finally, she was delivered of healthy twin boys. The first one to be born was named 'As (as) (Esau), which means rebellious. He was thick and strong and covered with reddish hair, a physical man. The second son was small and quiet, a man of thought who had an eye for beauty. He was named Ya'qub (as) because they say he held on to his brother's heel on his way into the world. *Ka'b* means heel but is also from the same root as Ka'ba and indicates a man of high station. Rifqa (rah) favored Ya'qub (as) while Ishaq (as) favored his firstborn, 'As (as).

The family lived in tents like Ibrahim (as) and they moved from place to place to find water and pasture for their herds. Wherever Ishaq (as) went, Allah helped him find water so that he was a blessing for all the people around him and they listened to what he told them about their Creator. He generated a large following. But the rulers in the area became jealous. They threatened him in order to take over his wells and to discourage people from listening to him. He did not fight back but simply moved on, leading his people on the path of peace. They would settle where Allah guided him and showed him the places to dig new wells. And wherever they went they prospered.

The brothers continued to disagree as they grew. As Ishaq (as) aged, unlike his father he became feeble and his eyesight dimmed. He knew he would be leaving this world soon so he called his firstborn son 'As (as) and told him to go hunting and bring him some meat. When he returned from the hunt, Ishaq (as) intended to give him his inheritance, his blessing and with it the prophethood. But Rifqa (rah) heard and she told Ya'qub (as) to sacrifice a sheep and prepare it with mountain herbs so that it would taste like wild game. Then she told him to cover himself with the sheep skin and take the roasted meat to his father pretending to be 'As (as). She wanted the blessing for the son she favored. Ya'qub (as) did as his mother advised. Ishaq (as) ate the meat and thought it was wild game. When he heard Ya'qub's (as) soft voice he was suspicious but when he reached out his hand to touch him, he felt the woolly sheepskin and was reassured that he must be 'As (as). In this way he was tricked into giving his blessing and the prophethood to Ya'qub (as). But of course, Allah is not blind and cannot be tricked. The honor of prophethood can only go to the one for whom it was intended.

However, 'As (as) felt that he had been robbed and he was furious and threatened to kill his brother. Ya'qub (as) fled for his life and for this reason the Muslims say he was given the name Isra'il – the one who flees in the night, *isra* being a night journey. The Jews, however, say that he fought with an angel and so is called Isra-el which they say means 'he fought with God'. He fled to Harran and lived with his uncle Laban, who was his mother's brother and his father's cousin. He worked for seven years in order to marry Laban's daughter Rahila (rah) (Rachel). But when he married and lifted the veil of his bride he found her older sister La'iqa (rah) (Leah). Laban had tricked Ya'qub (as) in the same way Ya'qub (as) had tricked his father Ishaq (as). He worked another seven years and finally was given Rahila (rah). Until the advent of Islam men were allowed to have two sisters as wives.

Ya'qub (as) had one daughter, Dinah, and twelve sons. Ya'qub (as) loved two of his sons more than the others, Yusuf (as) and Benyamin (as) who were born to Rahila (rah), because the light of prophecy shone strongly in them. The other ten sons were mothered by La'iqa (rah) and two concubines. Their names were Judah, Levi, Reuben, Simeon, Asher, Zebulun, Naphtali, Gad, Issachar, and Dan. Each of Ya'qub's (as) sons fathered a tribe, becoming the twelve tribes of Isra'il, known as the Children of (*Banu*) Isra'il. Each one of them had the spiritual station of a prophet although not of a messenger.

After many years, the brothers reconciled. 'As (as) was headstrong but repentant. They stood together to bury their father and they continued to live near each other. 'As (as) married his cousin Basima (rah) the daughter of Isma'il (as), and they had a son Ruel. 'As (as) also had four other sons by two other wives. He joined forces with the clan of Isma'il (as). He is considered to be the ancestor of three tribes of people, the Edomites, the Kenizzites, and the Amalekites. They were all tribes with whom the Banu Isra'il did not get along and in the Torah they are described as rough, red, and hairy.

Ishaq lived to be 180 years old, older than either his father or brother had lived. When his time came, Ya'qub (as) and 'As (as) together buried him in the cave at Hebron where Ibrahim (as), Sarah (rah) and Rifqa (rah) were already buried. The Qur'an says of them all: **And remember Our servants Ibrahim and Ishaq and Ya'qub, all men of strength and vision. We caused them to be devoted to Us through their sincere remembrance of the Final Home: with Us they will be among the elect, the truly good. And remember Our servants Isma'il, Alyas'a, and Dhu l-Kifl, each of them truly good. This is a reminder** (38:45-49).

The Maqams of Ishaq (as) and Rifqa (rah) in Hebron.
Courtesy Akram Reda.

The entrance to the *maqam* of Sarah (rah) in the mosque at Hebron.
Courtesy Akram Reda.

CHAPTER FORTY-SEVEN

Two Rivers

Sarah (rah)

Although Sarah (rah) is not mentioned by name in The Qur'an, her story is told and her voice is heard. She is mentioned in the Bible, however, more times than any other woman. She is the matriarch, a model of womanhood: beautiful, pure, devout, obedient, and strong. For the Jews she is perhaps the most prominent female figure, although there are many other examples of strong believing woman. She is the first of what are called seven prophetesses mentioned in the Torah. For both Christians and Muslims, Maryam (rah) the mother of 'Isa (as) has perhaps superseded Sarah (rah) in holiness but not replaced her.

Her beauty was legendary, second only to our common mother Hawwa (rah) the wife of the first prophet Adam (as). She was one of those very rare women who remain physically beautiful in every stage of life, even into extreme old age. But it was not her beauty that attracted the admiration of her husband or the believers or for which she is remembered and praised. In fact, her beauty served mostly as a trial and source of suffering, causing tyrannical men to try to take her for their own. However lovely her appearance, it was her inner beauty that most distinguished her.

She was ten years younger than Ibrahim (as). Being a relative of some sort she grew up near him. From her early childhood he had always been a part of her life. She never knew life without him. Being adorned with a true heart as well as a beautiful face she responded to Ibrahim's (as) call and was probably one of his first followers. Love for him came to her as naturally as the air she breathed. When he was forced to part company with family and home she did not grieve or worry. She followed him into the unknown, never doubting either his goodness or his guidance. He was her lover and her friend but he was also her shaykh and teacher. On every level she truly saw him and knew his true worth.

Ibrahim (as) was always gentle and kind but when it came to truth he knew no compromise. He was unbending in his devotion to his Lord and his great compassion did not allow him to remain silent when he saw others in error. This led them into conflict over and over again with the political and social world in which they lived. When he opposed the religion and customs of her people and her parents, she followed him. From place to place they moved as Allah directed and there was no one spot on earth for her to call home. Wherever they were together that was her home. She must have known that she did not just marry a man but she was marrying a mission and a force. He could never be entirely hers. He belonged first to Allah and then she would always have to share him with the world. But she was content with her lot and by her service to him she knew she was also serving her Lord.

She was devoted to Ibrahim (as) but she was also wise in her own right and strong. Whatever path he walked, she would walk beside him, without complaint or regret, helping him to carry the burdens of life. She ran the household, fed the stream of people he constantly brought home, watched over the families of their followers and retainers. She supported him in poverty and then later in wealth. She was a mother to the believers and a calm harbor for her husband. She supported him totally and the truth he stood for and she backed him up even when he was forced to lie. They say that Ibrahim (as) ministered to the men and Sarah (rah) to the women. She was for them an example and a teacher. She kept the material things of life running smoothly for a man who was capable of handing over all his possessions to three strangers for a prayer and then walking away with nothing. She enabled him to be true to his vision, completely in the service of Allah. She had already given up the world to walk through life at his side. It is said in the Midrash that wherever they lived "a cloud of glory" hung over her tent and a warm light glowed inside.

Perhaps her biggest test was the many years she remained childless. Even though Allah promised Ibrahim (as) children, it did not seem that she would be the one who would bear them. Eventually she even took upon herself the solution to the problem. Ibrahim (as) never expressed any desire for another wife and never even prayed for children from any woman other than Sarah (rah). She was the one who suggested that he take her servant Hajar (rah) as a wife. This turned into perhaps an even harder test for her. She was happy for her husband but another wife threatened the one and only thing that she had held on to all those years – her relationship with the man for whom she had given up everything else. We know also, through their own truthful accounts, of the pain and jealousy with which many of the righteous wives of the Prophet Muhammad (sas) had to wrestle.

Sarah (rah) matured into a woman of strong spirituality. As Ibrahim (as) was a leader of men, Sarah (rah) was a leader of women and sometimes she had her own inspirations and occasionally she initiated action. Allah answered her prayers against the predations of the Pharaoh over and over again. It was her inspiration to give her handmaid Hajar (rah) to Ibrahim (as) as a second wife and then it was her inspiration again to banish them into the far desert of Arabia. When Ibrahim (as) tried to object, it was Allah who confirmed that Sarah's (rah) inspiration was right.

Allah supported Sarah (rah) and blessed her. He removed her trial and sent His angels to announce to her personally the almost incredible news that in her old age she would have a son. And she laughed. This first laugh they say was out of disbelief that anyone would even suggest she could bear a child at ninety years of age. She exhibited her sincere humbleness by doubting that the Lord would work such a miracle for her. **She struck her face** [in astonishment] **and said, "A barren old woman** [like me]!" (51:29). And then she laughed a second time nine months later out of joy when she was delivered of a beautiful baby boy. She managed to carry her trials with patience and with humor. She became a sign for all people that anything and everything is possible if Allah wills, to never stop asking and never give up hope.

Sarai, the little princess of her parents, became Sarah (rah) a noble example and a blessing for the whole world. She would be the grandmother of prophets and kings and of a great people. The Banu Isra'il, the preservers of true belief in Allah Almighty for thousands of years, were the result of her patience and faith. It was through her that the royal line of King Dawud (as) descended and through her that eventually the prophet 'Isa (as) was born.

Hajar (rah)

Although Hajar (rah) also is never mentioned by name in The Qur'an, she is at the heart of Islam and the Prophet (sas) called her the mother of the Arabs. She was the means by which Allah would bring the greatest and last prophet, Sayyiduna Muhammad (sas), into the physical world. How extraordinary she must have been to be chosen from among all the women of the world for this honor. It was for her that Ibrahim (as), one of the five greatest prophets, was sent on a journey of many hundreds of miles, walking across hot sands to a strange land. It was for her that he had to endure the trial and humiliation of a tyrant king taking his first wife and not being allowed to defend either her or himself. It was to connect with this humble slave girl of unknown heritage that all this difficulty and hardship was necessary.

Some of the commentators claim that Hajar (rah) was also a princess, a daughter of pharaoh, who gave her to Sarah (rah) as a sign of his respect. In the Midrash it says that when Hajar (rah) saw how Allah protected Sarah (rah) from her father she declared "it is better to be a slave in Sarah's (rah) house than a princess in my own." And so like Asiya (rah), the wife of the pharaoh at the time of Musa (as), she chose a heavenly house over an earthly one (66:11). Others say that she was an Arab of the people of Thamud, a granddaughter of the prophet Salih (as), either given as tribute or captured in war. She was born of a family of believers already chosen and elevated. She was a believing servant of Allah before she even met Ibrahim (as) and Sarah (rah).

However it was, at the time she entered the life of Ibrahim (as),

Even though Hajar (rah) has no known tomb, her station is the *Hijr* beside Allah's Holy House.

Hajar (rah) was not a free woman. The People of the Book who discredit her for the fact she was not free, discredit themselves. The people among whom the ownership of others was common practice knew that but for God they could find themselves in the same situation. Slavery was the result of war or raiding, not lack of intelligence or character. Men and women of honor and ability could fall into the hands of enemies and be sold as property. Their lack of freedom did not diminish who they were. The prophet Yusuf (as), after all, was a slave for most of his early life through no fault of his own. Many of the most famous and honored companions of the Prophet (sas) were slaves, Zayd ibn Harithah (ra), Salman al-Farsi (ra), Bilal al-Habashi (ra), Baraka (rah). It was a strange custom to give people as gifts, yet we know that two and a half millennia later the Muqawqis of Egypt sent two beautiful slave girls as gifts in just this same manner to the Prophet Muhammad (sas), Maria (rah) and her sister Sirin (rah). Interestingly enough, along with them the Muqawqis sent one thousand measures of gold just as the Pharaoh of Ibrahim (as) sent one thousand coins of silver along with Hajar (rah). Maria (rah), by her beauty and her goodness, became a wife of the Prophet (sas) and he set her free. She is the only wife other than Khadijatu l-Kubra (rah) from whom Allah granted the Prophet (sas) a child. The son Sayyiduna Muhammad (sas) fathered from his Egyptian wife he named Ibrahim no doubt in memory of the marriage of the prophet Ibrahim (as) and his Egyptian wife Hajar (rah).

However, even as a slave in Egypt, Hajar (rah) must have been used to the ease of palace life in the wealthiest country in the area at that time: rich and varied foods, beautiful clothing, and the company of friends and perhaps family in a busy court life. She was forced to leave all of that to be a servant in the tents of a nomadic chief whose language and customs she did not even understand. Her new life was so different and her old life so far away. But she appreciated the goodness and kindness of her new family and, being a spiritual person in her own right, her heart recognized and responded immediately to the worship of the one God. She must have felt that finally she had found her place, the place where she belonged.

Then Ibrahim (as) married her and she became pregnant. Instead of confirming her sense of belonging, it turned into the exact opposite and became the cause of her estrangement and exile. In sorrow she fled from her only home with nowhere to run but to Allah. And Allah heard her cry and answered her directly with His messenger angel who made a well open out of the ground for her that she called Bir-Lahai-Roi, the well of the Living One who sees me. However, He ordered her back to her husband and to her mistress Sarah (rah) to have her baby. For although the two women were in conflict, each must have known the true worth of the other. They loved each other for Allah even if they had a hard time living together. Hajar (rah) obeyed without question.

Many millennia later Jibra'il (as) came to visit the Prophet Muhammad (sas) in Medina in the guise of a new Muslim. He asked, so all those listening would learn, "What is the meaning of *ihsan*, goodness?" The Prophet (sas) answered: "It is to serve Allah as if you see Him, for although you do not see Him, know that for certain He sees you." According to the Torah, after talking with the angel, Hajar (rah) said: "I have now seen the One who sees me." (Genesis 16:13). Of course she did not actually see Allah, because that is not possible, but she saw His heavenly Messenger and she heard His words and she submitted to them. She had her own connection to Allah and her own voice. Like her sister Sarah (rah), Hajar (rah) was a woman of God in her own right and Allah spoke to her individually.

Eventually Allah set Hajar (rah) free from Sarah (rah) and took her to a place that must have seemed like the end of the earth, a valley without water or any living thing. But what appears is not always what is. Allah showed her that, far from being the end, He had set her at the center of the world and it radiated with real life. For her and her son, a second well was made to pour out of the ground, the miraculous water of Zamzam. She became the focal point around which a whole community gathered. She, like Sarah (rah), ministered to their needs and instructed them in the worship of Allah. She became the mother and matriarch of a proud people who would guard the faith of Ibrahim (as) and the light of the Prophet Muhammad (sas) safely until, like Zamzam, it would be made to well out of the dry earth again, a miracle in the desert. Even the Jews cannot help but admire Hajar (rah) for being the recipient of two angelic visits and two miraculous sources of water.

She never doubted the guidance or sincerity of Ibrahim (as). When he left her in the desert she knew it was by Allah's will. She immediately recognized shaytan when he whispered that her husband wanted to kill her son and she chased him away with stones. She, along with Ibrahim (as) and Isma'il (as), helped to build the Ka'ba and establish the rites of Hajj. It was not destined for her to remain with Ibrahim (as) and serve his daily needs but, far away, in the place that was written for her, she remained faithful to him and to Allah.

She was tested with hardship and banishment, with loneliness and isolation. She was tested with abandonment and bereavement. In all this she remained loyal and faithful to God and to Ibrahim (as). She chose servanthood in Allah's house over being a princess in the house of the world and Allah Almighty showed his acceptance of her and her son by making His House their home, here and hereafter. As Sarah (rah) is buried in the cave which the Jews say is the entrance to Paradise, so Hajar (rah) is buried somewhere near the Ka'ba which is an opening to Heaven. She doesn't have a tomb of her own but the Holy House has become her maqam and that of her son and those who make pilgrimage remember and pray for them.

Both Sarah (rah) and Hajar (rah) became the vessels of God's true guidance. One conveyed the Jerusalem covenant of the Jews and Christians, the other the Meccan covenant of the Muslims. Two strong, spiritually mature women, each serving her Lord as it was written for her to do; each the channel for a sacred river carrying the blessings of a Merciful Lord from the only source to the only ocean.

CHAPTER FORTY-EIGHT
Three Images of Ibrahim (as)

Three images of Ibrahim (as) in particular emerge from his story. The first image is of a young man, a knight on the path of God, a warrior for truth. He challenged his people and his king to reconsider the foundations of their understanding of the world and the purpose of life while setting an example of righteousness and compassion. The second image is of the mature man, wealthy and established, a husband and father, a defender of the weak, a refuge for the needy, a practicing believer. He is a prophet of God and a shaykh in both its meanings, as a chief and leader and as a spiritual guide. In the third image he is a resident of the highest heaven, ever living, a continuing source of blessing and inspiration, a picture of love and submission, and a symbol of spiritual triumph and hope.

The young Ibrahim (as) is called in The Qur'an, *fata* (21:60). This means not just a young man but a chivalrous youth, noble and rightly guided. He bowed to no one but his Lord, standing strong, confident but humble in front of the tyrants and deceivers of the world. Ibrahim (as) is the first *fata* and is known among Sufis as *Abu l-Fityan*, the father of all noble youths. From his example was drawn the outline of what it

Ottoman miniature, 1583, showing several scenes from the life of Ibrahim (as), as *fata* and as father.

means to be a knight on the path of God. The attributes of chivalry are generosity, humility, loyalty and courage and being strict with oneself while remaining generous of spirit towards others. The qualities given Ibrahim (as) by Allah in The Qur'an are: *halim*, forbearing; *awah*, tender hearted; *munib*, devout; *hanif*, predisposed to truth; *bi-qalbin salim*, true hearted.

At a very young age he made a stand on the path of truth and never turned back. He stood firmly in opposition to idolatry and ignorance. He was intimately sure of the origin and truth of the guidance he received and yet humble and compassionate to those who were not. He could not, however, remain silent in the face of the foolishness of others. He pleaded with his father Azar, **"knowledge has come to me that has not come to you. Follow me, then; I will guide you to a perfect way"** (19:43). This appears to be a statement of youth that probably no father would respond to positively but in this case, a simple statement of truth without pride. He never took personal offense at his father's refusal to listen and he continued to pray for him to be guided.

Futuwwa is the name of a stage on the spiritual path of which it is said that Ibrahim (as) is its beginning, 'Ali ibnu l-Abi Talib (ra) its exemplar, and Sayyiduna Mahdi (as) its seal. Its way has been passed down from father to son, from master to disciple, and there was never a time when it did not exist. Ibrahim (as) was the first and both his sons Isma'il (as) and Ishaq (as) followed him. In fact, it is debated whether the son displayed even greater spiritual chivalry than his father in that Ibrahim (as) was willing to sacrifice his beloved child but his son was willing to give up his own life. From Ishaq (as) it passed to Ya'qub (as) and from him to Yusuf (as) (12:30). Then it arose again in Musa (as) and passed from him to Yusha (as) (18:60). Also mentioned in The Qur'an as *fityan* are the Sleepers in the Cave (18:10), followers of 'Isa (as) who fled from disbelief and dishonesty and who placed their reliance on Allah alone.

The Prophet Muhammad (sas) exhibited clearly the qualities of the *fata*. His generosity and selflessness are so complete that even on the Judgment Day when all the people will be totally absorbed with their own welfare, he will be concerned only with others. Even the other prophets when asked to intercede for their nations will decline out of shame and concern for their own fate. They will arise from their resting places murmuring "myself, myself". Only Muhammad (sas) Habib Allah, the Beloved, will rise saying *"ummati ummati"* – "my nation, my nation". These are the first words he is said to have spoken at the time of his birth and they will be his first words when he is born again.

The Prophet Muhammad (sas) said that he entered *futuwwa* following the example of his great grandfather Ibrahim (as) and that in like manner it radiated from his cousin and son-in-law 'Ali ibnu Abi Talib (ra). Perhaps the most famous and perfect example of Sayyiduna 'Ali's (ra) nobility was in one of the early battles. He was engaged in single combat, as was the custom of the Arabs before the general battle began. He had wounded his opponent and was standing over him ready to deal the final blow when the man spit in his face. At that point Sayyiduna 'Ali (ra) *Asad Allah*, the lion of God, sheathed his drawn sword and walked away. Later the man asked him why he had spared his life and Sayyiduna 'Ali (ra) replied that the man's action had made anger rise up inside of him to such an extent that if he had killed him then, he would have killed in anger and not in the name of Allah and justice. So rather than commit what he considered to be essentially an act of murder, he sheathed his physical sword and turned his spiritual sword against his own self and his anger. In this way he gave visible expression to the words of the Prophet (sas) that the battle with the ego is even greater than physical combat. The man was so impressed that, beyond his control, the tears streamed down his face and his heart opened. He later came to the Prophet (sas) with love and entered Islam.

The second image of Ibrahim (as) is as a mature man, a shaykh, guiding his people by means of his wise example and counsel, a political and spiritual leader of men. He is the father, the husband, the shepherd, the warrior, the peacemaker, the host. He is the man who gave up family and security to set out on the road of Allah. He is the one who gave away all he owned for the few words of divine praise spoken by the angelic Messenger. He is the one who was willing to even give his precious son in obedience to his Lord. And he is the one who having given it all up, had all of it and more returned to him by Allah. Symbolically and actually he is the builder of God's house on earth. Stone by stone, word by word, action by action, he established the worship of Allah – **the place whereon Ibrahim once stood; and whoever enters it finds inner peace** (3:97). This is the image of Ibrahim (as) the Patriarch, the father of faith, the father of all people of faith.

The third image is as he is now, in Paradise leaning with his back against the *Baytu l-Ma'mur*, the Heavenly House. He is called *hanif*, one inclining toward God, and so it is fitting that the Prophet (sas) found him reclining (*hanafa*) against the Inhabited House, the original Temple that is the Heart of all creation and in which it finds its *qibla* and its Lord. It is here that Sayyiduna Ibrahim (as) has found his eternal home. Allah has put under his kindly care the souls of all children who died in infancy, to be taught and raised under his eye. In much the same way that the Prophet (sas), as a child, used to see his grandfather, Abdu l-Muttalib (ra) sitting on a mat in the shade of the Ka'ba. And Muhammad (sas), was the only one of his many grandsons who was allowed to sit in the place of honor beside him. And it is to Ibrahim (as), into the "bosom of Abraham", that we will all be returned one day, God willing, as little children, clean and pure.

The Prophet Muhammad (sas) said, "Verily, every prophet has allies among the prophets, and my ally is my father and the close friend (*khalil*) of my Lord, Ibrahim (as)." (Tirmidhi). He also said that when he met Sayyiduna Ibrahim (as) in the seventh heaven he recognized him as being most like himself both spiritually and physically. He said that they resembled each other more closely than the other descendants of Ibrahim (as). We don't know if this means more closely than the other prophets of the Banu Isra'il that he met on his journey through the seven heavens or if he meant more closely than the Arabian Jews and Arabs who held claim to being his descendants. Most probably it means both. This statement encourages us to look with some confidence to the historical description of the Prophet (sas) in order to sketch out a picture of Ibrahim (as) that should closely approximate the truth.

The Prophet Muhammad (sas) is described as being neither very tall nor very short. He did not tower over the heads of others but his presence was so impressive as to make him appear taller compared to others when he was in a crowd. His shoulders were broad and straight. His hair and beard were black with a little bit of curl. His face was oval to round with light skin and some pink in his cheeks. His eyes were large and dark with thick long lashes. His mouth was full and his teeth very white.

His manner was gentle and serious. He smiled often but rarely laughed out loud. He always walked with intention, as if he knew exactly where he was headed and why. When someone spoke to him he turned his whole body towards them not just his eyes and he gave them his full attention. He sat among people as one of them. When he entered a gathering he did not have people move to make room for him but sat where there was space. He was open to people's questions and he loved to listen to their problems and try to find solutions. He asked for opinions and advice from others and then he made his own decision. He loved to spend time in the company of people, especially the very poor men living in the mosque who had left their homes for the sole purpose of learning their religion. He enjoyed the company of women, the scent of good perfume, and his delight was in prayer.

    He was thoroughly honest and his unparalleled generosity overwhelmed men who considered generosity the highest virtue. He lived simply, eating and dressing the same as everyone else and sleeping on a mat on the ground. He owned only a few changes of clothes which he mended and washed himself. When great wealth entered the community he distributed it among the needy with an open hand. He shouldered the heavy responsibility of his companions and community in peace and in war but he took no special favors or privileges in return.

    He was kind and compassionate with everyone except those who actively opposed Allah's message. With those who fought against Allah's word he was firm and unwavering but with those who hurt or insulted him personally he was forgiving and generous. Even those who were committed to fighting him had to acknowledge his trustworthy character and his fine manners.

    In all his busy daily life he never forgot his Lord. He spent his days teaching and his nights in solitary prayer. By his example he turned a nation of rough, egocentric, hardened men into a supportive community of upright brothers. By his perfect example he turned proud men and women, who worshipped stones and their own selfish desires, into thoroughly honest, compassionate, humble worshippers of the one God. Those who had the good fortune to see him were in awe of him and those who got to know him loved him more than they loved themselves. When some people, who did not have the chance to see the Prophet (sas) in life, asked what he was like, his wife Aisha (rah) said that he was like meeting

The Qur'an in person.

Sayyiduna 'Ali (ra) said that everyone agreed that they had never seen, before or after, anyone who was anything like him. The Prophet (sas), however, said that he saw the resemblance between himself and his forefather Ibrahim (as) Khalil Allah.

Ibrahim (as) greets the Prophet Muhammad (sas) in the 7th heaven. Persian 15th century.

The *maqam* of Ibrahim (as) in Hebron divided by bullet proof glass into a section for Jews and a section for Muslims.

CHAPTER FORTY-NINE

The Unwelcome Guest

It is recorded that Sayyiduna Ibrahim (as) lived for 175 years. All this time he remained healthy and vigorous. After Sarah (rah) and Hajar (rah) died and Ishaq (as) and Isma'il (as) had married, Ibrahim (as) took a third wife according to the Torah or perhaps even two wives or concubines. The one mentioned by name is Katura (rah), meaning 'sweet-smelling' and she gave him six more sons, Zimran, Jokshan, Medan, Midian, Ishbak, and Shuah. These sons fathered the Arab tribes to the south and east of Palestine, among them the Midianites of Sinai and northern Arabia, and the Shuites of Syria. A common understanding among the Jews, derived from the stories of the Midrash, is that Katura (rah) is actually another name for Hajar (rah). After the death of Sarah (rah) Isma'il (as) brought his mother back to live with his widowed father. She had been elevated by her long years of waiting faithfully and so received a new name. She continued to bear children for Ibrahim (as) and they lived happily into an even greater old age. The Muslim historians say that Ibrahim (as) married two Arab women, Katura daughter of Yaqtan (rah) and Hajur daughter of Arhir (rah) neither of whom was Hajar (rah) who had died earlier and was buried in Mecca. Katura (rah) had the six sons listed above although their names are spelled slightly differently. Hajur (rah) had five sons whose names were, Kaysan, Shawarukh, Amim, Lutan, and Nafis. All of them were the ancestors of various Arab tribes who were later to become enemies of the Banu Isra'il. Altogether, Sayyiduna Ibrahim (as) had either eight or thirteen sons before his time on earth was done.

When his time drew near, Allah Almighty, the Giver of life and death, sent the Angel 'Azra'il (as) to announce to Ibrahim (as) his coming departure. It is a pledge between Allah and His prophets that He does not take back their souls without informing them first and asking their permission. So in the Prophet Muhammad's (sas) last illness he was heard to make his choice by saying: **with those unto whom Allah has shown favor, the prophets and the saints and the martyrs and the righteous. The best of company are they** (4:69).

Now Ibrahim (as) greeted 'Azra'il (as) and was surprised at his beautiful appearance. He asked him if this is the way he appears to all men. 'Azra'il (as) shook his mighty head and answered that this attractive appearance was only for the prophets and chosen ones. So Ibrahim (as) asked to be shown in what form he would appear to other people. When the Archangel 'Azra'il (as) assumed his alternate appearance it was so terrifying that Ibrahim (as) asked him please to change back immediately. He said that the sight of him was enough to make any person die of fright.

Ibrahim (as) felt, however, that he was not quite ready to leave his earthly mission and requested some more time. He called all his family to gather around him. Isma'il (as) came with his wife and children, Ishaq (as) with his, and all the other sons and daughters joined them. Ibrahim (as) gave to each their inheritance. Isma'il (as) received Arabia and the lands to the south. Ishaq (as) received Palestine and ash-Sham. The other sons each received land on the Red Sea coast of Arabia and some in Syria.

'Azra'il (as) had departed but he had not given up his mission. He took a new and unfamiliar form - that of a very frail old man. Ibrahim (as) did not recognize him and thought he was just another weary traveler. So he invited him in and prepared a meal for him and sat down with him before the tray of steaming food. 'Azra'il (as), as the old man, reached out his hand for the food, trembling and shaking. He proceeded to take a piece of food and blindly stuff it in his ear. He took another piece, his hand trembling uncontrollably, and put it up his nose. Finally, on the third try he was able to find his mouth but then he had trouble chewing and swallowing. He coughed and sputtered, making inappropriate noises from up and from down. Ibrahim (as) watched in dismay. At last he asked his elderly guest how old he might be. 'Azra'il (as) answered that his age was one hundred and seventy-eight, just three years older than Ibrahim (as) himself. Ibrahim (as) then prayed to Allah to take his soul before he reached the same piteous state as his guest.

Another version of his death relates that 'Azra'il (as) came to Ibrahim (as) to inform him of his immanent death and Ibrahim (as) was not ready to accept. He asked the angel: "O 'Azra'il did you ever see a friend (*khalil*) ask for the life of his friend (*khalil*)?" And 'Azra'il (as) returned to Allah and told Him what His prophet had said. Allah Almighty ordered the angel to go back to Ibrahim (as) and say: "Have you ever known a friend (*khalil*) who refused to be reunited with his friend (*khalil*)?" And Ibrahim (as) smiled at that and happily gave up his soul to 'Azra'il (as). As he bowed his head to the ground in *sajda*, 'Azra'il (as) took his blessed soul as gently as it is possible to do.

Ibrahim Khalil Allah (as) was buried in the cave of Machpelah near his wife Sarah (rah). His two sons, Isma'il (as) and Ishaq (as), were united there to hear his last bequest, to carry his body to its final resting place and to pray over him. And much later, Ishaq (as) and Rifqa (rah) were also buried beside them in the cave. Their son Ya'qub (as) and his wife La'iqa (rah) were taken in their old age to live in Egypt with their son the prophet Yusuf (as) and there they died. But it is said that Yusuf (as), following his father's dying request, took their bodies back to Hebron to bury them there. Yusuf (as) later also died in Egypt. Because of the great love felt for him by all of the people, his sarcophagus was sunk into the middle of the Nile where it could not be claimed by any one particular group. Many generations later it resurfaced miraculously to enable Musa (as) to take it with him when he led his people out of slavery in Egypt. The wagon carrying the body of Yusuf (as) led the caravan of the Banu Isra'il through the opening in the sea, through forty years of wandering in the wilderness, and then finally into the Promised Land. At that time the prophet Yusha (as) interred the body of Yusuf (as) with his fathers in the cave of Machpelah. However, today there is a maqam for him in Nablus. Ismail (as) and Hajar (rah), Hala (rah), and Lut (as) and many other prophets, however, are buried in unmarked graves somewhere near the Ka'ba. And Ya'qub's (as) dear wife Rahila (rah) is said to be buried where she died, in Bethlehem. May Allah be pleased with all of them.

But the work of Sayyiduna Ibrahim (as) is not finished. When the Prophet Muhammad (as) was taken to visit the seven heavens on the Night Journey he met a different prophet in each of the levels of heaven. Sayyiduna Ibrahim (as) was in the seventh and highest heaven leaning back against the jeweled wall of the Baytu l'Ma'mur. Gathered at his feet was a crowd of little children and he was talking to them and teaching them. The Prophet (sas) was told that these are the children born to parents of every faith, who died before they were grown, children still in *fitra*, as pure and innocent as the day they were created. They have been given by Allah to Ibrahim (as) to raise because of his gentleness and patience.

The grave of Ibrahim (as) is in the city of Hebron/Halil in the state of Israel. It was the capital of Judah at the time of the king and prophet Dawud (as). The huge stone building that now serves as a mosque and temple was erected by King Herod for his Jewish subjects at the time of Sayyiduna 'Isa (as) in the first century. It is considered to be oldest intact place of prayer in continuous use in existence today. First a temple, then a church and then a mosque and now all three, the site has been considered a holy place for as long as people can remember. It is visited continuously by Muslim, Jewish and Christian pilgrims. The place where pilgrims pay their respects and pray, however, is several levels above the actual graves. Although there is a grate in the floor that enables them to peer down, the view is murky and not of the burial chambers themselves. The area of the actual graves has not been opened in hundreds of years. It can only be accessed through a small hole in the stone floor below the floor of the mosque that leads to a very narrow passageway down into the underground caverns themselves.

According to as-Suyuti, one of the earliest accounts of a visit to the actual tomb comes from a man named Abu Bakr al-Askafi sometime in the tenth century. He recounts slipping through the opening in the floor and descending seventy-two steps into the cave below. There on the right he saw a stone platform on which was lying the body of an old man dressed in green with a long black beard that curled over his cheeks. His guide told him this was the prophet Ishaq (as). Moving farther into the cave they came upon another man laid out on a stone platform. He was very old and all his hair was white, even the hair of his chest, face, and eye lashes. There was a small breeze, coming perhaps from Paradise at whose threshold the cave sits, that gently ruffled his long white hair. He was also dressed entirely in green. This was Sayyiduna Ibrahim (as). Al-Askafi in awe fell into *sajda* beside him. On the other side was another elderly man in green with a thick beard and a face browned by the sun. His guide told him that this was the prophet Ya'qub (as).

Then, as he started to move to the other side where the wives of the prophets are buried, he heard a voice coming from behind the wall warning him not to enter the private quarters (*harim*) of the women. Startled and alarmed, he and his guide clambered out of the cave chamber. A caretaker of the mosque in 1996 told the author of a *New Yorker* article that the tomb had not been entered in hundreds of years. He said that he had heard that six or seven hundred years ago, a doctor had made his way into the tomb without properly announcing his arrival. He had surprised a woman, whom he believed to be Sarah (rah), sitting on a rock slab combing her long hair. She screamed in shock and surprise. As a result of his indiscretion he became permanently blind.

Do not think of the prophets as being dead, cautioned the wise caretaker. Their bodies remain fresh and perfectly preserved. Their souls are in heaven but they can see, hear and respond to greetings and requests from the people in the world. **And say not of those who are slain on the way of Allah, "They are dead": nay, they are alive, but you perceive it not** (2:154).

Peace be upon Ibrahim (37:109).

The stairs leading to the burial caves of Hebron taken by people who broke in.

Alif , One, Allah.

CONCLUSION
Our God Is One

According to the Torah, when Ibrahim (as) was ninety-nine years old the angels came to him to announce the immanent birth of his son, Ishaq (as), and to establish a covenant between Allah and his descendants. At this time, they also relayed an astonishing command. Allah said to Ibrahim (as), "Walk before Me and be perfect (*tamam*)." (Genesis 17:1). It is impossible to imagine being ordered by Allah Almighty to be perfect in His sight. The strength and capacity of any man to receive and to carry such a command is almost inconceivable. In much the same way the Prophet Muhammad (sas) was commanded **So walk straight, as you were commanded…He sees what you do** (11:112). It is said that the Prophet (sas) got his first grey hair from the weight and mightiness of this order. Coincidently it is related that Ibrahim (as) also turned white soon after receiving his command.

We can say with some confidence that Sayyiduna Ibrahim (as) walked through life perfect in the eyes of his Creator, a model for mankind of true faith, *al-dini hanifa* (30:30). His was not an ordinary faith. There is nothing about a prophet that is ordinary. Among the things in the Torah that are surprising to a Muslim are the quite imperfect actions it ascribes to God's prophets – from drunkenness to incest. By definition, a man of the stature and station of a prophet is both incapable of, and protected from, such acts. This is why the three small, totally justifiable lies of Sayyiduna Ibrahim (as) are remembered and made much of. The standard to which a prophet is held is much higher than that of other men. His reality is different from our own.

The Prophet Muhammad (sas) was told by Allah to say to us: **I am only a human being, like you, to whom it has been revealed that your God is One – anyone who fears to meet his Lord should do good deeds and give no one a share in the worship due to his Lord** (18:110). In these few simple words perhaps, lie the secret. It is no ordinary thing to fear Allah and keep your actions, intentions and worship perfect in His eyes. And, however simple it might sound, it is far from an ordinary thing to know the full meaning of the Oneness of God. This is not the standard to which most of us are held. If it were, we would fail miserably, not just in our lives but in every moment of our lives and with every breath.

These men are chosen and their capacity is enormous and their hearts are vast and their sincerity is fathomless. It is said that Uways al-Qarani (ra) asked Sayyiduna 'Ali (ra) if he had seen the Prophet Muhammad (sas). Sayyiduna 'Ali (ra), who had lived his whole life in the company of the Prophet (sas), replied that he had only seen him once. He said that once he had been given a vision of him from his knees to his shoulders but where his feet extended and where his head soared, Sayyiduna 'Ali (ra) was unable to see. Each one of the 124,000 prophets that Allah has sent deserves his rank and our profound respect. Although each had his own style and his own personality, they each carried the same divine message, the same warning and reminder for mankind and they each knew, with a special kind of knowing, that our God is One.

The first and only religion of Allah is Islam and all prophets have been Muslim starting with Adam (as). Ibrahim (as) was a Muslim in the fundamental, literal meaning of the word, one who is submitted. Ibrahim (as) was one who subjected his ego, his *nafs*, to his will and who submitted his will to the Will of Allah. **When his Lord said to him 'Surrender (*aslim*)!' He said 'I have surrendered (*aslamtu*) to the Lord of the Worlds'** (2:131). This is clear. He obeyed his Lord no matter how personally painful or how enigmatic the command might seem. The command in itself was of little consequence. It was the act of submission that mattered. He was given knowledge while yet a child and he held on to it firmly throughout a very long life, never doubting and, most importantly, never turning back. He gave up all he had and when Allah gave it back, Ibrahim (as) was willing to give it up all over again. There was no love in his heart larger or greater than love of his Lord. As Ibn 'Arabi (q) wrote, he was permeated by, thoroughly drenched in divine love. He was a true friend, a servant completely submitted to his Lord.

Medieval Persian miniature of the Prophet Muhammad (sas) leading Ibrahim (as), Musa (as), 'Isa (as) and other prophets in prayer on the Night Journey.

It can also be said that Ibrahim (as) was a Muslim in the more specific meaning of the word. He fulfilled the requirements that are part of the message of the Prophet Muhammad (sas), the Five Pillars of Islam. 1. He testified to the oneness of God. When he was shown the millions of pilgrims who would answer his invitation for Hajj, he and his wives and children prayed for them, for the *Ummah* of Muhammad (sas). Therefore, it can be said that he also testified to the prophethood of Muhammad (sas). 2. Ibrahim (as) made *salat*, prostrating and bowing (14:40); 3. he fasted, although probably not the month of Ramadan which was only instituted the second year in Medina; 4. he gave *zakat* (21:73); and 5. he established and performed the pilgrimage in the same manner in which it was performed by the Prophet (sas), the way it continues to be performed today. The last advice which he left for his descendants was **"O my sons, indeed, Allah has chosen the religion for you, so do not die except as Muslims"** (2:132).

So how is it that today we have three major religious traditions and many smaller ones all claiming descent from Ibrahim (as)? The Qur'an states: **O men! Behold, We have created you all out of a male and a female, and have made you into nations and tribes, so that you might come to know one another. Verily, the noblest of you in the sight of Allah is the one who is most deeply conscious of Him (*taqwa*). Behold, Allah is all-knowing, all-aware** (49:13). So we cannot say that our differences are due to our mistakes or sins or that they are other than the way our Maker intended. The Qur'an elaborates: **Unto every one of you We have appointed a law and way. And if Allah so willed, He could surely have made you all one single community: But** [He willed it otherwise] **in order to test you by means of what He granted you. Compete then, one another in doing good works! Unto Allah you all must return and then He will make you truly understand all that on which you differed** (5:48).

This world is a testing ground. Allah sent us here to see how we will use the gifts He has so abundantly granted us; to see how we will deal with the sorrow and hardship that inevitably accompany them. Will we compete to do good, always returning love and thankfulness in the knowledge that everything good and even everything that might seem bad is a gift from Allah? Or will we set up others as gods and blame them for our troubles and waste our lives seeking to eradicate them? In other words, will we be Ibrahim (as) or will we be Namrud?

Unlike the Jews, Muslims do not believe that God left the world unfinished nor that it is the purpose of man to complete it. Unlike the Christians, Muslims do not believe that man is unforgiven on account of the actions of his father Adam (as) nor that it is the purpose of man to rebuild Paradise on Earth. Things are the way they are supposed to be, ordained by an All-Knowing Creator. Adam (as) was made in Heaven but his purpose from the beginning was clearly to be Allah's deputy on Earth. He was never meant to remain in Paradise although he is meant to return there. The cause of his so-called 'sin' or 'fall' was preprogrammed into his nature - weak, hasty, and forgetful but not intending to evil. It all played out according to Allah's plan.

"When a man has a wife and is her companion, he does not know that he loves her, for the love is hidden by the blessings and companionship. Wait until they fall into separation! It is then that friendship appears. Adam was the friend, but his friendship was hidden by the blessings of Paradise. So, when the veil of Paradise was lifted from Adam, the reality of his love became apparent. When satan was Iblis, no one knew he was satan, nor did he know. He appeared as a worshipper bound by the belt of his service, his face washed with the water of conformity. When his foot slipped, it became apparent that he was neither friend nor servant. Adam, the chosen, was the friend but the friendship was concealed by blessings. When his foot slipped, it became clear that he was both friend and servant." (*Kashf al-Asrar* tafsir for ayah 76:1).

Man is a creation with the ability to change and grow. He is not an angel. He has will and choice, ego and mind. He is made from both earth and heaven, an amalgam of dust and the breath of the Almighty. He needs to choose his path and find his balance. He needs to follow the examples that Allah has provided him, the Prophets and their Books. **There has certainly been an example in them for you, for anyone whose hope is in Allah and the Last Day** (60:6). But unfortunately man needs to experience things for himself and sorrow is the mother of wisdom. Man learns best when his foot slips.

Perhaps our fall from unity is Allah's plan to challenge us with the discomfort of diversity in order to make us long for His Unity. In the early days of Islam diversity was embraced. Acceptance of difference, within limits, was built into the very core of the religion itself and is reflected beautifully in the behavior of the Prophet Muhammad (sas) and his blessed companions (ra). After the coming of Sayyiduna Mahdi (as) and the winning of the great war, the prophet 'Isa (as) will rule the world in peace, without any dissension or dispute, all submitted under one law, Allah. But after forty short years it will be over. Clearly unity and peace have little or no permanent role to play in this world. However, putting up with dissension, disagreement, and difference – having patience and tolerance does.

If it is the knowledge of Oneness that makes a prophet who he is, then the story of Ibrahim (as) is the model of a life led by this principle. He clung staunchly and peacefully to his own truth in the face of a whole world of deniers. Musa (as) is the one who had the task of forming a community, building a nation, establishing a state. Ibrahim's (as) mission was not to collect people and build a nation. It was rather to be a nation in himself. **Verily, Ibrahim was a nation in himself (*ummah*), obedient to Allah, following the truth (*hanif*) and taking no God but God** (16:120). His order was to be perfect in himself, to erase any selfishness, any deceit, any love for other than Allah and to live that life to the fullest extent in order to become a radiant example for others. So those who came later and found they could not follow the religion of their fathers called themselves *hanif*. They took as their model Sayyiduna Ibrahim (as) and they searched the world for the traces of his way. The *ummah* they belonged to was that of Ibrahim Khalil Allah (as).

Ibn 'Arabi (q) coined a term for the relationship to Ibrahim (as) that is shared by the Jews, Christians, and Muslims. He calls Ibrahim (as) their 'milk father'. In Islam, the relationship between a wet nurse and her fosterlings is parallel to that of mother and child and the relationship between children who have nursed from the same mother is comparable to siblings, even to the extent that they are forbidden to marry. As a milk mother nurses her fostered children, so in a similar manner Ibrahim (as) nourishes the believers on the milk of his faith and his wisdom. He is not so much the progenitor as he is the one who nourishes.

To take this metaphor a bit farther, when Ibrahim (as) was a baby hidden in the cave he is said to have nursed from the four fingers of his right hand. From one issued butter, from one honey, from one water, and from one milk. Perhaps this is an indication that those who are nursed in turn by Ibrahim (as) each have received a different nourishment, a different wisdom. Milk was the heavenly drink chosen by the Prophet (sas) and it has come to symbolize Islam in general. It could be said that both water and butter are contained within milk, that they are one. But it can also be said that each has its own flavor and beauty, its own unique quality, and all of them are wholesome and good. Each is a gift bestowed by Allah the most Generous and conveyed to us by means of His prophet Ibrahim (as). By partaking of the legacy of Ibrahim Khalil Allah (as) we incur a filial obligation to him and a fraternal obligation to each other that is not based on blood but rather on knowledge. Let us become more knowledgeable then and in so doing, God willing, more brotherly.

"O Allah grace Muhammad and the people of Muhammad as you have graced Ibrahim and the people of Ibrahim, only You are worthy to be praised and glorified.

O Allah bless Muhammad and the people of Muhammad as you have blessed Ibrahim and the people of Ibrahim. In all the worlds only You are worthy to be praised and glorified."

Salatu l-Ibrahimiya.

Glossary

Abjad – The Arabic numerology system.

Abu Bakr (ra) – The father-in-law and close companion of the Prophet Muhammad (sas) and the first rightly guided khalif in Islam.

'Aisha (rah) – the Prophet's (sas) wife and the daughter of Abu Bakr (ra).

'Ali ibnu l-Abi Talib (ra) – The fourth rightly guided khalif and the cousin of the Prophet (sas) and his son-in-law.

Arhamu r-Rahimin – Epithet for Allah, the Most Merciful of the merciful.

'As (as) – Esau son of Isaac, brother of the prophet Jacob (as).

As-saddiq – A friend, one who testifies to the truth.

Ash-Sham – All the land within a radius of 6 days camel ride from Damascus. Canaan, Palestine, Mesopotamia.

Awliya – The plural of wali.

Ayyub (as) – The prophet Job.

'Azra'il (as) – Pronounced Azra-eel. One of the four Archangels called in The Qur'an the Angel of Death, Maliku l-mawt.

Banu Isra'il – The Children of Isra'il (as) or Jacob, the tribes descending from the 12 sons of Jacob (as). The Jews – a name derived from Judah (as) the oldest son of Jacob (as).

Book of Jubilees – An early book of the Jews that retells the stories of Genesis with emphasis on a solar calendar.

Buraq – The heavenly steed which carried the Prophet Muhammad (sas) on the Night Journey.

Canaan – Palestine, the Holy Land, Bilad ash-Sham.

Dawud (as) – The prophet David.

Dhabih – Sacrificial animal offering.

Dhu l-Qarnain (as) – A prophet mentioned in the The Qur'an, "the Possessor of the Two Horns", usually identified with Alexander the Great.

El – Earliest recorded name of the Creator.

Fata – A chivalrous youth.

Fitra – The natural state in which Allah made us, submitted to Him.

Gematria – The Hebrew numerology system.

Habib Allah – The Beloved of Allah – an honorific of the Prophet Muhammad (sas).

Habil (as) – pronounced Habeel – Abel, the son of Adam (as).

Hajj – The annual pilgrimage to Mecca.

Hadith – The transmitted and recorded words and actions of the Prophet Muhammad (sas) that have been ranked and rated by the scholars according to their veracity.

Hanif – Pronounce haneef from the root h-n-f – to incline towards. One inclining to truth, a true believer.

Hawwa (rah) – Eve, the first woman.

Ibrahim (as) – Pronounced Ibraheem. The prophet Abraham (as).

Iblis – Pronounced Iblees, The name of shaytan, the devil.

Idris (as) – The prophet Enoch.

Imam – One who stands in front, a leader, specifically the leader of prayer.

Iman – Meaning faith.

Ishaq (as) – Pronounced Is-haq. The prophet Isaac.

Isma'il (as) – Pronounced Isma-eel. The prophet Ishmael.

'Isra – A night journey, specifically the miraculous journey of the Prophet Muhammad (sas) from Mecca to Jerusalem.

Isra'il (as) – Pronounced Isra-eel. Israel, another name for the prophet Ya'qub, Jacob (as).

Israfil (as) – Pronounced Israfeel. The Archangel who will blow the trumpet at the end of time.

Jamarat – Pronounced jamaraat. The three pillars representing the devil towards which the pilgrims throw pebbles during the Hajj.

Jibra'il (as) – Pronounced Jibra-eel. The Archangel Gabriel who delivers God's words.

Kaffir – One who denies the truth – an unbeliever.

Khadijatu l-Kubra (rah) – Khadija the Great, the honorary title of the Prophet Muhammad's (sas) first wife and the mother of his children.

Khalil – Pronounced khaleel. Meaning intimate friend from the root kh-l-l meaning to penetrate, permeate.

Khalilu r-Rahman – Pronounced Khaleelu r-Rahmaan meaning friend of the All-Merciful.

Khidr (as) – A saint and prophet mentioned in The Qur'an in relation to Musa (as). Also known as the Green Man said to have been given eternal life. Sometimes associated with Ilyas (as) Elias.

La'iqa (rah) – Pronounced Laa-ika, Leah wife of Jacob (as).

Lut (as) – Pronounced Loot. The prophet Lot.

Luqman – A prophet or saint mentioned in The Qur'an sometimes identified with Aesop.

Madhhab – A school of Law. There are now only four accepted Sunni schools – Hanifi, Shafi'I, Maliki, and Hanbali. There used to be hundreds of others but they have no more followers. The Shi'a also have their own school. They come to different conclusions on matters of Shari'ah all based on The Qur'an and Hadith.

Mahdi (as) – A member of the Prophet's (sas) family who will fight the antichrist at Armageddon.

Midrash – Commentary on the Torah and stories of the Rabbis collected in the first ten centuries CE.

Mika'il (as) – Pronounced Mika-eel. The Archangel Michael who is responsible for the vegetation of the world and justice.

Mi'raj – The ascent to Heaven of the Prophet Muhammad (sas).

Muhammad Mustafa (sas) – Muhammad the Chosen one (sas).

Musa (as) – Pronounced Moosa – The prophet Moses (as).

Mushrik – Meaning idolater, one practices shirk, to worship other than Allah.

Muslim – One who is submitted. From the root s-l-m meaning peace, submission.

Nabi – Meaning prophet.

Nuh (as) – Pronounced Nooh, the prophet Noah.

Old Testament – It is divided into 39 Books which are a different ordering of the Books of the Torah and include the Book of Prophets and Wisdoms called the Tanakh by the Jews.

Palestine – Canaan, Ash-Sham. The land promised Ibrahim (as), Mesopotamia.

Qabil – Pronounced Qabeel – Cain the son of Adam (as).

Qarin - Pronounced qareen, meaning a companion but usually interpreted as a personal devil who encourages men to sin

Qibla – The direction faced in prayer.

Qira'a – The seven authentic ways the Prophet (sas) used to recite The

Qur'an. They entail some variation in pronunciation but not in meaning.

Qirba – A whole goat skin that is prepared to serve as a bag to hold water.

Quraysh – The tribe to which the Prophet (sas) belonged, descendants of Isma'il (as).

Rabb - Meaning Lord, Sustainer, the One who nourishes.

Rahila (rah) – Pronounced Raheela, Rachel wife of Jacob (as).

Rasul – Pronounced rasool, meaning messenger.

Rifqa (rah) – Rebecca wife of Isaac (as).

Ruku' – The act of bowing in the Muslim prayer.

Sadaqa - Charity.

Sajda – The act of prostration in the Muslim prayer.

Salah - Prayer.

Salam – Pronounced salaam. Meaning peace.

Salih (as) – An Arabian prophet only mentioned in The Qur'an, whose people, the Thamud, may have lived north of Mecca in Mada'in Salih.

Salman al-Farsi (ra) – One of the close companions of the Prophet Muhammad (sas) of Persian Zoroastrian origin who searching for the true religion was enslaved and brought to Medina where he met the Prophet (sas) and became Muslim.

Sam (as) – Son of Noah (as) ancestor of the Semites.

Sayyid – Master, lord.

Sayyida – Lady.

Sayyiduna – Pronounced sayyidina, our master.

Sayyidatuna – Pronounced sayyidaatina, our lady.

Shari'ah – Islamic Law derived from The Qur'an and Hadith by exceptional men of great learning and understanding.

Shaytan – Satan, the devil.

Shu'ayb (as) – An Arabian prophet of the people of Madyan whose daughter became the wife of the prophet Moses (as). He is sometimes identified as Jethro.

Sulayman ibn Dawud (as) – The prophet Solomon son of the prophet David.

Sunnah – The practices and example of the Prophet Muhammad (sas) as \ recorded in the Hadith.

Ta'if – A mountain city near Mecca.

Talmud – Rabbinical commentaries on Jewish the law and tradition written after the Babylonian exile.

Tanakh – What the Christians call the Old Testament consisting of the Torah, History, Prophets, and Wisdoms.

Tawaf – Circumambulation around the Ka'ba.

Torah – The Law as revealed to Moses in the 5 books of Moses – Genesis, Exodus, Leviticus, Numbers, and Deuteronomy called by Christians the Pentateuch, part of the Old Testament.

'Umar (ra) – Sayyiduna 'Umar ibnu l-Khattab (ra) a close companion of the Prophet (sas) and the second rightly guided khalif of Islam.

Ummah – Nation, community.

Uways al-Qarani (ra) – A companion of the Prophet (sas) who never physically met him but with whom he had a spiritual connection.

'Uzayr (as) – Pronounced Oozayr, the prophet Ezra.

Wali – A saint, a friend of Allah.

Walid – Pronounced waleed – birth parent.

Wudu' – Ablution, ritual washing in preparation for prayer.

Ya'qub (as) – Pronounced Ya-coob, the prophet Jacob.

Yunus (as) – The prophet Jonah.

Yusha (as) – The prophet Joshua.

Yusuf (as) – The prophet Joseph.

Zakah – tithe, tax, giving a prescribed amount of your wealth once a year to be used for those in need. Derived from the root meaning 'to grow'.

Bibliography

Abu Dawud. *Sunan Abi Dawud*. Accessed from: https://www.searchtruth.com/searchHadith.php

Adil, Hajjah Amina. *Lore of Light*. MI: Institute for Spiritual and Cultural Advancement, 2009

Adil, Hajjah Amina. *Muhammad – Messenger of Islam*. Washington D.C.: ISCA, 2002

Adil, Hajjah Amina. *Forty Questions*. Washington D.C.: ISCA, 2013.

Asmani, Ibrahim Lethome and Maryam Sheikh Abdi. *De-linking Female Genital Mutilation/Cutting from Islam*. USAID, 2008. Accessed from: https://www.unfpa.org (2018, May)

Beach, Bradley and Matthew Powell editors. *Interpreting Abraham: Journeys to Moriah*. Minneapolis: Fortress Press, 2014.

Brill, EJ *The First Enclycopaedia of Islam* 1913-1936. Accessed from: https://brill.com/view/db/ei1o

Al-Bukhari, Muhammad. *Sahih Bukhari*. Accessed from: https://www.searchtruth.com/searchHadith.php

Caspi, Mishael M. and John T. Greene. *Unbinding the Binding of Isaac*. Maryland: University Press of America, 2007.

Cohen, A. *Everyman's Talmud*. NY: Schocken Books, 1975.

Curry, Andrew, "Gobleki Tepe: The World's First Temple?" *Smithsonian Magazine*, November, 2008.

Dajani, Samer. "The Secret of the Salat Ibrahimiyya". Accessed from: https://beneficialilm.com/2017/12/07

Dirks, Jerald F. *Abraham: The Friend of God*. Maryland: Amana Publications, 2002.

Firestone, Reuven. *Journeys in Holy Lands: Evolution of the Abraham-Ishmael Legends in Islamic Exegesis*. Albany: State University of New York Press, 1990.

Feiler, Bruce. *Abraham: A Journey to the Heart of Three Faiths*. New York: HarperCollins, 2005.

Ginzberg, Louis. *Legends of the Bible*. Philadelphia: The Jewish Publication Society, 1956.

Haneef, Suzanne. *A History of the Prophets of Islam vol. I*. Chicago: Library of Islam, 2002.

Hertenstein, Stephen. "The Brotherhood of Milk". Accessed from: http://www.ibnarabisociety.org

Hoffman, Joel. "Five Mistakes in Your Bible Translation." Accessed from: https://www.huffingtonpost.com/dr-joel-hoffman/five-mistakes-bible-translation_b_1129620.html. 30/9/18.

Hujwiri. *The Kashf Al-Mahjub of Hujwiri*. Reynold A. Nicholson trans. London: Luzac and Company LTD. 1967.

Ibn Abbas, Abdullah. *Tanwir Al-Miqbas*. Accessed from: https://www.altafsir.com

Ibn 'Arabi, Muhiyiddin. *The Bezels of Wisdom*. R. W. J. Austin trans. NY: Paulist Press, 1980.

Ibn 'Arabi, Muhiyiddin. *The Meccan Revelations*. M. Chodkiewicz ed. NY: Pir Press, 2005.

Ibn Ishaq. *The Life of Muhammad*. A. Guillaume trans. Lahore: Oxford University Press, 1974.

Ibn Kathir, Ismail. *Stories of The Prophets*. Riyadh: Maktaba Dar-us-Salam, 2003.

Ibn Kathir, Ismail. *Qur'an Tafsir* accessed from: http://www.qtafsir.com

Al-Jilani, Abd al-Qadir. *The Sublime Revelation*. Muhtar Holland trans. Al-Baz Publishing Inc.

Al-Jilani, Abd al-Qadir. *Utterances*. Muhtar Holland trans. Malaysia: Al-

Baz Publishing Inc.

Al-Kashani, Abd ar-Razaq. *Tafsir.* Accessed from: https://www.altafsir.com

Kennedy, T. M. "The Date of Camel Domestication in the Ancient Near East". *Bible and Spade,* Fall, 2010.

Kisai, Muhammad ibn 'Abd Allah. *Tales of the Prophets.* Wheeler M. Thackston Jr. trans. USA: Great Books of the Islamic World, Inc., 1997.

Kotlatch, Alfred J. *The Jewish Book of Why.* NY: Penguin Press, 2003.

Lane, Edward William. *An Arabic-English Lexicon.* London: Islamic Texts Society, 1984.

Lings, Martin. *Muhammad His Life Based on the Earliest Sources.* Rochester VT: Inner Traditions International, 1983.

Lumbard, Joseph E. B. *Covenant and Covenants in the Qur'an.* Edinburgh: University Press, 2015.

Madani, Mufti Abdur Rahmaan Kauthar and Mufti Afzal Hoosen Elias. *The Virtues and Laws of Zamzam.* South Africa: EDI Publishers, 2011.

Mahmud, Muhammad Bin Kanvendshah Bin. *The Rauzat-Us-Safa.* E. Rehatske trans. London: Kessinger Publishing, 2010.

Malik, Imam. *Muwatta.* Accessed from https://www.searchtruth.com/searchHadith.php

Maybudi, Rashid al-din. *Kashf al-Asrar tafsir.* Accessed from: https://www.altafsir.com

McDaniel, Thomas F. Clarifying Baffling Biblical Passages. Chapter 3. "Ishmael: A Peacemaker Genesis 16:10-12." Accessed from: http://tmcdaniel.palmerseminary.edu/CBBP_Chapter_3.pdf. 9/1/18.

Muslim, ibn al-Hajjaj. *Sahih Muslim.* Accessed from: https://www.searchtruth.com/searchHadith.php

An-Nawawi, Imam Abu Zakariya Yahya. *Riyad As-Salihin.* Accessed from: https://sunnah.com/riyadussaliheen

Renard, John. "Images of Abraham in the Writings of Jalal ad-Din Rumi". Journal of the American Oriental Society vol. 106 no.4 (Oct. - Dec. 1986).

Al-Qushairi, Abd al-Karim. *Tafsir.* Accessed from: www.altafsir.com

al-Qubrusi, Shaykh Nazim. *To Be a Muslim*. Nikosia, Cyprus: Spohr Publishers Ltd., 2016

Sabzawari, Husayn Wa'iz. *The Royal Book of Spiritual Chivalry*. Trans. Jay R. Crook. Chicago: Great Books of the Islamic World, 2000.

Saltanat.org. The Official Site of Shakh Muhammad Nazim Al Haqqani Online Magazine. http://saltanat.org

Schimmel, Annemarie. *The Mystery of Numbers*. New York: Oxford University Press, 1993.

Silva, Phillip. The Geography and History of Tall el-Hammam. Accessed from: https://www.researchgate.net/publication/269930714 Sept. 1, 2018.

Sufi Live.com. The Media Gateway of the Naqshbandi-Haqqani Sufi Order in America. https://sufilive.com

As-Suyuti, Shamsu d-din. "Description of the Noble Sanctuary in Jerusalem in 1470." Guy Le Strange translator. Journal of the Royal Asiatic Society of Great Britain and Ireland for 1898. London: Forgotten Books, 2017.

As-Suyuti, Jalaluddin. *Tafsir al-Jalalayn*. Accessed from: https://www.altafsir.com

As-Suyuti, Jalaluddin. *Al-Itqan fi 'Ulum Al-Qur'an*. Translated by Muneer Fareed. Accessed from https://archive.org/stream/AlItqanFiUlumAlQuran/AlItqanFiUlumAlQuran-SuyutiEnglish_djvu.txt. September 2018.

al-Tabari, Abu Jafar Muhammad b. Jarir. *The History of al-Tabari vol. III*. W. M. Brinner trans. Albany: SUNY, 1991.

al-Tha'labi, Abu Ishaq Ahmad b. Muhammad Ibrahim. *'Ara'is al-Majalis Qisas al Anbiya or Lives of the Prophets*. W. M. Brinner trans. Leiden: E. J. Brill, 2002.

Taylor, Bayard. *The Lands of the Saracen*. N.Y.: G. P. Putnam and sons, 1855.

Al-Tustari, Sahl. *Tafsir al-Tustari*. Accessed from: https://www.altafsir.com

Al-Wahidi. *Asbab al-Nuzul*. Accessed from: https://www.altafsir.com

Wilentz, Amy. "Battling Over Abraham". The New Yorker: Sept 16, 1996 issue. p.46-50.

Williams, Rev. George. *The Holy City or Historical and Topographical Notices of Jerusalem*. London: John W. Parker, 1845.

Wheeler, Brannon M. *Prophets in The Qur'an: An Introduction to the Qur'an and Muslim Exegesis*. London: Continuum, 2002.

Wheeler, Brannon M. Arab Prophets of the Qur'an and Bible. Journal of Qur'anic Studies, vol. 8, no. 2 (2002). Edinburgh University Press. Accessed from http://www.jstor.org

Zangi, Nuruddin. "The Prophet Ibrahim's Father". Accessed from: https://beneficialilm.com/2013/01/25

Translations of The Qur'an

I have used all the following translations interchangeably throughout the text, sometimes one, sometimes another depending on which seems most appropriate or most graceful. Where it occurs I have taken the liberty to change archaic vocabulary, such as thou to you etc.

Abdel Haleem, M.A.S. trans. *The Qur'an*. Oxford: Oxford University Press, 2004.

Ali, A. Yusuf. trans. *The Holy Qur'an*. NY: Aftner Publication, 1946.

Asad, Muhammad trans. *The Message of the Qur'an*. Gibraltar: Dar al-Andalus, 1980.

Pickthall, Marmaduke trans. *The Meaning of the Glorious Qur'an*. London: Allen & Unwin Ltd., 1930.

Picture Credits

Cover - adrianadefernex, Shutterstock.

p.32 - iAzeem, Shutterstock.

p.38 – abu_zeina, Shutterstock.

p.64 - Fedor Selivanov, Shutterstock.

p.73 – muratart, Shutterstock.

p.79 – sueleymancoskun, Shutterstock.

p.84 - Akram Reda. Photoshopped by Aminah Alptekin.

p.102 - Miqrodesign, Shutterstock.

p.114 - Anna Kubyshina, Shutterstock.

p.122 - Gregory Zameli, Shutterstock.

p.128 - Marzolino, Shutterstock.

p.130 - Akram Reda.

p.246 - Akram Reda.

p.154 - Kylie Nicholson, Shutterstock.

p.160 - lian_2011, Shutterstock.

p.164 - Sergio Ponomarev, Shutterstock.

p.172 - Roberto Binetti, Shutterstock.

p.197 - https://majesticislam.wordpress.com/2011/07/06/family-tree-from-adam-to-prophet-muhammed-as/

p.214 - A-Gallery, Shutterstock. Andy Magee, Shutterstock.

p.222 - Rudmer Zwerver, Shutterstock.

p.227 - yod67, Shutterstock. Photoshopped by Aminah Alptekin.

p.263 - Akram Reda.

p.264 - Akram Reda.

p.269 – Sufi, Shutterstock.

p.280 - Akram Reda.

p.285 - https://www.breakingisraelnews.com/81859/secret-hidden-chambers-hebrons-cave-patriarchs-finally-revealed-photos/

p.287 - https://st2.myideasoft.com/idea/bg/03/myassets/products/269/elif-tablo.jpg?revision=1490945443

www.ingramcontent.com/pod-product-compliance
Lightning Source LLC
Chambersburg PA
CBHW042127160426
43198CB00021B/2931